Pam Bono Designs

Quick Rotary Cutter
Quilts

Oxmoor
House®

Quick Rotary Cutter Quilts from the *For the Love of Quilting* series

© 1994 by Oxmoor House, Inc.
Book Division of Southern Progress Corporation
P.O. Box 2463, Birmingham, Alabama 35201

Published by Oxmoor House, Inc., and Leisure Arts, Inc.

Library of Congress Number: 93-085407
Hardcover ISBN: 0-8487-1149-1
Softcover ISBN: 0-8487-1412-1
Manufactured in the United States of America
First Printing 1994

Editor-in-Chief: Nancy J. Fitzpatrick
Senior Crafts Editor: Susan Ramey Wright
Senior Editor, Editorial Services:
    Olivia Kindig Wells
Art Director: James Boone

Quick Rotary Cutter Quilts

Editor: Patricia Wilens
Copy Editor: Susan Cheatham
Designer: Emily Albright
Editorial Assistant: Wendy L. Wolford
Copy Assistant: Leslee Rester Johnson
Senior Photographer: John O'Hagan
Photostylist: Katie Stoddard
Illustrator: Karen Tindall Tillery
Production Manager: Rick Litton
Associate Production Manager: Theresa Beste
Production Assistant: Marianne Jordan
Senior Production Designer: Larry Hunter
Publishing Systems Administrator: Rick Tucker

Dedicated to my husband, Robert, who has supported me, worked by my side, and given me strength when I needed it. Because of this book, he discovered untapped talents he never knew he possessed. From this book comes a new Bono husband-and-wife team. We are making music in our own way.

Special thanks to:
My life-long friend, *Lynn Mara Isenberg,* for her wonderful contributions to this book. Lynn is an occupational therapist who works with learning-disabled children. Her design talents surfaced long before mine, and I am pleased to present her work in this book. She produced a monumental number of designs in a short time, while working a full-time job. I am greatly appreciative and proud of her accomplishments.

Janet Frane, who was Lynn's right hand. Janet contributed to every quilt that Lynn made. Janet is a jewel, and her dedication is appreciated.

The owners of *The Brass Bed* of Homewood, Alabama, for the bed pictured on page 25 and to *Lord & Lockridge* of Birmingham for the bed pictured on page 168.

Designers
Pam Bono: *Baby Bunnies, Chili Pepper Tablecloth, Friends, Best Friend Doll, Safari Path, South of the Border, Stained Glass Floral, Which Came First?*
Pam and Robert Bono: *Blue Stars, Country Hearts, Seminole Flower Bed, Trellis, Tuxedo Cats, Water Lily*
Lynn Isenberg: *Amish Triangles, Black-Eyed Susan, Celtic Rose, Formal Garden, High Summer, Moo-vable Feast, Mountain Greenery, Oriental Desire, Paw of the Bear, Stars & Stripes, Till the Cows Come Home*

Contributors
Nancy Birger
Janet Frane
Curé of Ars Quilt Group
Judy DeVries
Dotty's Quilt Shop
Cindy Jochims, Iowa Quilting
Debbie McCormac
Barbara Morgan, Animas Quilts
Mother of the Universe Quilt Group
Melissa Mullgardt
Wanda Nelson
Barbara Roddy
Ella Roth
Elizabeth Smith
Fern Stewart
Gail Thomson
Marquleta Westbrook

Rotary Cutters and Cutting Tools
EZ International
P.O. Box 895
Saddle Brook, NJ 07662

Fiskars, Inc.
7811 West Stewart Avenue
Wausau, WI 54401

Fabric
Stained Glass Floral
VIP Fabrics
1412 Broadway
New York, NY 10018

Table of Contents

quilt \kwilt\ *vt:* to sew together, in a creative manner, layers of fabric and batting to make a product of any size that is used for warmth, decoration, and/or attire.

quick \kwick\ *adj* **1:** acting or capable of acting with speed; done or taking place with rapidity; **2:** marked by speed or promptness; **3:** capable of being easily and speedily prepared; **4:** hastened or accelerated beyond the norm.

Throughout my career, I designed and made mostly appliqué quilts. As a beginner, the thought of all those little pieces in a patchwork quilt boggled my mind and, as my time to complete each project was limited, I avoided pieced quilts. Looking over the procedures required to make a patchwork quilt, I became convinced that I'd never finish one—templates had to be made for every pattern piece, and cutting was a major ordeal. For someone not adept with scissors, it was agony! Accuracy was essential.

But the pieces that I cut with scissors never seemed to fit together properly.

The introduction of rotary cutting and quick piecing opened up a whole new world of quilts to me. Developed by talented professionals, these tools and techniques are among the greatest innovations of all time for quiltmakers.

Using these methods, I was pleasantly surprised how quickly I could cut out and sew all those little pieces together. Now we can approach patchwork with a new attitude and finish a quilt in half the time it took only a few years ago.

Today's lifestyle generally does not allow us the precious time we'd like to spend on quilting. But with the speedy techniques in this book, we can save time and get the quality results our grandmothers expected. You'll find a variety of designs to make quilts for every room in your house—bed quilts for young and old, wall hangings, holiday projects, baby quilts, pillows, shams, and tablecloths. Whichever project you choose, I hope to make your quilting a faster, more rewarding experience with projects that you will be proud to give as gifts or treasure for years to come.

Before beginning any project in this book, read the Workshop chapter so that you will understand the presentation of the instructions and methods used to make each one. Five basic quick-piecing techniques are used to make the quilts in this book. Each quilt employs one or more of these methods. Practice these quick techniques—it doesn't take long to become proficient, and the time spent will yield spectacular results.

To create something is the greatest feeling in the world.

Happy quilting!

Pam Bono

Workshop

Tools & Supplies

The selection of most quiltmaking tools is a personal choice. Quilters are different—some have good eyesight, some don't; some have large hands, while others have small or even arthritic hands. Choose the tools that are most comfortable for you.

The following list of tools and supplies is by no means exhaustive. There are many amazing gadgets available today. I've mentioned the tools that I believe will help you successfully make the quilts in this book in the fastest and most accurate way possible.

Rotary Tools

Rotary Cutter. A rotary cutter has a round blade attached to a handle and comes in two sizes. I find the larger cutter is more efficient, easier to control, and the blades seem to last longer. Select a cutter that is comfortable in your hand, as it will spend a lot of time there. Some quilters feel a curved handle puts less strain on their wrists.

Change the blade frequently. A dull blade tends to skip and be less accurate. Always retract the blade when the cutter is not in use—this protects the blade as well as everyone's fingers. *Keep the cutter out of the reach of small children.*

To keep the blade of your rotary cutter running smoothly, oil it periodically by loosening the tension screw and

placing one drop of sewing machine oil between blade and sheath. Wipe excess oil with a clean cloth to avoid staining the fabric.

Cutting Mat. Always use a heavy-duty, self-healing cutting mat. A 24" x 36" mat is a good, all-purpose size. (Smaller mats require you to move the fabric too frequently.) The best mats are marked in a 1" grid with two 45° angles. These lines are helpful in aligning fabric and squaring blocks. Always store the mat flat. Avoid exposing the mat to excessive heat.

Rulers. Rulers used with rotary cutters are made of clear, 1/8"-thick acrylic. The basic ruler should be marked in 1/8" increments as well as 45° and 60° angles. The most versatile ruler is 6" x 24", a good length for cutting long strips. A large square ruler, used with the 24" ruler, helps to keep cuts straight. You will also need small rulers, because a big ruler can get in your way when making small cuts. Other rulers that make cutting easier include those with light print for dark fabrics, rulers with dark print for lighter fabrics, and a 1" x 6" ruler to keep near the sewing machine for checking the accuracy of seams. An 18"-long plastic ruler is helpful for drawing grids.

To keep your ruler from slipping, cut 3/8" squares of self-sticking sandpaper (available at most hardware stores) and place them on the back of your ruler at the corners.

Basic Supplies

Sewing Machine. Any basic straight-stitch machine is adequate. You will want a more sophisticated machine if you intend to try machine appliqué or machine quilting. Keep your machine in good working order. If the tension is not properly adjusted, you'll get puckered or distorted seams. The machine should make an evenly locked stitch that looks the same on front and back. Clean and oil the machine as directed by the manufacturer and take it to your dealer periodically to be serviced.

Be sure to use a throat plate that has a small, round needle hole designed for straight stitching. A wide, oblong needle hole (intended for zigzag stitching) lets the needle push the fabric down into the throat plate as you stitch. Replace the throat plate if necessary.

Sewing Machine Presser Feet. Special feet that measure a 1/4" seam allowance are available for most machines. These are especially helpful when sewing patchwork. If you don't have one, see page 14 for other ways to mark an accurate seam allowance.

Sewing Machine Needles. The needle most recommended for machine piecing is size 80/12.

If you hear a popping noise when sewing, the machine's needle may be dull. Replace it to maintain stitch quality and to avoid snags in the fabric.

Sewing Thread. Use either 100% cotton thread or the stronger cotton-wrapped polyester thread. Use a light neutral color (ivory or taupe) when sewing light fabrics and a dark neutral (gray) thread when piecing dark fabrics.

Seam Ripper. This invaluable tool is much more efficient than the tips of small scissors for removing unwanted stitches. A seam ripper is also useful in several of these quilts where you are instructed to remove a square from a pieced sashing strip or border.

Pins and Pincushions. Use long, thin dressmaker's pins. Sharp, rustproof pins with round heads are preferable. I like a magnetic pin holder on my wrist, but any type of pincushion will do.

Scissors. You need sharp dressmaker's shears for cutting the occasional appliqué shape and for trimming batting and backing. Use sharp embroidery scissors for snipping threads. If your project requires a template, you will also need small utility scissors for cutting paper or plastic.

Iron and Ironing Board. Use an iron that has both dry and steam settings. An iron with an automatic shut-off will probably be a nuisance—in the pauses between quilting and pressing, I find the iron shuts off just when I need it. For steam, use distilled water to keep your iron free of foreign particles that can cause spotting. An ironing board that adjusts to different heights will make your work more comfortable.

Fabric Sizing Spray. I use a light spray after prewashing fabric to give the fabric some stiffness. This is especially helpful when working with bias seams to prevent stretching.

Zip-top Plastic Bags. Resealable bags are essential for storing cut pieces. One box of sandwich bags should see you through several quilts. See page 13 for more details.

Pencils and Markers. Use pencils to mark grids and pattern shapes on fabric. Keep pencils sharp and make thin lines. A good mechanical pencil that holds 0.5-mm (thin) lead is an excellent investment. For marking quilt tops, try a silver drawing pencil or chalk marker that shows well on both light and dark fabrics and washes out easily. Water-erasable markers are easy to use, but the chemicals from these sometimes remain in the fabric even after a cold water rinse, causing permanent discoloration. I use a mechanical pencil to *lightly* mark quilting lines on most fabrics. Whatever product you choose, test it on scraps first to be sure it will wash out.

Use permanent fabric marking pens when you want the lines to remain forever. I used three colors of fine-tipped permanent fabric marking pens on the *Friends* quilt and doll. These pens are useful for signing and dating your quilts.

Template Plastic. Available in sheets of lightweight plastic, this material is transparent enough to allow you to see the pattern through it and trace the pattern directly onto it. It is thin enough to cut with scissors, but strong enough to withstand repeated use. Templates are used for appliqué shapes and for marking faces on the *Friends* quilt.

Tear-Away Stabilizer. This lightweight, nonwoven material is placed under the background fabric to keep it from slipping during machine appliqué.

Eraser. A white plastic eraser called Magic Rub is available at most art supply stores. This eraser, used by professional drafters and artists, cleanly removes carbon smudges left by pencil lead without fraying the fabric or leaving eraser crumbs.

Fabric Glue. After pressing under ¼" on appliqué pieces, I apply a bit of fabric glue to hold the edges in place while I pin and stitch the fabric.

Safety Pins. Purchase rustproof, 1"-long, nickel-plated safety pins to pin-baste quilt layers together for machine quilting. You will need approximately 350–500 safety pins for a large quilt.

Thimble. Hand quilting is difficult and painful without a thimble on the middle finger of your sewing hand to keep the needle from digging into your fingertip. Use a thin rubber thimble if you want to feel the needle.

Quilting Needles. Purchase a packaged assortment of "sharps" for general hand stitching and a package of "betweens" for hand quilting. Sharps are longer and have a larger eye than betweens. For hand quilting, select the between that is most comfortable to use. I use a size 10 between for hand quilting, but size 7 or 8 is better for beginners.

Quilting Thread. For hand quilting, purchase good-quality quilting thread. Most fabric stores and quilting shops have a wide range of colors. Quilting thread is heavier than sewing thread and is coated to prevent tangling. Throw away an old spool of quilting thread if it has become brittle.

For machine quilting, load the bobbin with regular sewing thread that matches the backing. For the top thread, use sewing thread that coordinates with the quilt top, or use monofilament (a clear nylon thread for machine quilting). The nylon thread blends with any fabric and tends to camouflage irregularities in the stitching. When using regular thread in the bobbin and nylon thread on top, adjust the top thread tension to prevent bobbin thread loops from showing.

Bicycle Clips. For machine quilting, use these metal or plastic bands to hold the rolled edges of the quilt in place. These clips are sold in quilt shops and fabric stores.

Walking Foot. This special presser foot is excellent for machine quilting straight lines or grids as well as for applying binding and for stitching large, simple curves. While it is not essential, this foot certainly makes these tasks easier. It is an even-feed foot; that is, it feeds the top fabric through the machine at precisely the same rate that the feed dogs move the bottom fabric. Some machines have a built-in even-feed feature.

Quilting Hoops and Frames. A quilting hoop has deeper sides than an embroidery hoop to accommodate the three thicknesses of a quilt. For hand quilting you can carry anywhere or work in your lap, use the size hoop you find most comfortable or practical. The most popular hoops are from 14"–22" in diameter. A quilting frame is large and heavy and more or less permanently fixed in place while the quilting is in progress. Inquire at your local quilt shop or study mail order sources for the best style, price, and size to fit your needs.

Fabric

Lightweight, 100%-cotton fabric is the traditional choice of most quiltmakers. It is easy to sew and to handle. A sturdy and durable fabric, it has a slight nap that helps keep the pieces from slipping while stitching. Neither too stretchy nor too tightly woven, it has some give, which is helpful in piecing and in appliqué. Cotton takes a crease well, so that patchwork seams are easy to press.

Buy only good-quality fabric. Avoid fabrics that feel stiff, loosely woven and stretchy, or are misprinted. You want your quilt to last, so put quality goods into it.

Choosing Fabrics

Fabric selection seems to be the toughest hurdle for many quilters. You have selected a beautiful design from the book and have read its precise instructions . . . you have practiced the techniques and know how to assemble the project . . . but the colors shown just aren't right for you. How do you choose fabrics to make that design work?

Don't be afraid to trust your own instincts. Go with what *you* like, especially if you're making the quilt for yourself. Ask yourself several questions about the project before you go to the fabric store. Who is the quilt for? How and where will the project be used?

If you need help with your selection, several resources are available. Some mail-order sources offer sets of coordinating prints and solids. Employees of quilt shops and fabric stores are often glad to assist. Take this book with you to the store—having the design in front of you is helpful and enables the shop's experts to make suggestions.

I exhaust the people at my favorite quilt shops. When I'm finished, there is a stack of bolts piled up to be put back on the proper shelves. I put different combinations together on a large table and—this is very important—I step back as far as I can go and squint. This gives me a good look at the overall mix of values and textures. If one fabric doesn't look right, I replace it.

Create a Mood. The choice of fabric colors and patterns will affect the mood of any design. The soft pastel fabrics of *Formal Garden*, for example, evoke gentle spring breezes and delicate flowers. Bright, strong colors would convey a very different feeling. It's up to the maker to establish the quilt's personality.

Look at *Safari Path* for another example. Dramatic fabrics in rich browns and mellow golds suggest the size and strength of animals of the African plains. The same design becomes a whimsical fantasy quilt when you substitute pink elephants and yellow lions with orange manes.

Even if you're making a Christmas project, you can still vary the mood. Bright red and green mixed with sparkling white looks crisp and new. Soft beige, rich burgundy, and forest green suggest a country, Victorian, or old-fashioned atmosphere.

Big floral prints are excellent for Victorian and English Country looks. Don't be afraid to cut those bold prints into small pieces, as they create an interesting variety of textures. Amish-style quilts combine solid colors and black. Country themes often use warm colors, small prints or plaids, and tea dyeing to create an old-fashioned look. Oriental-style prints add sophistication to even the simplest designs.

Choose a Color Scheme. Take a design you like and visualize it with different color schemes and applications in mind. Don't limit yourself to what I did. I've been to many quilt shows where I've seen my designs made in different color choices and I usually say, "Wow! That's great!"

Tea Dyeing

To get an antique look, tea-dye some of the light and medium fabrics to obtain the sepia-toned appearance of age. (The stain isn't dark enough to affect dark fabrics.) Tea dyeing accomplishes the goals of prewashing, so it's not necessary to do both.

To tea-dye yardage, use the biggest pot you have. (Our family has Italian ancestry, so it's natural for us to have *large* spaghetti pots.) Fill the pot about ¾ full with water. Add two tea bags per quart of water. (Add more tea bags for a slightly darker stain.) When the water boils, remove the tea bags.

Immerse the fabric in the boiling water. Don't put too much fabric in the pot—the fabric should be completely covered and you should be able to stir it easily. If you have a lot of fabric to dye, do it in batches.

Let the fabric simmer, using a wooden spoon to stir frequently. After 20 minutes, rinse the fabric in cold water, stirring it in the pot to remove excess tea. Wring the water from the fabric; then heat-set it in the dryer.

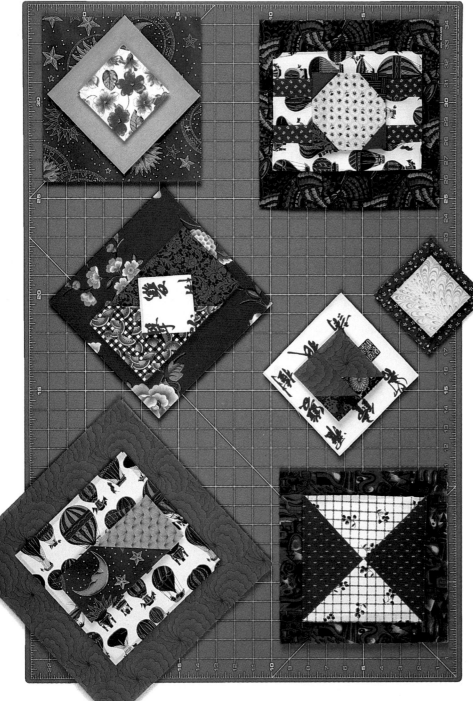

where it is important to mix small and large prints as well as dark and light values. Mix a solid fabric among the prints. Too many prints create a confusing surface, making design elements difficult to see. Solid fabrics help create the visual contrast that defines the design elements.

A rule of thumb for creating good balance in any quilt is to use at least one fabric both in the central design and at the outside edges. My quilt borders usually repeat one or more fabrics used in the main design. When I chose a dark print for the *Trellis* border, I felt it necessary to pull that print into the center for balance. So I used that fabric for all the flower centers. I also like to use one of the dominant colors in the binding.

How Much to Buy

Each materials list gives the amount of fabric needed to make the quilt. Yardages stated are based on 42"-wide fabric after prewashing.

The Fabric Bug. Anyone who loves fabric is eventually bitten by the fabric bug. Once bitten, you may be compelled to buy fabric even when you don't need it. As the disease progresses, try to balance the limits of your purse and storage space with the inalienable right to invest in yourself and your creativity. Don't let guilt keep you from building a nice inventory of fabric for your quilts. I can usually take one or two fabrics from my stockpile and use them with new fabrics to make a quilt.

Finders Keepers. When buying fabric, remember that you may never find it again. If you see a fabric that you really like, buy a lot! Chances are, when you return to the shop to get more, that fabric won't be there anymore. Even worse, that fabric may never be available again. It's better to have extra for future scrap quilts than not enough. All the dolls in *Friends* were made from my scraps. I purchased background and sashing fabric, but I already had plenty of pinks and blues to make the dolls, and it was fun to mix and match.

The blue *Stained Glass Floral* makes a nice bedroom ensemble, but how would that design work as a Christmas table runner? Try flowers of dark red print and solid red with pale gold centers, forest green leaves, an ivory background, and solid burgundy for the center square and border.

You can always rely on formal color relationships such as monochromatic, analogous, and complementary. There are several excellent books available that explain the applications of these theories in quiltmaking.

Combining Fabrics. A simple approach to combining fabrics for a quilt is to choose one fabric that contains several colors and then select fabrics in coordinating colors.

But color is not the only factor to consider. In fabric, visual texture is the combination of elements that creates the overall look. These elements include pattern, scale, contrast, and color. A good balance of texture, value, and pattern scale is essential for an attractive quilt. This is particularly true in a monochromatic color scheme,

I buy fabrics in ¼-yard, 1-yard, 3-yard, or 6-yard cuts. I buy small pieces just to have them for scrap quilts. If a fabric is a good accent, I'll buy 1 yard. It's 3 yards if that fabric will make a great background someday and 6 yards if the fabric is on sale and it's a sure-fire candidate for major design elements and borders.

Directional Prints. Always buy extra fabric when using stripes or other directional prints. These are effective in some designs, but cutting them to keep the direction consistent can be wasteful. (If the stripes don't go in the right direction, your quilt can have a chaotic appearance.) Do not use a directional print for background fabric. See page 12 for more on directional prints.

Prewashing

Wash, dry, and iron all fabrics before cutting. Washing removes excess dye and sizing from the fabric and may shrink it. Wash light and dark colors separately in warm water using a mild detergent or, preferably, Orvus Paste (a mild soap originally developed for washing livestock, which is now available at many quilt shops). Before washing, snip a ¼" triangle off each corner of the fabric. This helps prevent raveling.

Avoid Dry Cleaning. Many people prefer to work on unwashed fabric and subsequently have the finished quilt dry-cleaned. But this tempts fate because the fabrics could run if they happen to get wet in the course of normal use. Also, chemicals used in dry cleaning may prove detrimental to long-term preservation of a quilt. If you take the time to prewash, there is less chance of damage being done to a quilt that will be used for years to come.

Test for Colorfastness. Many dark fabrics bleed excessively during washing. To test for colorfastness, add a clean scrap of white fabric to the load of dark fabrics each time you rinse. Continue rinsing until the white scrap remains white; then the fabric is colorfast. If a fabric bleeds after repeated rinses, do not use it in your quilt.

Dry and Press. Dry prewashed fabrics at a medium or permanent-press setting in the dryer. Press them with a steam iron set at the appropriate setting for the fabric. A light spray of fabric sizing makes it easier to get wrinkles out and adds body. Fold the fabric lengthwise in fourths to store it. Store your fabric neatly, according to color, preferably in boxes to protect it from light.

Rotary Cutting

Rotary cutting is faster and more accurate than conventional scissor cutting. It's fast because you can measure and cut multiple layers with a single stroke, skipping the time-consuming steps of making templates and marking fabric. It is more accurate because the fabric stays still and flat as you cut, instead of being raised by the scissor blade. If you are new to rotary cutting, practice on scraps before beginning a project. Once you master the cutter, you'll appreciate the accuracy and time it saves.

The best work surface for me is kitchen-counter height. Experiment to find the best work area and height for you. Stand with the mat directly in front of you, centering your body over the cutting line for maximum control.

The Right Direction

The interwoven lengthwise and crosswise threads of a fabric are called straight grain. The following are some things to know about grain direction before you cut. Cotton fabric can be stable or stretchy, depending on how it is cut.

Dare to Be Different

Try new fabrics and ideas. When you experiment, you won't get all things right all the time. Even professionals know failure as well as success. Let your talent evolve. My early quilts show a great difference in my taste and style. I'd like to remake some of them with different moods and colors. You, too, will improve with each quilt. Practice is important. It may not solve every problem, but it certainly helps.

Selvage. The lengthwise finished edges of the fabric are the selvages (Diagram 1). These edges are more tightly woven than the rest of the fabric and are often unprinted. Do not include selvage in cut pieces.

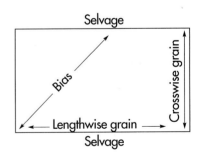

Diagram 1

Grain. Lengthwise grain, parallel to the selvages, is most stable and has the least give. Crosswise grain, perpendicular to the selvages, has a little more stretch. Most strips are cut on the crosswise grain. Long strips for sashing and borders are best cut lengthwise for more stability. For small pieces, either direction is acceptable.

Bias. True bias is at a 45° angle to the selvages, on the diagonal between the lengthwise and crosswise grains. Bias-cut fabric has the most stretch.

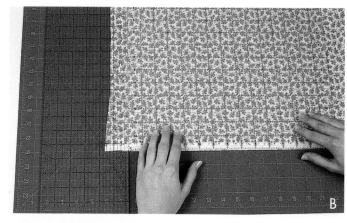

Squaring Up the Edge

Most new fabric has jagged edges or is folded off-center. In order to cut straight strips, you must refold the fabric and trim the ends to make them perpendicular to the center fold.

1. Fold and press the fabric with selvage edges matching. Place the folded fabric on a cutting mat, with the folded edge nearest you. Fold the fabric in half again as shown in Photo A, aligning the selvage with the fold, making four layers. This makes your fabric only 11" wide—the narrower width is easier to cut accurately. If you have a long length of fabric, accordion-fold the yardage to your right, leaving the end that you are going to cut on the mat. This conserves space and makes it easier to keep the fabric straight as you cut.

2. For a straight cut, use two rulers to establish a baseline perpendicular to the fold. Begin with a large square ruler, aligning its edge with the bottom fold so the side of the ruler is approximately 1" from the left edge of the fabric (Photo B). Butt a long ruler against the side of the square, overlapping the

fabric edge. Keeping the long ruler in place, remove the square.

3. To keep the ruler stable, spread the fingers of your left hand on the ruler as shown in Photo C. Keep your fingers away from the cutting edge. Release the cutter's safety guard. Keeping a firm grip on the handle, hold the cutter blade against the side of the ruler at the bottom of the mat. Begin rolling the cutter before it meets the fabric, moving it away from you. Use firm, even pressure, keeping the blade against the ruler. If necessary, lift your left hand (don't slide it) and reposition it farther up the ruler. Be careful not to shift the ruler. Do not lift the cutter from the fabric until it has cut through the folded edge.

Directional Fabrics. Directional fabrics include stripes as well as many fabrics that seem to be printed in a random manner but actually have motifs arranged in straight or diagonal rows.

These designs are rarely printed on the true grain. So, if you follow the rules and cut a piece on the straight of the grain, the printed motifs will seem to fall off the edge. To avoid this problem,

fold and square off the fabric using the motifs as guidelines. Then you can cut strips and smaller pieces that are aligned with the motifs, even though the fabric is off-grain. This is fine for small pieces, but directional fabrics are not recommended for borders or backgrounds.

First Cut

Rotary cutting usually begins with cutting long strips of fabric, which are then cut into smaller pieces. In this book, cutting instructions for the first cut (designated by ♦) specify the number and width of strips needed. The strips needed are 42" wide, cut on the crosswise grain. Instructions for the second cut (designated by •) state the quantity, size, and unit number of the smaller pieces to cut from these strips. The 1/4" seam allowances are included in measurements given for all strips and pieces.

1. To measure the correct strip width, position the ruler on the left edge of the fabric as shown in Photo D and cut. The blade will cut easily through all four layers.

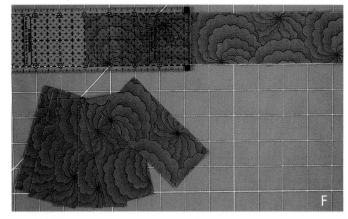

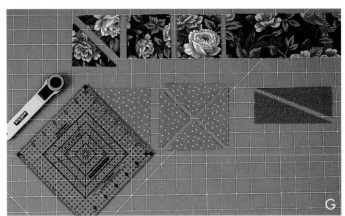

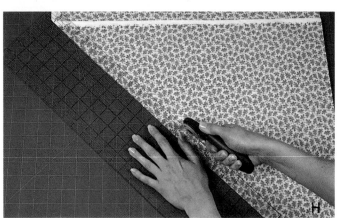

2. Open the cut strip. If the trimmed edge was not accurately perpendicular to the fold, the strip will bow in the center, as shown by the bottom strip in Photo E. Straighten the edge as described at left and cut another strip.

3. Using the ruler and rotary cutter, trim about ³⁄₈" from the strip ends to remove the selvage.

Second Cut

To cut squares and rectangles from a strip, align the desired measurement on the ruler with the strip end and cut across the strip as shown in Photo F.

For right triangles, the cutting instructions may say to cut a square in half or in quarters diagonally, as shown in Photo G. This technique works with rectangles, too. The edges of the square are straight grain, so the triangle sides cut on the diagonal are bias. On these pieces, carefully run a line of stay-stitching ⅛" from the bias edge to keep the fabric from stretching as you work with it.

Cutting Bias Strips

You will occasionally need to cut bias strips. If you need a small number of relatively short strips, cut a square in half diagonally as shown in Photo G—since the diagonal edges are bias, cutting parallel to the diagonal edge of each triangle will yield bias strips.

To cut bias strips from yardage, begin with a squared edge on one end of the fabric. Open the fabric to a single layer. Bring the bottom left corner up to the selvage on the opposite side as shown in Photo H, making a 45° angle along the fold. Trim ½" from the fold and then cut desired strips parallel to the cut edge.

Organize Cut Pieces

Some projects have many pieces, and you'll be easily confused unless they are neatly stored and organized as you work (especially if, like most people, you sew over a long period of time and are constantly moving your work on and off the kitchen table). It's important to be able to identify which piece is which when you're cutting so many.

In this book, the diagrams that illustrate each project show the design broken down into numbered units. I recommend that you place all same-numbered cut pieces in a zip-top plastic bag. Label each bag with masking tape, printing the number (and measurement, if applicable) of the unit on the tape. You can see the fabric through the bag, which will help you to locate the pieces as you work. If your project takes several weeks, the pieces sealed inside the bags won't get lost, mixed up, or dirty. Keep the bags in order by unit number and close to your sewing machine for easy access. Take out pieces as you need them.

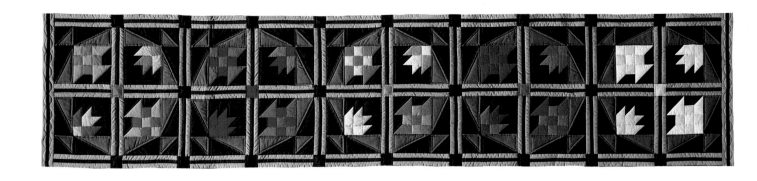

Patchwork Basics

The ¼" Seam Allowance

In patchwork, all seam allowances are ¼" wide. Maintaining an accurate and consistent ¼" seam is essential. If each seam in a block is off by as little as ¹⁄₁₆", the error multiplies quickly. If your blocks end up different sizes, it will be difficult to join them and your quilt top may be lopsided.

Measure the Seam. Some sewing machines have a line on the throat plate to designate the ¼" seam allowance, while others have presser feet that measure ¼" from the needle to the outside edge of the foot. Some let you adjust the needle position as desired. Whichever feature you have, stitch a sample seam and measure it carefully to make sure it is precisely ¼" wide. If it is not and the needle position cannot be adjusted, purchase a presser foot that measures a true ¼" seam.

Mark a Seam Line. Another method for making accurate seams is to mark the throat plate with tape. To do this, use a sharp pencil to draw a line ¼" from the edge of a piece of paper. (The thick line made by a dull pencil can affect the measurement.) Put the paper under the presser foot and lower the needle through the line. Lower the foot and adjust the paper so it is parallel with the edge of the foot as shown in Photo A. Lay a strip of masking tape along the paper's edge.

Stitch a seam, using the tape as a guideline; then check it. If the seam gets wider or narrower as you sew, the tape is not straight. Adjust the tape as needed until the seam is accurate. You may want to build up layers of tape so the ridge prevents the fabric from sliding over it.

Machine Piecing

Set the stitch length on your sewing machine to 12 stitches per inch.

Chain Piecing. This method of joining pieces saves time as well as thread. When joining many sets of the same unit, stack units in pairs with right sides facing. Join the first pair as usual. At the end of the seam, do not backstitch, cut the thread, or lift the presser foot. Just feed in the next pair—the machine will stitch on air before the needle strikes the next piece. Continue in this way until all pairs are joined as shown in Photo B. Keep the chain intact to hold the units together until you are ready to use them.

Pressing. Careful pressing is necessary for precise piecing. As you build a unit, press each seam as you go. Set the iron for cotton, checking on a scrap to be sure the heat won't scorch or glaze the fabric. Set a small ironing board next to your machine at table height so you won't have to spend time getting up and down.

Pressing—which differs from ironing—should set seams and remove wrinkles without distorting the fabric. Ironing (sliding the iron back and forth) can push seams out of shape.

To press, use an up-and-down motion, lifting the iron from spot to spot. First, press the seam flat on the wrong side. Open the piece and, on the right side, press both seam allowances to one side (usually toward the darker fabric). Do not press seams open as in dressmaking, as this weakens the seam and lets batting fibers escape through the finished quilt.

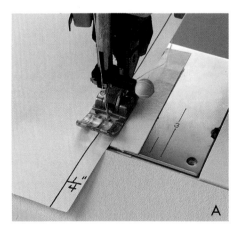

Matching Opposing Seams. To make neat corners and points, matching seams must align precisely. Begin by pressing seam allowances that need to match in opposite directions as shown in Photo C. (This is more important than whether seam allowances are pressed toward the dark or light side of the seam.) With right sides facing and seams aligned, stitch the joining seam, sewing over the seam allowances to lock them in place.

Pinning. Pin pieces together with right sides facing. Place pins perpendicular to the seam being sewn, with the heads toward the fabric edge. Pin the ends of the seam, then the center, and along the length as needed. As you stitch the seam, remove each pin just before the needle reaches it. If the needle hits a pin, either one could break and send bits of metal flying at you.

Small units require little or no pinning. It is essential, however, to pin long seams, especially where opposing seams must align.

Pin Matching. Using pins to align seam lines is called pin matching. When joining units, first place pins where the seams must match. With right sides facing, align opposing seam allowances. On the top piece, push a pin through the seam line about ½" from the top edge. The pin should go through the seam of the bottom piece in the same manner. Push the pin back through both layers, staying on the seam lines, about ¼" from the edge. When matching seams are pinned, then pin the rest of the seam line as needed.

Stitching Sharp Points. When two triangular or diagonal pieces are joined, the stitching lines cross in an X formation on the back. Watch for this X as you sew these units to other units—if the joining seam goes through the exact center of each X, you'll have nice sharp points on the front (Diagram 2).

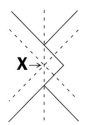

Diagram 2

Easing Fullness. Sometimes two units that should be the same size are slightly different. When joining such units, first pin-match opposing seams. Put the pinned unit under the presser foot with the shorter unit on top (Diagram 3). As you sew, the feed dogs will ease the fullness on the bottom piece. This is sometimes called sewing with a "baggy bottom."

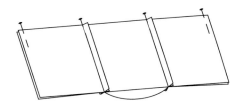

Diagram 3

If units are too dissimilar to ease without puckering, check each one to see if the pieces were correctly cut and that the seams are ¼" wide. Remake the unit that varies most from the desired size.

Appliqué

Appliqué is the process of sewing (applying) a cut fabric shape on top of a background fabric. In this book, there are some projects that have appliqué embellishments.

Hand Appliqué. Trace the appliqué pattern onto tracing paper or template plastic, including the seam allowance; then cut out the pattern. Pin or trace the pattern onto the right side of the fabric; cut out the appliqué.

Turn under the seam allowance around the appliqué piece and press. Clip curves and corners just inside the sewing line. On rounded shapes, baste the seam allowance to hold it down or use a little fabric glue to secure it. Pin the appliqué in place on the background fabric.

Use one strand of thread in a color that matches the appliqué fabric to make tiny slipstitches around the edge of the shape. Working from right to left, pull the needle through the base fabric and catch just a few threads on the fold of the appliqué. Reinsert the needle into the base fabric, keeping the needle under the top thread on the appliqué edge to keep the thread from tangling (Diagram 4).

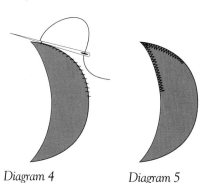

Diagram 4   *Diagram 5*

Machine Appliqué. Test the length and width of the zigzag or satin stitch before starting a project. Practice making points and curves. An open-toed presser foot is recommended.

Make a pattern for the appliqué shape, omitting seam allowances. Trace the pattern onto paper-backed fusible webbing and apply the webbing to the wrong side of the appliqué fabric as directed. Cut out the appliqué. Place tear-away stabilizer under the background fabric behind the appliqué. Machine-stitch the appliqué edges (Diagram 5). Remove the stabilizer when appliqué is complete.

Quick-Piecing Techniques

When Elias Howe invented the sewing machine in 1846, he changed the dynamics of home sewing forever. Quiltmakers immediately recognized the added speed and accuracy made possible by the machine. We like to imagine pioneer women stitching by hand, but many also used sewing machines.

In recent years, quiltmakers have developed time-saving techniques uniquely suited to machine piecing. Combined with the rotary cutter and a myriad of companion rulers, these techniques take us a long way from traditional one-piece-at-a-time methods.

All the quilts in this book are made using one or more of the techniques explained here. These methods differ from traditional patchwork in that they help you to make multiple units with fewer steps.

Practice is essential to become adept at any new technique. When you feel ready, begin a selected project by making one block to learn how the techniques are applied. Then you will feel comfortable piecing the remaining blocks asssembly-line style.

Diagonal Corners

This technique is used for many projects in this book as an easy way to add triangle corners to squares or rectangles. This technique is particularly helpful if the corner triangle is very small, because it is easier to cut and handle a square than a small triangle.

With right sides facing, match a square to the corner of the base square or rectangle. On the wrong side of the square, draw a diagonal line from corner to corner. (If you prefer, you can press the square in half diagonally and use the crease for a stitching line.) With practice, you will be able to stitch small squares (up to 1½") by eye without having to mark a sewing line.

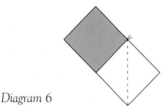

Diagram 6

Stitch on the drawn line as shown in Diagram 6. Next, trim excess fabric *from the diagonal-corner fabric only*, leaving ¼" seam allowance (Diagram 7). Press the triangle open so the pieced corner covers the corner of the base fabric. Pin layers together.

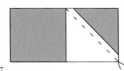

Diagram 7

If diagonal corners overlap, join the first diagonal corner as usual and press it out. Then join the second fabric to the same corner of the square or rectangle in the same manner. The result is a pieced or double diagonal corner (see *Oriental Desire*, page 46).

Diagonal Ends

This method eliminates difficult measuring, cutting, and sewing of trapezoids. The technique is basically the same as for diagonal corners except a rectangle (instead of a square) is sewn to the corner of the base rectangle.

To stitch diagonal ends, position the top rectangles perpendicular to the base rectangle with right sides facing (Diagram 8a). Mark a diagonal line across the end of the top rectangle in the same manner as for diagonal corners, beginning in the corner where the two fabrics meet and angling upward to the opposite corner of the base rectangle at a 45° angle. Stitch on the marked line; then cut away the excess fabric from the corner seam allowance.

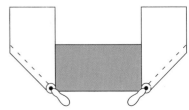

Diagram 8a

When diagonal ends need to be made in mirror image sets, as shown in Diagram 8b, be careful to draw your sewing line in the right direction.

Diagram 8b

Half-Square Triangles

Squares and right triangles are the shapes most often used in patchwork. Many designs are made by joining two contrasting triangles on the diagonal (hypotenuse) to make a square. Each of these triangles is called a half-square triangle.

The grid method of sewing half-square triangles is used in many projects in this book. In each case, the instructions illustrate a grid that is the secret weapon for making lots of triangle-squares quickly and easily.

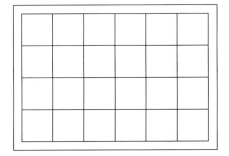

Diagram 9

1. Draw the grid on the *wrong* side of the lighter fabric. Use a sharp pencil or fine-tipped marker. Say, for example, the instructions call for a 4 x 6 grid of 2" squares. Draw an 8" x 12" rectangle and then divide it into four 2" squares vertically and six 2" squares horizontally (Diagram 9). When making a grid, be sure to measure and draw the squares carefully and accurately. The size of the drawn square is always ⅞" larger than the desired *finished* size of the triangle-square.

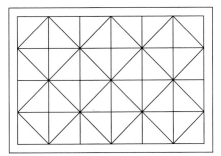

Diagram 10

2. Draw diagonal lines through all squares (Diagram 10). In most cases, diagonal lines alternate directions in adjacent squares. Only one diagonal line is drawn through each square.

3. If your presser foot accurately measures a ¼" seam, use it as a guide to stitch seams on both sides of each *diagonal* line. If the foot does not measure an accurate seam allowance, then you must draw a stitching line ¼" on each side of all diagonal lines.

4. Place the fabric on which the grid is drawn on top of the piece that is the other part of the triangle-square, with right sides facing.

5. Start at an outside point near the top left corner of the grid (blue arrow on Diagram 11). Stitch an accurate ¼" seam, making a complete circuit of the grid indicated by the blue line. At the end of one diagonal line, stitch into the border beyond the grid as shown. Keep the needle down but raise the presser foot and pivot the fabric; then continue along the next line in the same manner. When you return to the starting point, you will have stitched on one side of all diagonal lines.

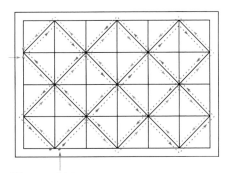

Diagram 11

6. Begin again at another outside point (red arrow on sample grid) and repeat stitching on opposite side of the diagonal lines. When all diagonal stitching is done, gently press fabric to smooth stitching.

7. Using a rotary cutter and ruler, cut on *all* grid lines to separate the triangle-squares (Diagram 12). Each square of the grid yields two triangle-squares. Press triangle-squares open, pressing the seam allowance toward the darker fabric. Trim the points at the end of each seam (Diagram 13).

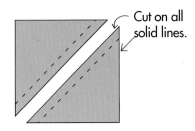

Cut on all solid lines.

Diagram 12

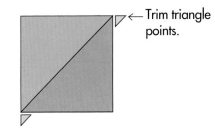

← Trim triangle points.

Diagram 13

Quarter-Square Triangles

When a square is made up of four right triangles, each triangle is called a quarter-square triangle. The grid method for making these units is the same as for half-square triangles except that the grid squares are 1¼" larger than the desired *finished* size of the unit. However, after the grid is stitched and cut apart, the resulting triangle-squares require a few more steps to transform them into four-triangle squares.

On the wrong side of one triangle-square, draw a diagonal line from corner to corner that bisects the seam line as shown in Photo A. Match this square with another triangle-square, right sides facing, matching seams and fabrics as directed. Stitch on both sides of the drawn diagonal line. Cut the units apart on the drawn line as shown in Photo B and press each new unit.

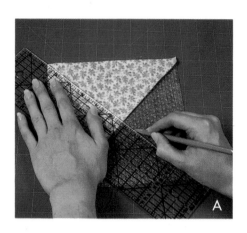

Strip Piecing

For some projects, you'll sew different-colored strips together to make 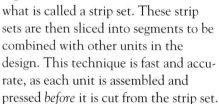 what is called a strip set. These strip sets are then sliced into segments to be combined with other units in the design. This technique is fast and accurate, as each unit is assembled and pressed *before* it is cut from the strip set.

Throughout the instructions, each strip set is illustrated, and the project directions specify how to cut and join the strips.

To keep strips straight as you sew, practice what I call anti-directional stitching. This is important when you have three or more strips in a strip set. As you add strips to the set, stitch each new seam in the *opposite* direction from the last one (Diagram 14). This distributes the tension evenly in both directions and keeps the strips from getting warped and wobbly.

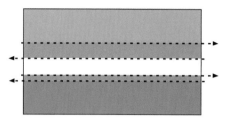

Diagram 14

When the strip sets are assembled and pressed, you will be directed to slice them into segments as shown in Photo C. These segments will then be joined with those cut from other strip sets to make a design unit.

Seminole Patchwork

This technique is the ultimate use of strip piecing, practiced and perfected by the Seminole Indians of Florida. Using a variety of strip sets, segments are rejoined in different combinations to make intricate designs. An example of Seminole patchwork in this book is *Seminole Flower Bed.*

Instructions for sewing strip sets are given with each project, followed by directions to cut the strip sets into segments. In Seminole piecing, specific

points (usually seams) on each segment are designated as match points to align and join adjacent pieces to make an off-set, stair-steplike pieced strip.

With right sides facing, align two segments as directed. Pin and check alignment; then stitch the joining seam. Use assembly-line sewing to save time when joining the many segments this type of patchwork usually requires.

Build on each unit, first making pairs (Diagram 15) and then joining pairs to make a four-segment set. Continue in this manner until the unit reaches its desired length (Diagram 16).

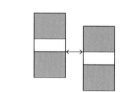

Diagram 15

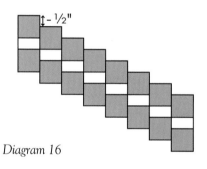

Diagram 16

With the patchwork faceup, align the long edge of an acrylic ruler with the line of the innermost raw edges along the top of the strip (Diagram 17). Use a rotary cutter to trim the excess fabric. Repeat at the bottom edge of the strip. The pieced strip is then ready to stitch into a block or sashing unit.

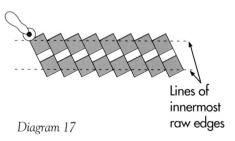

Lines of innermost raw edges

Diagram 17

Putting It All Together

Borders

Project instructions specify whether border corners should be straight or mitered. In all cases, measurements given for border strips include seam allowances and are slightly longer than necessary to allow for piecing variances. Most borders in this book are pieced in order to conserve fabric. Border instructions are included with each project.

Measure First. Because seams may vary and some fabrics may stretch a bit, opposite sides of the assembled quilt top may not measure the same. You should correct this when adding borders.

Measure the length of each side of the quilt top. Trim the assembled border strips to match the *shorter* of the two sides. Join borders to the quilt as described below, easing the longer side of the quilt to fit the border. Measure and trim borders for top and bottom edges in the same manner.

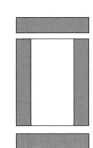

Diagram 18

Match Centers. Side borders are usually added first (Diagram 18). With right sides facing and raw edges aligned, pin the center of one side border strip to the center of one side of the quilt top. Pin the border to the quilt at each end and then pin along the side as desired.

Machine-stitch with the border strip on top. Backstitch at the beginning and end of these long seams. Press the seam allowance toward the border. Add the border to the opposite side; then add top and bottom borders in the same manner.

Marking the Quilting Design

The best time to mark the top is after it is pressed and before it is layered with the batting and backing. The quilting design is an integral part of any quilt, so choose it with care. The hours you spend connecting the layers of your quilt create shadows and depths that bring the quilt to life, so make the design count.

Stencils. Many beautiful designs are available as stencils in today's quilt shops. To transfer a design to the quilt top, position the stencil on the quilt top and mark through the slits in the stencil as shown above. Connect the lines after removing the stencil.

To make your own stencil, use transparent template plastic. Lay the plastic over the design and trace it onto the plastic with a permanent felt-tip pen. Cut the plastic with a craft knife.

Marking a Grid. Many quilts feature a grid of squares or diamonds as a quilting design in the background areas of the quilt. Use an acrylic ruler to mark a grid. To mark the first line of a diagonal grid of squares, align the 45° angle marked on the ruler with the horizontal seam line of the border. Continue marking parallel lines, spacing them as desired (usually 1" apart). Align the 45° angle of the ruler with the seam of the vertical border to mark the first line in the opposite direction. Continue until all background areas are marked as desired.

Quilting Without Marking. Some quilts can be quilted in-the-ditch (right in the seams), outline-quilted (1/4" from the seam line), or echo-quilted (lines of quilting rippling outward from the design like waves on a pond). These methods can be used without any marking at all.

If you are machine quilting, you can use the edge of your presser foot and the seam line as guides for outline quilting. If you are hand quilting, by the time you have pieced a quilt top, your eye may be practiced enough for you to produce straight, even quilting without the guidance of marked lines. If not, use narrow drafting tape as a guideline between the seam and the quilting line.

Other Options. Throughout the U.S., there are businesses that offer quilting services. Using large, industrial quilting machines, they can stitch an overall pattern on your quilt. If quilting is not your thing or if you want to make a lot of quilts in a relatively short time, you should check out a local quilting service. Some have machines that can do more refined or specific quilting such as outline quilting or free-motion quilting. Prices for these services will vary according to the size of the quilt and complexity of the quilting desired.

If you are doing your own machine quilting, you can try your own freehand quilting designs, letting the needle go where the mood takes you. In plain blocks or background areas, you might try stippling—meandering lines of quilting, worked closely together to fill space and outline designs. This can be done by hand or by machine.

Batting

Each quiltmaker has her own preference as to the type of batting she uses. When selecting a batt, read the product information on the batting packages. You need to consider the desired loft, washability, and fiber content.

Loft. Loft is the height or thickness of the batting. To achieve the traditional flat look, choose a low-loft batt. Because it is so thin, this batt is best for hand quilting, particularly if the quilting is elaborate. For tied comforters or fluffy baby quilts quilted by machine, a higher loft is better. Refer to the chart below for the characteristics of some available brands of batting.

Cotton. When using cotton batting, rows of quilting should be no farther than 1" apart, or the cotton will separate and bunch up. Although some people say that it is harder to quilt and provides less warmth, cotton gives the flat look of antique quilts. Cotton batting shrinks slightly when washed, giving that wrinkled look characteristic of old quilts, so always wash quilts with cotton batting in cold water to prevent excessive shrinking.

Polyester. Look for the word "bonded" when selecting polyester batting. Bonding helps to keep the loft of the batt uniform and minimizes the effects of bearding (the migration of loose batting fibers through the quilt top). Polyester batting should be quilted at 3"–6" intervals, depending on the brand. Polyester batting is easy to

Batting Comparison Chart	Fiber	Loft	Finished	Sizes Available				
				Crib 45"x60"	Twin 72"x90"	Full 81"x96"	Queen 90"x108"	King 120"x120"
Mountain Mist								
Bleached Cotton	Cotton	Low	Glazed	-	-	x	x*	-
Blue Ribbon Cotton	Cotton	Very Low	Punched	x	-	-	x	-
Polyester	Polyester	Medium	Glazed	x	x	x	x	x
Quilt-Light	Polyester	Low	Glazed	x	-	x	x	-
Fatt Batt	Polyester	High	Glazed	x	x	x	x	-
Hobbs								
Polydown	Polyester	Medium	Bonded	x	-	x	x	x
Polydown DK	Polyester	Medium	Bonded	-	-	-	x	-
Thermore	Polyester	Low	Bonded	-	-	-	x**	-
Heirloom	Cotton	Low	Punched	-	-	-	x	-
Cloud Lite	Polyester	Low	Bonded	x	x	x	x	x
Cloud Loft	Polyester	High	Bonded	x	-	x	x	x
Fairfield Poly-Fil								
Traditional	Polyester	Medium	Punched	x	x	x	x	x
Extra-Loft	Polyester	High	Bonded	x	x	x	x	x
Ultra-Loft	Polyester	High	Punched	x	x	x	x	-
Low-Loft	Polyester	Low	Bonded	x	-	x	x	x
Hi-Loft	Polyester	High	Bonded	x	-	-	x	-
Cotton Classic	Cotton/Polyester	Low	Bonded	-	-	x	-	-
Crafter's Cabin	Polyester	Medium	Bonded	x	-	x	-	-
Warm & Natural	Cotton	Low	Punched	-	-	-	x	-

*81" x 108"   **Also available in 27" x 45", 54" x 45", and 45"-wide rolls.

needle and can be machine-washed with little shrinkage.

At least one brand of polyester batting is available in gray, which is recommended for quilts with dark fabrics.

Poly/cotton. A blend offers the best of both cotton and polyester batts. It has the flat look of an old quilt, as well as easy needling and resistance to bearding. Soak a blended batt in warm water to preshrink it before using it. Dry the batt in the same manner as you will the finished quilt.

Fleece and Flannel. Fleece is the thinnest of all low-loft batts. It is recommended for use in clothing, table runners, or wall hangings. A single layer of prewashed cotton flannel is good for tablecloths.

Making a Quilt Backing

Most fabric shops sell 90"- and 108"-wide cotton sheeting that eliminates the need to piece narrower fabric, which is often very wasteful. In this book, yardage is given for 44"-wide fabric, but you should always check to see if sheeting is a more practical option.

A quilt wider than 42" requires a pieced backing if you use 44"-wide fabric. For quilts up to 78" wide, you need an amount of fabric equal to two times the desired *length* of the unfinished backing. (The unfinished backing should be at least 3" larger on all sides than the quilt top.)

The simplest method of making a backing is to cut the fabric in half widthwise (Diagram 19) and then sew the two panels together lengthwise. The result is a backing with a vertical center seam. Press the seam allowances to one side.

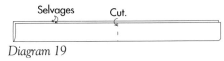

Diagram 19

If the quilt is wider than 78", it is most economical to cut the fabric into three lengths that are the *width* of the quilt, plus 6". Join the three panels so that the seams are horizontal to the quilt, rather than vertical.

Layering

After the quilt top and backing are made, the next steps are layering and basting in preparation for quilting.

Prepare a large working surface where you can spread out the quilt—a large table, two tables pushed together, or an uncarpeted floor. Center the backing wrong side up on the work surface and secure it tautly on all sides with masking tape. Place the batting (which has been out of its package for several days so it can "relax") on top of the backing, smoothing away wrinkles and lumps.

Lay the quilt top wrong side down on top of the batting and backing. Make sure edges of the backing and quilt top are parallel (Diagram 20).

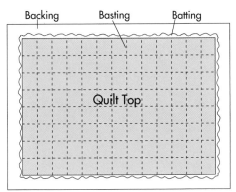

Diagram 20

Basting

Knot a long strand of sewing thread and use a long (darning) needle for basting. Begin basting in the center of the quilt and baste out toward the edges. The basting stitches should cover enough of the quilt so that the layers will not shift during quilting (Diagram 20).

For machine quilting, use 1" nickel-plated safety pins for basting so there will be no basting threads to catch on the presser foot. Insert the pins every 2"–3" all over the quilt. Wait to close the safety pins until they are all in place, as the closing action can pucker the backing if you close as you go. When the safety pins are in place, remove the masking tape at the quilt edges. Gently, but firmly, tug the backing as you close the safety pins so that you do not pin any pleats underneath. Safety pins can be used by hand quilters, too.

The Quilting Stitch

Quilting is the process of stitching the three layers of a quilt together, by hand or machine, usually using a straight or running stitch. Consider the design, intended use, and your personal preference to decide whether to quilt a project by hand or machine.

Hand Quilting. Stitches should be evenly spaced, with the spaces between stitches about the same length as the stitches themselves. The number of stitches per inch is less important than the uniformity of the stitching. Don't worry if you take only five or six stitches per inch; just be consistent throughout the project.

1. Start by placing your work in a frame or hoop. Sit in a comfortable chair near good light. Have a thimble, scissors, thread, and quilting needles at hand. Position yourself so that the line of quilting angles from upper right to lower left, so that you can quilt toward yourself. (Reverse directions if you are left-handed.)

2. Use a short needle called a "between." If you are a beginner, try a size 7 or 8; because betweens are much shorter than other sewing needles, they may feel awkward at first. As your skill increases, a smaller needle will help you make smaller stitches.

3. To keep the thread from snarling as you stitch, thread the needle *before* you cut the thread from the spool. Cut an 18"–24" length and make a small knot in the cut end.

4. Insert the needle through the quilt top, about 1" from the quilting line. Slide the needle through the batting, but do not pierce the backing. Bring the needle up at the beginning point and pull the thread until the knot stops on the surface. Tug the thread gently to pop the knot through the top into the batting. If it does not slip through, use the needle to gently separate the fabric threads and then tug again.

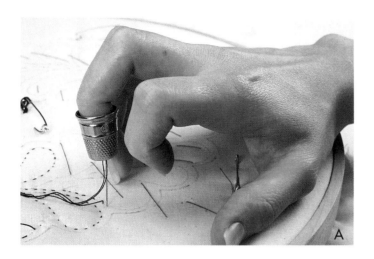

5. With your non-sewing hand under the quilt, insert the needle with the point straight down as shown in Photo A, about 1/16" from the start. With your underneath finger, feel for the point as the needle comes through the backing. With practice, you will be able to find the point without pricking your finger.

6. Push the fabric up from below as you rock the needle to a nearly horizontal position. Using the thumb of your sewing hand as shown in Photo B and the underneath hand, pinch a little hill in the fabric and push the tip of the needle back through the quilt top.

7. Rock the needle to an upright position to take another stitch before pulling it through. At first, load only two or three stitches on the needle. As you gain experience, try more stitches at one time, but take no more than a quarter-needleful before pulling the needle through.

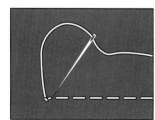

Diagram 21

8. End the thread when you have 6" left. Tie a knot in the thread close to the quilt surface (Diagram 21). Pop the knot through the top as before, and clip the tail. Rethread the needle and continue quilting.

When quilting is complete, trim backing and batting the same size as the quilt top.

Machine Quilting. For machine quilting, the backing and batting should be 4" larger all around than the quilt top, because quilting pushes the quilt top fabric outward.

Thread the bobbin with sewing thread (not quilting thread) in a color to match the backing. Use a top thread color to match the quilt top or use monofilament (clear nylon thread). Set the machine to make a long stitch—6 to 8 stitches per inch.

A walking foot is most helpful for machine quilting. It feeds all the quilt's layers through the machine at the same speed. It is possible to machine-quilt without this foot, but it will be easier *with* it.

1. Roll both sides of the quilt toward the center. Leave a center section open, securing the rolled sides with bicycle clips.

2. Start stitching at the top center (Diagram 22). Begin by stitching in place several times to lock the stitches.

Diagram 22

3. Straight-line quilting is the easiest machine quilting. The seam lines for blocks and sashing form a grid across the quilt. These are the longest lines of quilting, and they should be done first. Quilt down the center, from edge to edge.

4. Begin the next row at the bottom. Alternating the direction of quilting lines keeps the layers from shifting. Continue quilting half of the quilt, unrolling it until you reach the edge.

5. Remove the quilt from the machine and reroll the completed side. Turn the quilt and work out from the center again to complete the quilting on the other half.

6. When you have completed the vertical quilting lines, reroll the quilt in the other direction to quilt the horizontal lines in the same manner. When quilting is complete, trim backing and batting to the same size as the quilt top.

7. Some projects do not have vertical and horizontal quilting lines. Instead, the lines may be diagonal or follow the patchwork. Always machine-quilt the longest lines first.

Binding

The best binding for quilts is a double-layer binding often called French-fold binding. Double-layer binding wears well and is easy to make and apply. An even-feed or walking foot is helpful when sewing binding to the quilt.

Straight-grain strips. Most instructions in this book allow enough fabric to cut 3"-wide straight-grain strips that will yield a ⅝"-wide finished binding. Each project states the number and width of the strips required to make binding for that quilt.

Straight-grain binding is best for quilts with straight sides. Make bias binding only when your quilt is an irregular shape or has rounded corners.

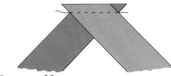

Diagram 23

Preparation. Join straight-grain binding strips end-to-end. Join bias strip ends on the diagonal as shown in Diagram 23. Trim points from the seam allowances.

With wrong sides facing, press the binding strip in half lengthwise so that it is 1½" wide. Roll up the binding as you go to make it easy to handle.

Application. Binding is applied to the front of the quilt first. Begin anywhere on the edge of the quilt except at a corner.

1. Matching raw edges, lay the binding on the quilt. Fold down the corner of the binding at a 45° angle, align the raw edges, and pin (Diagram 24).

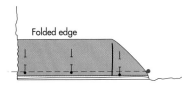

Diagram 24

2. Starting at the folded end, machine-stitch the binding to the quilt. Stop stitching ¼" from the corner and backstitch. Fold the binding strip diagonally away from the quilt, making a 45° angle (Diagram 25).

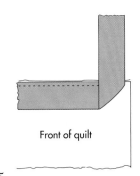

Diagram 25

3. Fold the binding strip straight down along the next side to be sewn, making a pleat in the corner (Diagram 26). Position the needle at the seam line of the new side, ¼" from the top edge. Make a few stitches, backstitch, and then stitch the seam. Continue around the quilt. Overlap the binding end over the beginning fold and stitch 2" beyond it. Trim any excess binding.

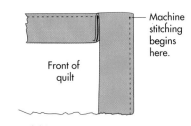

Diagram 26

4. Turn the binding over the raw edge of the quilt. Slipstitch the fold in place on the back, using thread that matches the binding.

5. At each corner, fold the binding to form a miter. Handstitch the miters closed if desired (Diagram 27).

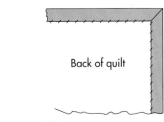

Diagram 27

Option for nonmitered corners. Prepare binding as for mitered binding. With raw edges aligned, match binding to one side of the quilt from corner to corner. Machine-stitch binding to that side; trim the excess binding. Repeat for the opposite side. Turn the binding over the raw edge and slipstitch it on the back, using thread to match binding.

To bind the top edge of the quilt, begin at the top left corner. Matching edges of binding and quilt, wrap 1" of binding around the corner to the back (Diagram 28) and pin it. On the front, pin the binding across the top edge to the opposite corner. Trim the excess binding, leaving 1" to wrap around the corner to the back. Stitch the binding to the quilt. Turn the binding over to the back, encasing raw edges and corners. Slipstitch the binding to the backing. Repeat for the bottom edge.

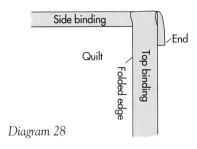

Diagram 28

Hanging Sleeve

Quilts that are hung for display often have a sleeve on the back. A dowel or curtain rod, slipped through the sleeve, can hang from wall brackets.

1. Cut a 6"-wide fabric piece that measures the width of the quilt plus 2". Turn under ¼" hem on both ends and press; then turn under 1" more. Press and topstitch.

2. With wrong sides facing, join long edges. Press the seam allowances open, centering the seam on one side of the tube. With the seam facing the quilt backing, place the sleeve just below the binding at the top of the quilt, centering it between the sides (Diagram 29).

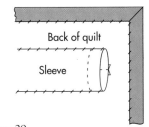

Diagram 29

3. Slipstitch the top and bottom edges of the sleeve to the quilt backing only, making sure no stitches go through to the quilt top.

How to Use These Instructions

✔ At the beginning of each project, icons identify the quick-piecing techniques used to make that quilt. Refer to the general instructions for each technique before beginning the project.

✔ All yardages given are based on 44"/45"-wide fabrics unless otherwise stated.

✔ A color key accompanies each materials list, matching each fabric with the color-coded illustrations given with the project directions.

✔ All seam allowances are ¼". Cutting instructions include seam allowances.

✔ Cutting instructions are given for each fabric. In most cases, the first cutting requirement is a specified number of cross-grain strips. The first cut is indicated by a ♦. Second cuts, indicated by a •, specify how to cut those strips into smaller pieces. The identifying unit number of each piece follows in parentheses. These unit numbers correspond to the assembly diagram given for each block. For pieces used in more than one unit, several unit numbers may be given. When organizing the pieces in zip-top bags, be sure to label all unit numbers.

✔ The largest pieces, such as sashings and borders, are usually cut first to be sure that you have enough fabric for the remaining cuts.

✔ To eliminate waste, you may be instructed to cut some pieces from a first-cut strip and then cut the strip down to a narrower width to cut additional pieces.

✔ Cutting instructions identify triangle-square units in the same way, but the piece cut is large enough to sew the grid as directed in the project instructions. Each piece allows for a border around the grid at least ¾" wide.

✔ Cutting and piecing instructions are given in a logical step-by-step progression. Follow this order in all cases to avoid confusion.

✔ Every project has one or more block designs. Each block is illustrated in the instructions, showing the numbered units and fabric colors.

✔ For most blocks, an assembly diagram is also given. Each numbered unit is isolated, with + symbols indicating how units are joined. Follow the instructions to be sure to join units in the proper sequence. Some of the more complex blocks are further divided into sections, which are joined according to instructions.

✔ Some blocks have mirror images. Illustrations for both blocks are given for assembly reference.

✔ In the assembly diagram, each unit has an identifying number. The main part of the unit is indicated with the number only. A diagonal line represents a seam where a diagonal corner or end is attached. Each diagonal piece is numbered with the main unit number plus a letter (such as 1a).

✔ Some units have multiple diagonal corners or ends. When these are the same size and cut from the same fabric, the identifying letter is the same.

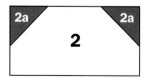

✔ If the unit has multiple diagonal pieces that are different in size or color, the letters are different. These pieces are joined to the main unit in alphabetical order.

✔ Triangle-squares are shown with a diagonal line separating the triangles and the unit number in the center of the square.

✔ For pieced, or double, diagonal corners, join the first one to the main unit. Press the seam allowances; then join the second diagonal corner.

✔ Each strip set is identified and illustrated. The segments to cut from each set are also shown.

✔ Piecing instructions for blocks are given for one block. Make the number of blocks specified to complete the project as shown or the number needed for projects of your own design, such as accessory pillows or wall hangings.

✔ Practice the quick-cutting and quick-piecing methods with scrap fabrics before beginning a project. Refer to assembly diagrams frequently, following the unit identification system carefully. Organizing your work as suggested will minimize confusion and save time.

✔ The quilts in this book were made in a relatively short time because of the quick methods used. But remember that each person works at his or her own speed—don't feel like you're racing the clock to get your quilt finished. Relax and enjoy the creative process.

Rotary Cutter
Quilt Collection

25

Tuxedo Cats

All of the twenty spiffy felines, posed in a garden of hearts and flowers, are made using the same fabrics and techniques, but half are mirror image. To create the interwoven pattern, follow assembly diagrams carefully to position blocks correctly. Make extra blocks to create decorative throw pillows.

Quick-Piecing Techniques:

Finished Size

Blocks: 20 cat blocks, 15" square
     49 flower blocks, 5" x 15"
     30 heart blocks, 5" square

Quilt: 85" x 105"

Materials

	Fabric I (gray-on-black print)	3½ yards
	Fabric II (gray print)	3½ yards
	Fabric III (white-on-white print)	2 yards
	Fabric IV (peach mini-print)	4 yards
	Fabric V (dark green print)	2 yards
	Fabric VI (medium green solid)	¾ yard
	Fabric VII (burgundy solid)	½ yard
	Fabric VIII (barn red print)	½ yard
	Backing fabric	8 yards

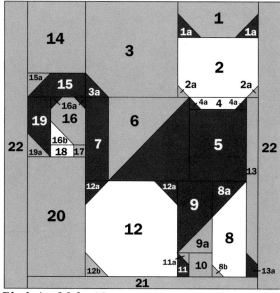

Block A—Make 10.

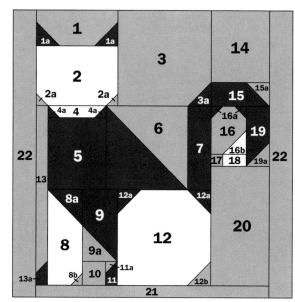

Block B—Make 10.

Cutting

From Fabric I, cut:
- Ten 3" x 42" strips for binding.
- Seven 2⅜" x 42" strips.
  From these, cut:
  - Eighty 2⅜" squares (A-8a, B-8a, H-1b).
  - Twenty 2⅜" x 4¼" (A-9, B-9).
- Four 4¼" x 42" strips.
  From these, cut:
  - Twenty 3⅝" x 4¼" (A-5, B-5).
  - Sixty 1⅜" x 4¼" (H-2).
- Twelve 1¾" x 42" strips.
  From these, cut:
  - 100 1¾" squares (A-1a, A-3a, A-12a, B-1a, B-3a, B-12a).
  - Forty 1¾" x 3⅝" (A-15, A-19, B-15, B-19).
  - Twenty 1¾" x 4⅞" (A-7, B-7).
  - Forty 1⅛" x 1¾" (A-11, A-13a, B-11, B-13a).
- Fourteen 1⅛" x 42" strips.
  From these, cut:
  - Sixty 1⅛" x 5½" (H-3).
  - 200 1⅛" squares (A-4a, A-16a, B-4a, B-16a, H-1a).
- One 12" x 28" for triangle-squares (A-6, B-6).

From Fabric II, cut:
- Five 2⅜" x 42" strips.
  From these, cut:
  - Twenty 2⅜" x 4⅞" (A-1, B-1).
  - Twenty 2⅜" x 3" (A-16, B-16).
  - Twenty 2⅜" squares (A-9a, B-9a).

- Twenty 1¾" x 42" strips.
  From these, cut:
  - Forty 1¾" x 15½" (A-22, B-22).
  - Eighty 1¾" squares (A-10, A-12b, A-15a, A-19a, B-10, B-12b, B-15a, B-19a).
- Six 3⅝" x 42" strips.
  From these, cut:
  - Twenty 3⅝" x 6¾" (A-20, B-20).
  - Twenty 3⅝" x 4¼" (A-14, B-14).
- Fourteen 1⅛" x 42" strips.
  From these, cut:
  - Twenty 1⅛" x 9¼" (A-13, B-13).
  - Twenty 1⅛" x 13" (A-21, B-21).
  - 100 1⅛" squares (A-2a, A-8b, A-11a, A-17, B-2a, B-8b, B-11a, B-17).
- Three 5½" x 42" strips.
  From these, cut:
  - Twenty 5½" squares (A-3, B-3).
- One 12" x 28" for triangle-squares (A-6, B-6).

From Fabric III, cut:
- Seven 3⅝" x 42" strips.
  From these, cut:
  - Twenty 3⅝" x 4⅞" (A-2, B-2).
  - Sixty 2⅜" x 3⅝" (H-1).
  - Twenty 1⅛" x 3⅝" (A-4, B-4).
- Four 5½" x 42" strips.
  From these, cut:
  - Twenty 5½" squares (A-12, B-12).
  - Twenty 2⅜" x 5½" (A-8, B-8).

- Two 1¾" x 42" strips.
  From these, cut:
  - Twenty 1¾" squares (A-16b, B-16b).
  - Twenty 1⅛" x 1¾" (A-18, B-18).

From Fabric IV, cut:
- Fourteen 2⅜" x 42" strips.
  From these, cut:
  - Forty-nine 2⅜" squares (F-5).
  - Ninety-eight 1¾" x 2⅜" (F-3, F-8).
  - Ninety-eight 2⅜" x 3" (F-12, F-14).
- Twelve 1¾" x 42" strips.
  From these, cut:
  - Forty-nine 1¾" x 3" (F-6).
  - 196 1¾" squares (F-9a, F-17a).
- Seventy-one 1⅛" x 42" strips.
  From these, cut:
  - Ninety-eight 1⅛" x 15½" (F-19).
  - Ninety-eight 1⅛" x 3" (F-11, F-15).
  - Ninety-eight 1⅛" x 4¼" (F-18).
  - 539 1⅛" squares (F-1a, F-2a).

From Fabric V, cut:
- Six 3" x 42" strips.
  From these, cut:
  - Ninety-eight 1⅛" x 3" (F-10, F-16).
  - Forty-nine 2⅜" x 3" (F-13).
- Four 2⅜" x 42" strips.
  From these, cut:
  - Forty-nine 1⅛" x 2⅜" (F-4).
  - Forty-nine 1¾" x 2⅜" (F-7).

- ◆ Two 1⅛" x 42" strips.
  From these, cut:
  - • Forty-nine 1⅛" squares (F-2b).
- ◆ One 26" square for triangle-squares (F-9, F-17).

From Fabric VI, cut:
- ◆ One 26" square for triangle-squares (F-9, F-17).

From Fabric VII, cut:
- ◆ Six 2⅜" x 42" strips.
  From these, cut:
  - • Ninety-eight 2⅜" squares (F-1).

From Fabric VIII, cut:
- ◆ Six 2⅜" x 42" strips.
  From these, cut:
  - • Ninety-eight 2⅜" squares (F-1, F-2).

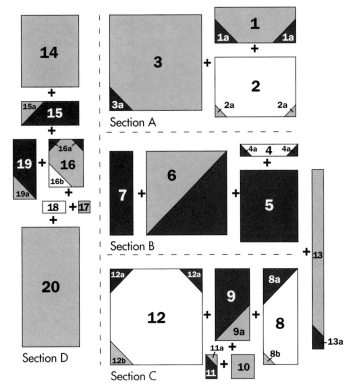

Block A Assembly

Piecing the Cat Blocks

1. Referring to Block A Assembly diagram, use diagonal-corner technique to make one each of units 1, 2, 3, 4, 8, 9, 11, 12, 15, 16, and 19. Use diagonal-end technique to make one of Unit 13.

2. To make Unit 6, see page 17 for instructions on half-square triangles. On wrong side of 12" x 28" piece of Fabric II, draw a 2 x 5-square grid of 5¼" squares. With right sides facing, match marked fabric with 12" x 28" piece of Fabric I. Stitch grid as directed on page 17. Cut 20 triangle-squares from the grid, one for each cat block.

3. To assemble Section A, join units 1 and 2; then add Unit 3 as shown.

4. To assemble Section B, begin by joining units 4 and 5. Add Unit 6 and then Unit 7 as shown.

5. To assemble Section C, begin by joining units 10 and 11. Join this combined unit to bottom of Unit 9; then add Unit 8 and Unit 12 to each side as shown.

6. Join sections B and C. Join Unit 13 to side of combined sections as shown.

7. To assemble Section D, begin by joining units 17 and 18. Add Unit 16 to top edge of combined unit; then join Unit 19 to side as shown. Join units 14

and 15; then join both combined units. Complete Section D by joining Unit 20 at bottom.

8. Join Section A to top of combined BC unit. Join Section D to side of ABC.

9. Join Unit 21 at bottom of block; then join one of Unit 22 to each side as shown in Block A diagram.

10. Block B is made in the same manner as Block A, but it is a mirror image. Most units are made exactly the same as for Block B, but some require opposite positioning of fabric colors and angles. Be sure to consult Block B diagram carefully when making units 8, 9, 11, 12, 13, 16, and 19.

Piecing the Heart Block

1. Use diagonal-corner technique to make two of Unit 1. *Note that these are mirror images, so be careful to position each 1b piece as shown.*

2. Join the two halves of Unit 1 as shown. Add a Unit 2 strip to top and bottom edges of Unit 1. Join one of Unit 3 to each side as shown.

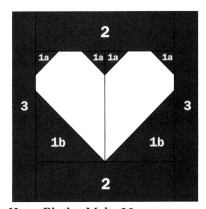

Heart Block—Make 30.

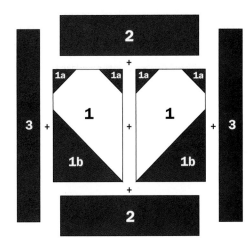

Heart Block Assembly

Piecing the Flower Block

1. Referring to Flower Block Assembly diagram, use diagonal-corner technique to make two of Unit 1 with Fabric VII centers and one of Unit 1 with Fabric VIII center. Make one of Unit 2. Join these units as shown to complete flower section.

2. The combined 6-7-8 unit is made using diagonal-end technique as shown below. Begin by joining pieces 6 and 7; trim excess fabric from seam allowance and press seam. Add piece 8 to end of combined unit in the same manner. Trim and press.

3. Make combined 12-13-14 unit in the same manner.

4. To make units 9 and 17, see page 17 for instructions on half-square triangles. On wrong side of 26" square of Fabric VI, draw a 7 x 7-square grid of 3⅜" squares. With right sides facing, match marked fabric with square of Fabric V. Stitch grid as directed on page 17. Cut 98 triangle-squares from the grid. Add diagonal corners (9a, 17a) to each triangle-square as shown below. When completed, designate 49 squares as Unit 9 and 49 as Unit 17.

5. Join units 3, 4, and 5 in a row; then join assembled 6-7-8 unit to bottom edge of this row. Join this combined unit to bottom of flower section.

6. Join units 9, 10, and 11 in a row; then assemble another row of units 15, 16, and 17 as shown. Join remaining assembled units to flower block as shown.

7. Join one of Unit 18 at top and bottom of block; then join a Unit 19 strip to each side as shown in Flower Block diagram.

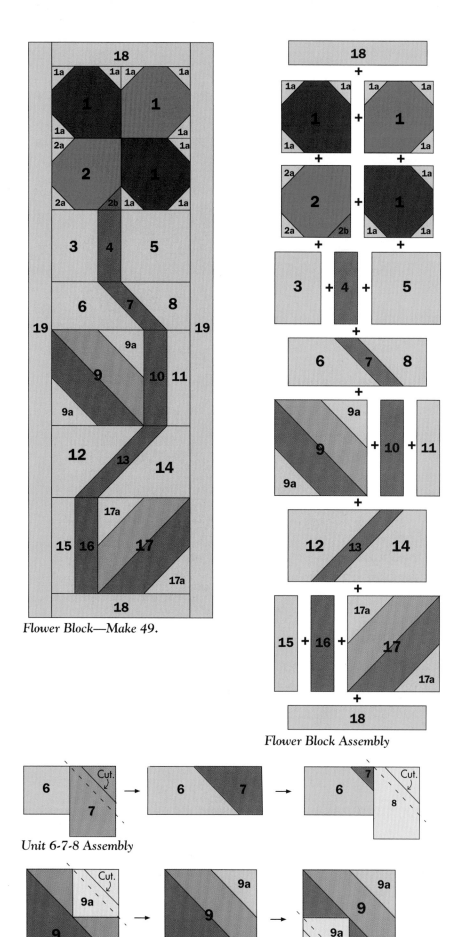

Flower Block—Make 49.

Flower Block Assembly

Unit 6-7-8 Assembly

Unit 9-17 Assembly

Quilt Assembly

1. Referring to Row Assembly diagrams, join blocks in rows as shown. Make three of Row 1 and two of Row 2. Join remaining flower and heart blocks in a horizontal row as shown at top of Row 2.

2. Starting with a Row 1, join all rows, alternating row types in a 1-2-1-2-1 sequence.

3. Join remaining sashing row to bottom of last row. *Note:* The positions of the flowers follow a regular pattern when assembled as shown in the Row diagrams. But when this quilt was made, one flower block got turned the wrong way. Can you find the one that breaks the pattern? Hint: It's at one of the corners.

Quilting and Finishing

Outline-quilt patchwork and borders or quilt as desired.

Make 380" of binding. See page 23 for directions on making and applying straight-grain binding.

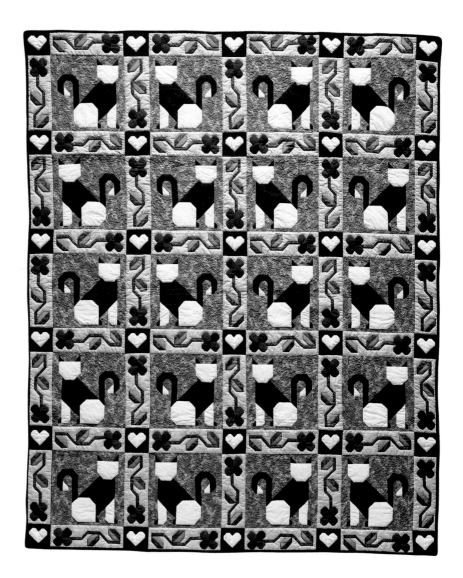

Row 1

Row 2

Row Assembly

High Summer

A meadow of luxurious green surrounds bright summer flowers, interpreted in an easy-to-piece geometric design. The optical illusion of circles within the different-colored blocks creates the sense of separate beds of pretty posies. The blocks are random combinations of light, medium, and dark values. As you sew, vary the placement of values within the blocks any way you like to create a garden uniquely yours.

Quick-Piecing Techniques:

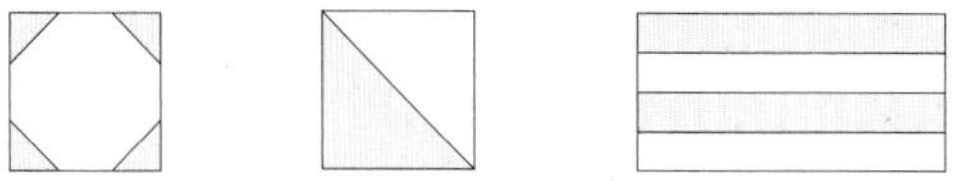

Finished Size

Blocks: 15 blocks, 20" square   Quilt: 68" x 112"

Materials

	Fabric I (15 assorted light solids)	⅛ yard each
	Fabric II (15 assorted light-medium solids)	⅛ yard each
	Fabric III (15 assorted medium solids)	⅛ yard each
	Fabric IV (15 assorted dark solids)	⅛ yard each
	Fabric V (light green solid)	2¾ yards
	Fabric VI (medium green solid)	2 yards
	Fabric VII (dark green solid)	5¼ yards
	Backing fabric	6¾ yards

Cutting

Refer to diagrams on page 34 to identify blocks and units designated in cutting list.

From each Fabric I, cut:
♦ One 2" x 42" strip.
   From this, cut:
   • One 2" x 4" (4).
   • Two 2" squares (5a).
   • One 2" x 8" (8).

From each Fabric II, cut:
♦ One 2" x 42" strip.
   From this, cut:
   • Two 2" squares (11a).
   • One 2" x 4" (12).
   • One 2" x 8" (13).

From each Fabric III, cut:
♦ One 3⅞" x 42" strip.
   From this, cut:
   • One 3⅞" square (10).
   • Two 2" x 8" (8, 13).
   • Four 2" squares (9a).

From each Fabric IV, cut:
♦ One 2½" x 42" strip.
   From this, cut:
   • One 2½" square (15).
   • Two 2" x 4" (4, 12).
   • Four 2" squares (6a).

From Fabric V, cut:
♦ Twenty 1¼" x 42" strips for mitered borders.
♦ Fifty-two 1¼" x 42" strips (14, sashing).

From Fabric VI, cut:
♦ Three 14⅝" x 42" strips.
   From these, cut:
   • Fifteen 7⅜" x 14⅝" (2, 3). Cut these rectangles as shown in Cutting diagram to get eight triangles from each piece for a total of 120 triangles.*
♦ Two 18" squares for triangle-squares (1).

From Fabric VII, cut:
♦ Ten 3" x 42" strips for binding.
♦ Ten 1" x 42" strips for mitered borders.

♦ Three 14⅝" x 42" strips.
  From these, cut:
  • Fifteen 7⅜" x 14⅝" (2, 3).
    Cut these rectangles as shown in
    Cutting diagram to get eight trian-
    gles from each piece for a total of
    120 triangles.*

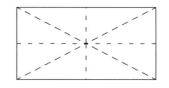

Cutting

♦ Two 2½" x 42" strips.
  From these, cut:
  • Thirty 2½" squares for sashing.
♦ Twenty-six 1" x 42" strips
  (14, sashing).
♦ One 18" x 42" strip.
  From this, cut:
  • Two 18" squares for triangle-
    squares (1).
♦ Fifteen 2" x 42" strips.
  From these, cut:
  • 180 2" x 3½" (5, 6, 9, 11).

♦ Three 3½" x 42" strips.
  From these, cut:
  • Thirty 3½" squares (7).
♦ Two 3⅞" x 42" strips.
  From these, cut:
  • Fifteen 3⅞" squares (10).

* *Note:* Each rectangle yields eight
triangles, four of which point to the left
and four to the right. Designate "lefties"
for Unit 2 and "righties" for Unit 3.
Trim ⅞" from tip of all these triangles.

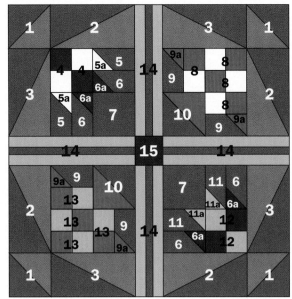

High Summer Block—Make 15.

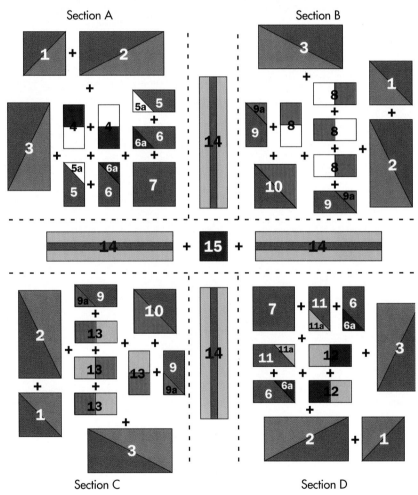

Block Assembly

Piecing the Blocks

1. See page 17 for instructions on half-square triangles. On wrong side of each 18" square of Fabric VI, draw a 4 x 4-square grid of 3⅞" squares. With right sides facing, match each marked fabric with an 18" square of Fabric VII. Stitch each grid as directed on page 17. Cut 32 triangle-squares from each grid (60 for Unit 1 and four extra).

2. Referring to Block diagram, join lefty triangles of fabrics VI and VII to make Unit 2. The resulting rectangle will measure 3½" x 6½". Make 60 of Unit 2. Using righties, make 60 of Unit 3 in the same manner.

3. For each block, join one 2" x 4" piece of Fabric I and one 2" x 4" piece of Fabric IV to make a strip set. From this, cut two 2"-wide segments for Unit 4. Repeat, using 2" x 4" pieces of fabrics II and IV, to make two of Unit 12.

4. For each block, join one 2" x 8" strip of Fabric I and one 2" x 8" strip of Fabric III to make a strip set. From this, cut four 2"-wide segments for Unit 8. Repeat, using 2" x 8" strips of fabrics II and III, to make four of Unit 13.

5. For each block, use diagonal-corner technique to make two each of units 5 and 11 and four each of units 6 and 9.

6. For Unit 10, draw a diagonal line on wrong side of each 3⅞" square of Fabric III. With wrong sides facing, match each marked square with a square of Fabric VII. Stitch a ¼" seam on both sides of drawn line. Cut on drawn line to get two triangle-squares. Make two of Unit 10 for each block.

7. Referring to Unit 14 as shown in Block Assembly diagram, join long strips of fabrics V and VII. Make 26 of this strip set. Cut four 9½"-wide segments from each strip set (104 total). Set aside 60 segments for Unit 14 and 44 segments for quilt sashing.

8. To assemble Section A, begin by joining two of Unit 4 as shown in Block Assembly diagram, turning one unit upside down. Join one Unit 5 and one Unit 6; then add this to bottom of Unit 4 pair. To assemble right half of flower, join remaining units 5 and 6 to Unit 7 in a vertical row as shown. Join halves to complete flower. Join Unit 3 to left side of flower; press seam allowances toward Unit 3. Join units 1 and 2 as shown; press seam allowances toward Unit 2. Join 1-2 unit to top of flower to complete Section A.

9. To assemble Section B, join three of Unit 8 in a vertical row, turning units as shown in Block Assembly diagram. Join one of Unit 9 to bottom of this row. Join remaining Unit 8 to remaining Unit 9; then add this to top of Unit 10, positioning triangle-square as shown. Join both rows to complete flower. Join Unit 3 to top of flower; then press seam allowances toward Unit 3. Join units 1 and 2 as shown; press seam allowances toward Unit 2. Join 1-2 unit to right side of flower section to complete Section B.

10. To assemble Section C, join three of Unit 13 in a vertical row, turning units as shown in Block Assembly diagram. Join one of Unit 9 to top of this row. Join remaining Unit 13 to remaining Unit 9; then add this to bottom of Unit 10, positioning triangle-square as shown. Join both rows to complete flower. Join Unit 3 to bottom of flower; then press seam allowances toward Unit 3. Join units 1 and 2 as shown; press seam allowances toward Unit 2. Join 1-2 unit to left side of flower to complete Section C.

11. To assemble Section D, begin by joining two of Unit 12 as shown. Join one Unit 11 and one Unit 6; then add this combined unit to left side of Unit 12 pair. To assemble top of flower, join remaining units 6 and 11 to Unit 7 in a row as shown. Join halves to complete flower. Join Unit 3 to right side of flower; press seam allowances toward Unit 3. Join units 1 and 2 as shown; press seam allowances toward Unit 2. Join 1-2 unit to bottom of flower section to complete Section D.

12. Referring to Block Assembly diagram, join sections A and B with one Unit 14 between them. Press seam allowances toward Unit 14. Join sections C and D in the same manner.

13. Join Unit 15 between two of Unit 14 as shown. Stitch top and bottom halves of block to opposite sides of 14-15 unit as shown in Block Assembly diagram. Press seam allowances toward Unit 14. Make 15 High Summer blocks.

Quilt Assembly

1. Referring to Sashing Unit diagram, join all remaining sashing strips in pairs with a Fabric VII sashing square between each pair. You will have eight sashing squares left over.

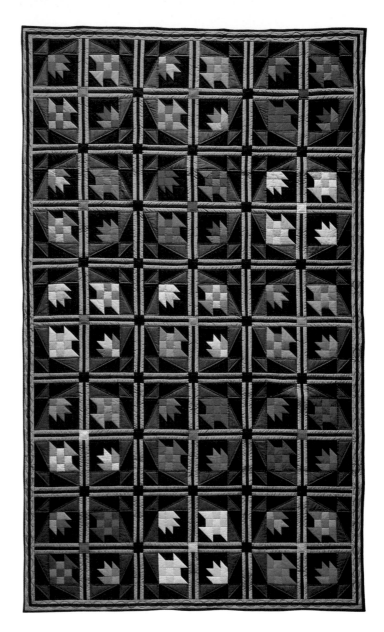

2. Referring to quilt photograph, arrange blocks as desired in five horizontal rows of three blocks each. Position a sashing unit between blocks in each row as shown. Join blocks in rows.

3. Referring to photograph, assemble remaining sashing units in four horizontal rows of three units each, adding sashing squares between units.

4. Assemble block rows and sashing rows, alternating row types as shown in photograph.

5. To assemble borders, join border strip of fabrics V and VII in strip sets in the same manner as for sashing. Join three strip sets end-to-end for each side border and two strips sets each for top and bottom borders.

6. Matching centers of each quilt side and border strip, join borders to assembled quilt top. Miter border corners.

Quilting and Finishing

Outline-quilt patchwork and borders or quilt as desired.

Make 380" of binding. See page 23 for directions on making and applying straight-grain binding.

Sashing Unit

Country Hearts

Lavish fringe decorates the edges of this linen throw. When made with cotton fabrics, it can be bound traditionally to make a cozy lap quilt. The combination of two solids and one print makes the fabric selection easy in any color scheme.

Quick-Piecing Techniques:

Finished Size
Blocks: 24 blocks, 11" square   Throw: 48" x 70", plus fringe

Materials*

Fabric I (cranberry solid)		2¼ yards
Fabric II (cranberry plaid)		1⅜ yards
Fabric III (cream solid)		2½ yards
Backing fabric		2⅛ yards

* Throw pictured is made with upholstery linen. Yardages given are for 54"-wide linen. To make the same size throw with 44"-wide cotton fabric, add ¾ yard to each fabric.

Cutting
Refer to diagrams on page 38 to identify blocks and units designated in cutting list.

When using 44"-wide fabric, cut additional strips as necessary to cut number of pieces specified.

From Fabric I, cut:
- Two 2½" x 72" lengthwise strips and two 2½" x 46" crossgrain strips for borders.
- Six 1" x 48" strips.
  From these, cut:
  - 288 1" squares (1d, 6a, 9a).
- Three 1¼" x 48" strips.
  From these, cut:
  - Ninety-six 1¼" squares (5).
- Twenty-four 1½" x 48" strips.
  From these, cut:
  - 192 1½" x 2¼" (6b, 9b).
  - 192 1½" x 3½" (7, 11).
- Two 8" x 48" for fringe. (If using cotton fabric, use these pieces to make binding.)

From Fabric II, cut:
- Nine 2" x 54" strips.
  From these, cut:
  - Ninety-six 2" x 3" (1).
  - Ninety-six 2" squares (2).
- Six 1½" x 54" strips.
  From these, cut:
  - 192 1½" squares (1c, 13).
- Five 1" x 54" strips.
  From these, cut:
  - Ninety-six 1" squares (8a).
  - Ninety-six 1" x 1½" (17a).
- Eight 1¼" x 54" strips.
  From these, cut:
  - Ninety-six 1¼" x 1¾" (14).
  - Ninety-six 1¼" x 2½" (16).

From Fabric III, cut:
- Thirty-four 1" x 54" strips.
  From these, cut:
  - 672 1" squares (1a, 2a, 7a, 11a).
  - Ninety-six 1" x 3½" (8).
  - Ninety-six 1" x 1½" (10).
  - Ninety-six 1" x 4" (12).
  - Ninety-six 1" x 2" (17).
- Five 2" x 54" strips.
  From these, cut:
  - Ninety-six 2" x 2½" (1b).
- Six 1¼" x 54" strips.
  From these, cut:
  - Ninety-six 1¼" x 2" (3).
  - Ninety-six 1¼" squares (4).
- Seventeen 1½" x 54" strips.
  From these, cut:
  - 192 1½" x 2¾" (6, 9).
  - Ninety-six 1½" squares (7b).
  - Ninety-six 1½" x 2" (11b).
- Four 1¾" x 42" strips.
  From these, cut:
  - Ninety-six 1¾" squares (15).

Country Hearts Block—Make 24.

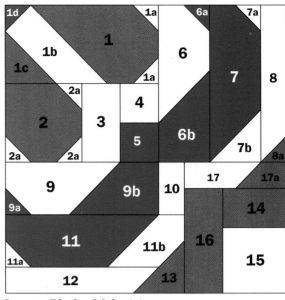

Quarter Block—Make 96.

Piecing the Blocks

1. Referring to Section A of Quarter Block Assembly diagram, use diagonal-corner technique to add 1a pieces to two adjacent corners of piece 1 as shown. Use diagonal-end technique to add 1b to opposite side of piece 1. Join pieces 1c and 1d as diagonal corners. Make four of Unit 1 for each block.

2. Using diagonal-corner technique, make units 2, 7, and 8 as shown. Use diagonal-end technique to make Unit 17.

3. Units 6, 9, and 11 are made with both diagonal-corner and diagonal-end techniques. Make each unit as shown.

4. To assemble Section A, begin by joining units 2 and 3. Join units 4 and 5 and then join it to Unit 3 as shown. Complete Section A by joining Unit 1 to top of assembled section.

5. To make Section B, join units 6, 7, and 8 as shown.

6. To make Section C, begin by joining units 9 and 10 as shown. Next, join Unit 12 to the bottom of Unit 11. Add Unit 13 to the combined 11-12 piece as a diagonal corner. Complete Section C by joining assembled units.

7. To make Section D, begin by joining units 14 and 15. Add Unit 16 to one

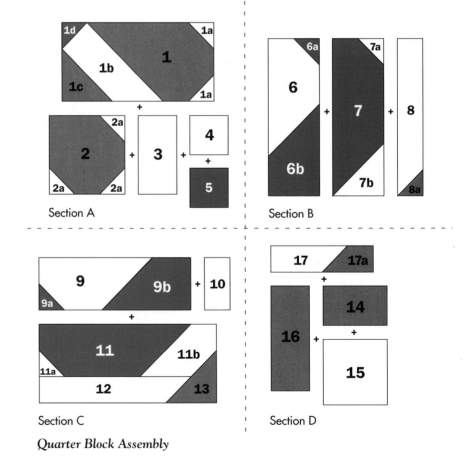

Quarter Block Assembly

side as shown. Complete Section D by adding Unit 17 to top of assembled section.

8. Join sections A and B; then join sections C and D. Complete quarter block by joining top and bottom halves.

9. Make four quarter blocks for each block. Join quarter blocks in pairs, rotating as necessary to position 1d triangles at center. Join pairs to complete each block.

Quilt Assembly

1. Referring to photograph, join completed blocks in six horizontal rows of four blocks each. Join rows.

2. Join short border strips to top and bottom edges of throw. Press seam allowances and trim excess border length. Add side borders in the same manner.

Finishing

1. With right sides facing, center one linen fringe piece at top edge of throw, matching long raw edges. (Throw should extend at least ¼" beyond fringe piece on each side.) Topstitch edge. Repeat at bottom edge of throw. *Note:* If using cotton fabric, omit fringe and set aside this fabric to make binding.

2. With right sides facing, join backing to throw, stitching a ¼" seam around all edges. (Be sure to keep sides of fringe piece out of seam.) Leave a 10" opening in one side for turning. Trim excess backing fabric from seam allowances.

3. Turn throw right side out. Press. Slipstitch opening closed.

4. Fray fringe pieces by pulling out horizontal threads up to the edge of the throw. Separate vertical threads into equal sections as desired. Knot each section close to throw edge.

5. Tie throw with cream-colored pearl cotton if desired.

6. If using cotton fabric, quilt throw as desired. Make 245" of binding. See page 23 for directions on making and applying straight-grain binding.

Paw of the Bear

Traditional Bear's Paw blocks alternate with pieced polar bears in this contemporary version of a favorite classic. The blocks are set on the diagonal, framed with borders of green and strip-pieced patchwork made to look like stacked bricks. We recommend this project for experienced quiltmakers.

Quick-Piecing Techniques:

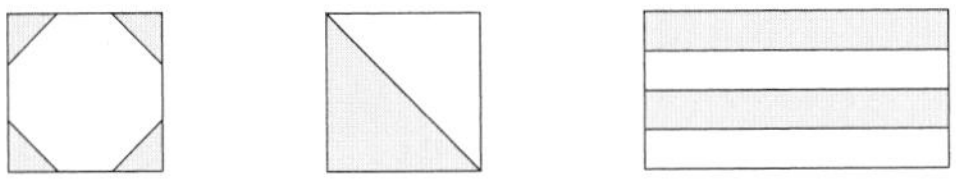

Finished Size
Blocks: 10 Bear blocks, 12" square
       12 Bear's Paw blocks, 12" square

Quilt: 66" x 100"

Materials

▢	Fabric I (white marbled-look print)	1⅜ yards
◼	Fabric II (cranberry print)	2 yards*
▨	Fabric III (green-on-green print)	3¼ yards*
◼	Fabric IV (navy print)	2 yards
▨	Fabric V (light gray mini-print)	2⅝ yards
	Backing fabric	6⅛ yards
	¼"-diameter cording for optional pillow	2⅛ yards

Add ½ yard of these two fabrics for each optional pillow. Other fabrics should have enough scraps left over to make two more bear blocks.

Cutting
Refer to diagrams on page 42 to identify blocks and units designated in cutting list.

From Fabric I, cut:
♦ Three 4" x 42" strips.
  From these, cut:
- Ten 4" x 9⅜" (1).

♦ Two 2" x 42" strips.
  From these, cut:
- Twenty 2" x 3¾" (2).

♦ One 2¼" x 42" strip.
  From this, cut:
- Ten 2¼" squares (3b).

♦ One 2⅝" x 42" strip.
  From this, cut:
- Ten 2⅝" squares (4a).

♦ One 1½" x 42" strip.
  From this, cut:
- Ten 1½" squares (3a).
- Twenty 1¼" squares (3c, 4b).

♦ Two 7" x 42" strips for pieced borders.

From Fabric II, cut:
♦ Ten 1" x 42" strips.
  From these, cut:
- Twenty 1" x 9½" (9).
- Twenty 1" x 10½" (10).

♦ One 6⅞" x 42" strip.
  From this, cut:
- Three 6⅞" squares.
    Cut these in quarters diagonally to get four triangles (7) from each square (includes two extra).
- Three 6⅛" squares.
    Cut these in quarters diagonally to get four triangles (6) from each square (includes two extra).

♦ One 9½" x 42" strip.
  From this, cut:
- Three 9½" squares.
    Cut these in quarters diagonally to get four triangles (22) from each square (includes two extra).
- Three 1½" x 12" and one 1¼" x 12".
    From these, cut:
      • Eighteen 1½" squares (18).
      • Ten 1¼" squares (2a).

♦ Two 3¾" x 42" strips.
  From these and scraps, cut:
- Ten 3¾" x 3⅞" (3).
- Ten 3" x 3¾" squares (4).

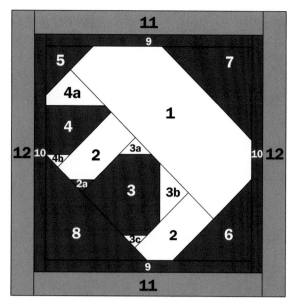

Block A—Make 10.

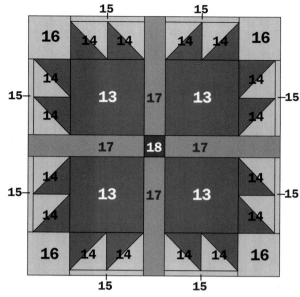

Block B—Make 12.

♦ One 7⅝" x 42" strip.
From this, cut:
  • Three 7⅝" squares.
    Cut these in quarters diagonally to get four triangles (8) from each square (includes two extra).
  • Three 4⅛" squares.
    Cut these in quarters diagonally to get four triangles (5) from each square (includes two extra).
♦ Two 7" x 42" strips for pieced borders.

From Fabric III, cut:
♦ Eight 3" x 42" strips for binding.
♦ Eight 2" x 42" strips for inner border.
From six of these, cut:
  • Six 2" x 29½".
  • Four 2" x 7½".
♦ Eight 3" x 42" strips for outer border.
From two of these, cut:
  • Six 3" x 14".
♦ One 2½" x 42" strip.
From this, cut:
  • Eight 2½" squares for pieced border corners.
♦ Twenty-six 1½" x 42" strips.
From these, cut:
  • Twenty 1½" x 10½" (11).
  • Twenty 1½" x 12½" (12).
  • Ten 1½" x 12" (25).
  • Ten 1½" x 13" (26).
  • Forty-eight 1½" x 6" (17).

From Fabric IV, cut:
♦ Six 4" x 42" strips.
From these, cut:
  • Fifty-four 4" squares (13).
♦ One 25½" x 42" strip.
From this, cut:
  • Four 10" x 25½" for triangle-squares (14).
♦ Two 7" x 42" strips for pieced borders.

From Fabric V, cut:
♦ One 25½" x 42" strip.
From this, cut:
  • Four 10" x 25½" for triangle-squares (14).
♦ Two 4" x 42" strips.
From these, cut:
  • Ninety-six ¾" x 4" (15).
♦ Nine 2½" x 42" strips.
From these, cut:
  • Forty-eight 2½" squares (16).
  • Ten 2½" x 8¾" (23).
  • Ten 2½" x 10¾" (24).
  • Six 2¼" squares (19).
♦ One 8" x 42" strip.
From this, cut:
  • Three 8" squares.
    Cut these in quarters diagonally to get four triangles (20) from each square.
♦ Four 1½" x 42" strips.
From these, cut:
  • Twelve 1½" x 12" (21).
♦ Two 7" x 42" strips for pieced borders.

Piecing the Bear Blocks
1. Referring to Diagram 1, trim two corners of Unit 1 as shown.
2. Using diagonal-corner technique, make one Unit 2 for bear's front leg, joining pieces 2 and 2a as shown in Block A Assembly diagram. Referring to Diagram 2, trim one corner from another 2 piece for back leg.
3. Using diagonal-corner technique, make one of Unit 3.
4. Using diagonal-corner technique, make one of Unit 4 as shown in Diagram 3. Trim bottom left corner as shown.

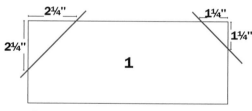

Diagram 1

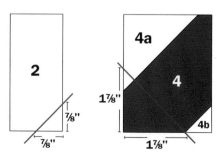

Diagram 2   Diagram 3

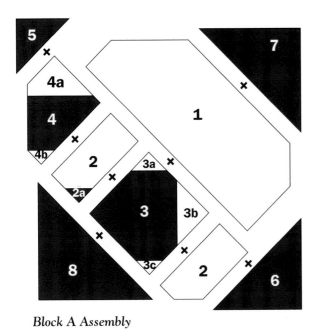

Block A Assembly

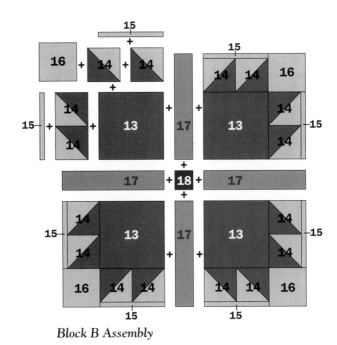

Block B Assembly

5. Join both of Unit 2 to sides of Unit 3 as shown in assembly diagram. Add Unit 4 to end of row as shown.

6. Join Unit 1 to top of combined units. Press seam allowances toward Unit 1.

7. Join triangles 5, 6, 7, and 8 to center unit in numerical order, centering each one carefully. Press seam allowances toward triangles. Bear block should now be 9½" square.

8. Join a Unit 9 to top and bottom edges of block; then add a Unit 10 to each side. Press seam allowances toward edge of block. Join units 11 and 12 in the same manner to complete block. Make 10 of Block A.

Piecing the Bear's Paw Blocks

1. See page 17 for instructions on half-square triangles. On wrong side of each 10" x 25½" pieces of Fabric V, make a 3 x 9-square grid of 2⅝" squares. With right sides facing, match each marked fabric with 10" x 25½" piece of Fabric IV. Stitch each grid as directed on page 17. Cut 54 triangle-squares from each grid (216 total) for Unit 14.

2. Referring to Block B Assembly diagram, join two pairs of Unit 14. (Be careful to position fabrics as shown for each pair.) Add a Unit 15 to top edge of both pairs.

3. Join one 14-15 unit to left side of Unit 13 as shown. Press seam allowances toward Unit 13. Join Unit 16 to left side of remaining 14-15 unit; press seam allowances toward Unit 16. Combine units to complete one paw section.

4. Make four paw sections for each block.

5. Positioning paw sections as shown in assembly diagram, join two blocks in a horizontal row with one Unit 17 between sections. Press seam allowances toward Unit 17.

6. To make center strip, join a Unit 17 to opposite sides of one Unit 18. Press seam allowances toward Unit 18.

7. Combine three sections to complete block. Make 12 of Block B.

Piecing the Setting Triangles

1. Referring to Setting Triangle X Assembly diagram, make six paw sections as you did for Bear's Paw blocks, omitting Unit 15 and substituting Unit 19 for Unit 16.

2. To prevent stretching, stay-stitch diagonal edges of Unit 20 as described on page 13.

3. Positioning paw section as shown in assembly diagram, join Unit 20 to top and left side of each

paw section. Triangles are slightly smaller than paw section, so align corners as shown in assembly diagram. Press seam allowances toward Unit 20.

4. Join one Unit 21 to right side of triangle as shown. Press seam allowances toward Unit 21. Add Unit 18 to another Unit 21; press seam allowance toward Unit 21. Join 18-21 strip to bottom of triangle. Unit 21 will extend past triangles.

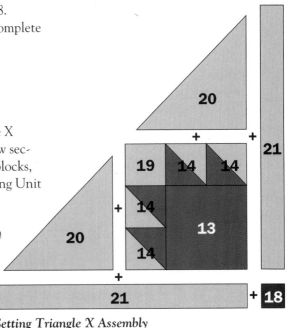

Setting Triangle X Assembly

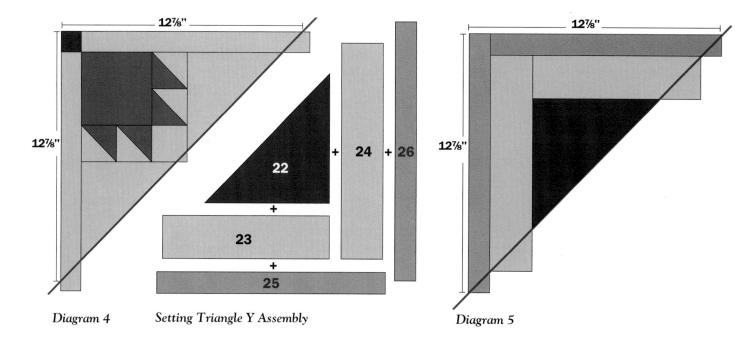

Diagram 4	Setting Triangle Y Assembly

Diagram 5

5. Referring to Diagram 4, align a long ruler with diagonal edges of Unit 20 triangles. With a rotary cutter, trim tip of Unit 19 and ends of each Unit 21 as shown. Legs of trimmed setting triangle should measure approximately 12⅞". Make six of Setting Triangle X.

6. Stay-stitch diagonal edges of Unit 22 triangles.

7. To assemble Setting Triangle Y, join units in numerical order as shown in Setting Triangle Y Assembly diagram.

8. Referring to Diagram 5, align a long ruler with diagonal edge of Unit 22. With a rotary cutter, trim ends of units 23, 24, 25, and 26 as shown. Legs of trimmed setting triangle should measure approximately 12⅞". Make 10 of Setting Triangle Y.

Quilt Assembly

1. Referring to Quilt Assembly diagram and photograph, join blocks and setting triangles in diagonal rows as indicated. Join rows.

2. Join three 2" x 29½" strips of Fabric III end-to-end to make an 87½"-long inner border for each side. Join 2" x 7½" strips to both ends of each 42"-long border strip to make top and bottom borders.

3. Measure quilt top length, measuring through middle rather than along sides. Measuring from center, trim long borders to this length. Sew borders to quilt sides, matching centers and easing as necessary. (See page 15 for tips on easing.) Press seam allowances toward borders.

4. Measure quilt width through middle of quilt top. Trim short borders accordingly; then join borders to top and bottom edges of quilt.

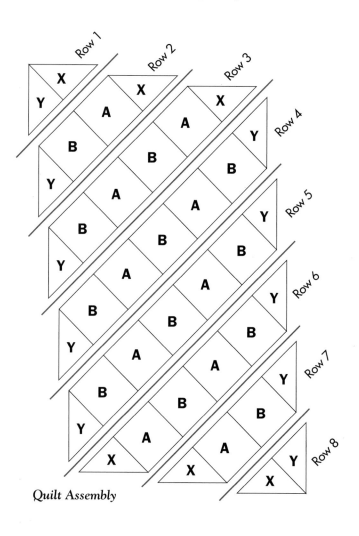

Quilt Assembly

Making the Strip-Pieced Borders

1. Referring to diagram of Strip Set 1, join 7" x 42" strips of fabrics I, IV, V, and II as shown. Make two strip sets. From these, cut twenty-four 2½"-wide segments. (Because this strip set is so wide, you will have to fold it to accommodate your longest ruler.)

2. Join three segments end-to-end, keeping fabrics in the same sequence. Join this strip to top of quilt. Trim pieced strip even with quilt sides.

3. Join two more strip-set segments to end of piece left over from top border. Join this strip to bottom edge in the same manner.

4. Starting with leftover piece, join three more segments end-to-end. Trim bottom of combined strip to match length of quilt side. Join Fabric III border squares to both ends of side border; then join border to one side of quilt. Repeat for opposite quilt side.

5. Repeat steps 2, 3, and 4 to make second row of pieced borders. Join borders to each edge in the same sequence, staggering fabrics so combined borders resemble stacked bricks.

6. Join 3" x 42" strips of Fabric III to both ends of a 14"-long strip to make a 97"-long outer border for each side. Join 3" x 14" strips to both ends of a 42"-long strip to make top and bottom borders.

7. Measure quilt top length as before; then trim side borders to match. Sew borders to quilt sides, matching centers and easing as necessary. Press seam allowances toward borders.

8. Measure quilt width and trim short borders accordingly. Join borders to top and bottom edges of quilt.

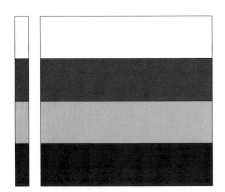

Strip Set 1—Make 2.

Quilting and Finishing

The quilt shown is outline-quilted around patchwork, with haunches and an ear added to each bear. The same bear outline is quilted in Setting Triangle Y. A pawprint is quilted in each paw section. Concentric triangles fill the sides of each Setting Triangle X. The three outer borders are quilted with parallel lines, spaced 2" apart, that are perpendicular to the quilt edges. Make stencils and mark quilt before layering and basting. Quilt as desired.

Make 345" of binding. See page 23 for directions on making and applying straight-grain binding.

Oriental Desire

This quilt mixes prints in rich blues, blushing pinks, and vibrant rose to create the exotic look of oriental porcelain. Many quilt shops now carry blue-and-white fabrics with traditional Far Eastern motifs like the fan print used here.

Quick-Piecing Techniques:

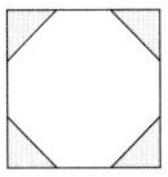

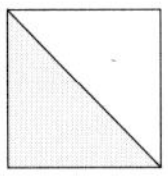

Finished Size
Blocks: 20 blocks, 20" square   Quilt: 87" x 107"

Materials

	Fabric I (medium blue print)	3¼ yards
	Fabric II (dark blue print)	1¼ yards
	Fabric III (dark blue print)	2 yards
	Fabric IV (medium blue print)	¾ yard
	Fabric V (medium rose print)	⅞ yard
	Fabric VI (light rose print)	1¾ yards
	Fabric VII (bright blue print)	¼ yard
	Fabric VIII (dark blue print)	1¾ yards
	Fabric IX (dark blue print)	¼ yard
	Fabric X (medium blue print)	1½ yards
	Fabric XI (medium rose print)	1½ yards
	Fabric XII (dark rose print)	1 yard
	Fabric XIII (navy solid)	1¼ yards
	Backing fabric	8 yards

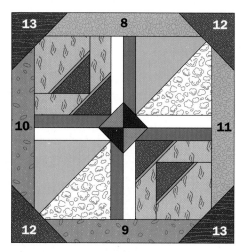

Oriental Desire Block—Make 20.

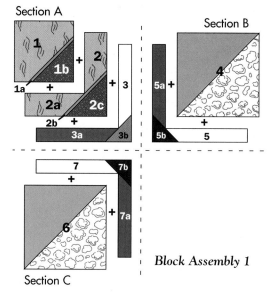

Block Assembly 1

Cutting

From Fabric I, cut:
- Ten 3" x 42" strips for binding.
- Ten 1" x 42" strips for middle border.
  From four of these, cut:
  - Four 1" x 23".
  - Four 1" x 12".
- Nine 5½" x 42" strips.
  From these, cut:
  - Forty 5½" squares (1).
  - Forty 2½" x 5½" (2).
- Three 7½" x 42" strips.
  From these, cut:
  - Forty 2½" x 7½" (2a).

From Fabric II, cut:
- Nine 4½" x 42" strips.
  From these, cut:
  - Eighty 4½" squares (1a, 2b).

From Fabric III, cut:
- Eight 3¾" x 42" strips.
  From these, cut:
  - Eighty 3¾" squares (1b, 2c).
- Six 5½" x 42" strips.
  From these, cut:
  - Forty 5½" squares (12).

From Fabric IV, cut:
- Three 7½" x 42" strips.
  From these, cut:
  - Eighty 1½" x 7½" (3, 5, 7).

From Fabric V, cut:
- Three 8½" x 42" strips.
  From these, cut:
  - Eighty 1½" x 8½" (3a, 5a, 7a).

From Fabric VI, cut:
- Three 18" x 42" strips.
  From these, cut:
  - Five 18" squares for triangle-squares (4, 6).

From Fabric VII, cut:
- Three 18" x 42" strips.
  From these, cut:
  - Five 18" squares for triangle-squares (4, 6).

From Fabric VIII, cut:
- Three 2½" x 42" strips.
  From these, cut:
  - Forty 2½" squares (3b).

From Fabric IX, cut:
- Three 2½" x 42" strips.
  From these, cut:
  - Forty 2½" squares (5b, 7b).

From Fabric X, cut:
- Twenty 2½" x 42" strips.
  From these, cut:
  - Twenty 2½" x 16½" (9).
  - Twenty 2½" x 20½" (10).

From Fabric XI, cut:
- Twenty 2½" x 42" strips.
  From these, cut:
  - Twenty 2½" x 16½" (8).
  - Twenty 2½" x 20½" (11).

From Fabric XII, cut:
- Six 5½" x 42" strips.
  From these, cut:
  - Forty 5½" squares (13).

From Fabric XIII, cut:
- Twenty-two 2" x 42" strips for inner and outer borders.
  From 10 of these, cut:
  - Six 2" x 25".
  - Four 2" x 22".
  - Two 2" x 19".

Piecing the Blocks

1. To begin Section A, make a diagonal corner on piece 1 with 1a. Trim and press. Make another diagonal corner on the *same* corner with piece 1b to complete Unit 1. Add Unit 2 to right side of Unit 1 as shown in Section A Assembly diagram; then join Unit 2a to bottom of combined unit. Repeat

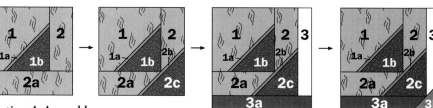

Section A Assembly

double diagonal corner with 2b and 2c as shown. To complete Section A, join units 3 and 3a; then add diagonal corner 3b. Make 40 of Section A.

2. See page 17 for instructions on half-square triangles. On wrong side of each 18" square of Fabric VI, draw a 2 x 2-square grid of 7⅞" squares. With right sides facing, match each marked fabric with an 18" square of Fabric VII. Stitch each grid as directed on page 17. Cut 8 triangle-squares from each grid (40 total—20 for Unit 4 and 20 for Unit 6).

3. Assemble Section B in the same manner as for Unit 3 of Section A. To begin, join Unit 5 to blue side of Unit 4. Join Unit 5a to rose side of Unit 4. To complete Section B, add diagonal corner 5b. Make 20 of Section B.

4. Section C is made in the same manner as Section B, but Unit 6 is turned around. Follow Block Assembly 1 diagram carefully. Make 20 of Section C.

5. Referring to Block Assembly 2 diagram, join sections A and B in pairs and sections C and A as shown. Turn blocks as shown in diagram for correct fabric placement. Join two halves as shown.

6. Join units 8 and 9 to top and bottom edges of block as shown in Block diagram; then join units 10 and 11 to sides.

7. Join diagonal corners 12 and 13 as shown to complete block.

Quilt Assembly

1. Referring to photograph, join completed blocks in five horizontal rows of four blocks each. All blocks are positioned in the same manner, with Fabric XII corners at top left. Join rows.

2. To piece each inner side border, join a 19" strip of Fabric XIII between two 42" strips to make two 102"-long border strips. To piece inner top and bottom borders, join a 22"-long strip onto both ends of two 42" strips to make two 85"-long borders.

3. Matching centers of quilt side and border strip, join long borders to sides of quilt. Press seam allowances and trim excess border fabric at ends. Add borders at top and bottom edges in the same manner.

4. To piece each middle side border, join two 42" strips of Fabric I; then join a 12" strip onto both ends of each strip to make two 106"-long border strips. To piece top and bottom borders, join a 23" strip onto both ends of each remaining 42" strip to make two 87"-long strips.

5. Add middle side borders to quilt top; then add top and bottom borders.

6. To piece each outer side border, join a 25" strip of Fabric XIII between two 42" strips to make two 108"-long border strips. To piece outer top and bottom borders, join a 25" strip onto both ends of two 42"-long border strips to make two 91"-long borders. Join side borders to quilt top in the same manner as inner border; then join top and bottom borders.

Quilting and Finishing

Outline-quilt patchwork or quilt as desired.

Make 400" of binding. See page 23 for directions on making and applying straight-grain binding.

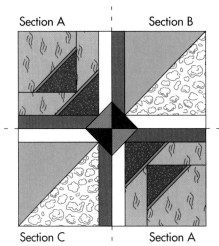

Block Assembly 2

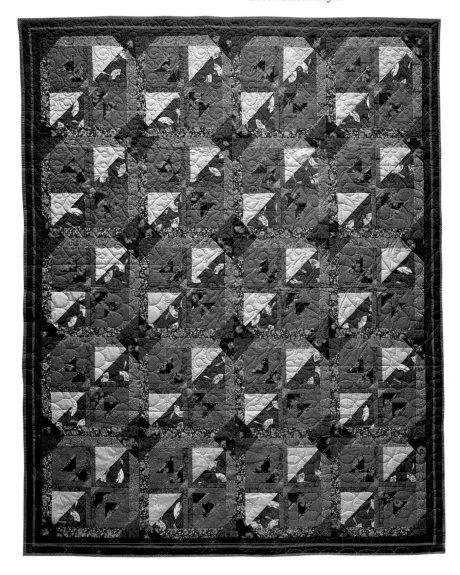

Celtic Rose

Strip piecing makes this garden bloom quickly and easily. For the
roses, pick the color of your favorite flower; then surround it with
garden greens and the background color of your choice.

Quick-Piecing Techniques:

Finished Size
Blocks: 80 blocks, 8" square

Quilt: 90" x 110"

Materials

	Fabric I (dark blue print)	3 yards
	Fabric II (medium rose print)	1 yard
	Fabric III (plum print)	1½ yards
	Fabric IV (medium green print)	1¼ yards
	Fabric V (light green print)	5¾ yards
	Backing fabric	8¼ yards

Block X—Make 40.

Cutting

Note: Most of these strips are not cut down into smaller segments until after they are joined into strip sets. Then segments cut from each strip set become individual units. In this cutting list, strips are identified by unit, not strip set.

From Fabric I, cut:
♦ Ten 3" x 42" strips for binding.
♦ Twenty-one 2½" x 42" strips (1, 3, 5, 9, 11).
♦ Three 4½" x 42" strips (12).
♦ Two 2½" x 42½" strips.
   From these, cut:
   • Nineteen 2½" squares for sashing and borders.

From Fabric II, cut:
♦ Five 2½" x 42" strips (1).
♦ Three 4½" x 42" strips (11).

From Fabric III, cut:
♦ Five 2½" x 42" strips.
   From these, cut:
   • Forty 2½" x 4½" (2).
♦ Three 4½" x 42" strips (3).
♦ Three 6½" x 42" strips (12).

From Fabric IV, cut:
♦ Six 4½" x 42" strips (4, 5).
♦ Seven 2½" x 42" strips (6, 10).

♦ Three 2½" x 42" strips.
   From these, cut:
   • Forty 2½" squares for sashing and borders.

From Fabric V, cut:
♦ Six 2½" x 42" strips (4, 5).
♦ Five 6½" x 42" strips (6).
♦ Eleven 8½" x 42" strips.
   From these, cut:
   • Forty 4½" x 8½" (7).
   • Ninety 2½" x 8½" (8).
♦ Six 8½" x 42" strips (9, 10).

Piecing the Blocks

1. Referring to strip set diagrams at right, join 2½"-wide strips of fabrics I and II to assemble five of Strip Set A. Press seam allowances toward Fabric I. From these strip sets, cut eighty 2½"-wide segments for Unit 1.

2. Join 2½"-wide strips of Fabric I to 4½"-wide strips of Fabric III to make three of Strip Set B. Press seam allowances toward Fabric III. From these strip sets, cut forty 2½"-wide segments for Unit 3.

3. Join 2½"-wide strips of Fabric V to 4½"-wide strips of Fabric IV to make three of Strip Set C. From these strip sets, cut forty 2½"-wide segments for Unit 4.

Strip Set A—Make 5.

Strip Set B—Make 3.

Strip Set C—Make 3.

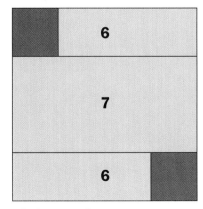

Block Y—Make 40.

4. Join 2½"-wide strips of fabrics I and V to 4½"-wide strips of Fabric IV as shown to make three of Strip Set D. From these strip sets, cut forty 2½"-wide segments for Unit 5.

5. Join 2½"-wide strips of Fabric IV to 6½"-wide strips of Fabric V to make five of Strip Set E. From these strip sets, cut eighty 2½"-wide segments for Unit 6.

6. Referring to Block X Assembly diagram, join two of Unit 1 to make a four-patch. Join Unit 2 to right side of joined Unit 1 as shown; press joining seam allowance toward Unit 2. Add Unit 3 to bottom of assembled units. Join Unit 4 to right side of center square as shown; press seam allowance toward Unit 4. Join Unit 5 to bottom of block as shown. Make 40 of Block X.

7. Referring to Block Y Assembly diagram, join two of Unit 6 to opposite sides of Unit 7. Make 40 of Block Y.

Strip Set D—Make 3.

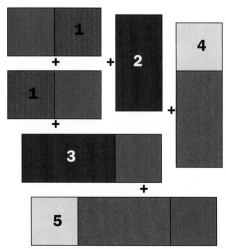

Strip Set E—Make 5.

Block X Assembly

Piecing the Sashing and Borders

1. Referring to diagrams at right, assemble strip sets F and G as shown. Press seam allowances toward Fabric V.

2. From Strip Set F, cut fifty-six 2½"-wide segments for Unit 9.

3. From Strip Set G, cut thirty-two 2½"-wide segments for Unit 10.

4. Assemble strip sets H and J as shown. Press seam allowances toward Fabric I.

5. From Strip Set H, cut thirty-six 2½"-wide segments for Unit 11.

6. From Strip Set J, cut thirty-six 2½"-wide segments for Unit 12. When these segments are cut, most of the third strip set will be left over. Pull out the stitching in this leftover segment to separate fabrics I and III. From the Fabric III piece, cut four 2½"-wide segments for outer borders.

Quilt Assembly

1. Referring to Row Assembly diagram, join four of Block X and four of Block Y to make Block Row A, positioning blocks as shown and adding a Unit 8 sashing strip between blocks. Complete Row A with Unit 8 and Unit 11 sashing strips on each end of the row. Make six of Block Row A.

2. Referring to diagram to position blocks correctly, make four of Block Row B in the same manner.

3. To make Sashing Row 1, join eight of Unit 9 end-to-end as shown. At right end of assembled row, join one Fabric I square and then one Fabric IV square.

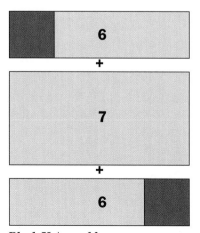

Block Y Assembly

Strip Set F—Make 4.

Strip Set G—Make 2.

Strip Set H—Make 3.

Strip Set J—Make 3.

Complete row by joining one Fabric IV square to left end as shown. Make two of Sashing Row 1.

4. To make Sashing Row 2, join four of Unit 9 and four of Unit 10 as shown. Add squares of fabrics I and IV to row ends. Make five of Sashing Row 2.

5. To make Sashing Row 3, join five of Unit 9 and three of Unit 10 as shown. Add squares of fabrics I and IV to row ends. Make four of Sashing Row 3.

6. To assemble top half of quilt, join sashing and block rows in the following sequence: 1, A, 2, B, 3, A, 2, B, 3, A. Repeat same sequence to make bottom half. Join top section to remaining

Sashing Row 2. Then turn bottom section upside down so that its Row 1 is at bottom and Block Row A is at top. Join this Block Row A to Sashing Row 2 at bottom of top section.

7. To make Border Row 1, join eight of Unit 12 end-to-end as shown. Press seam allowances toward Fabric I. Complete row by joining one 2½" x 6½" piece of Fabric III to right end as shown. Make two of Border Row 1.

8. To make Border Row 2, join eight of Unit 11 with Fabric IV squares between units. Press seam allowances toward Fabric IV. End row with squares of fabrics I and IV at both ends as shown. Make two of Border Row 2.

9. Join a Border Row 2 to top and bottom edges of assembled quilt top; then add Border Row 1 in the same manner.

10. To make side borders, repeat assembly of Border Row 1, using 10 of Unit 12 and one 2½" x 6½" piece of Fabric III. Complete row by adding a Fabric I square to both ends. Add one border strip to each side of quilt top.

Quilting and Finishing

Mark a 6"-diameter quilting design in each Block Y and a 1½" x 7" design in each Fabric V sashing unit. Quilt marked designs and outline-quilt each Block X. Quilt borders as desired.

Make 415" of binding. See page 23 for directions on making and applying straight-grain binding.

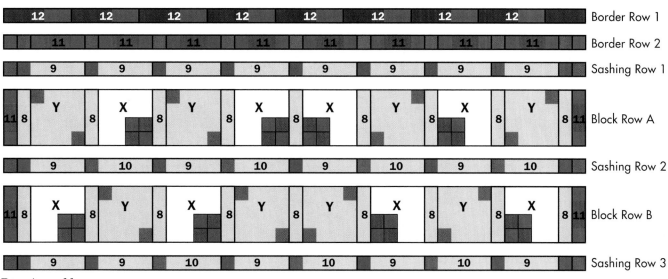

Row Assembly

Baby Bunnies Crib Set

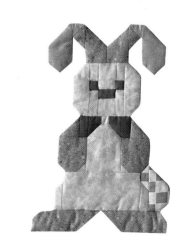

Quick cutting and piecing techniques make the little pieces in this bunny block a snap to cut and stitch. In less time than ever before, you can make this cute nursery ensemble using fabrics of sweet pastels or bright primaries. We've given separate yardage requirements for the wall hanging and the crib bumpers if you wish to make them without the crib quilt.

Quick-Piecing Techniques:

Finished Size
Blocks: 9 bunny blocks for quilt, 8" x 12"
     2 bunny blocks for wall hanging, 8" x 12"
     6 heart blocks for quilt, 6" square
     1 heart block for wall hanging, 6" square

Quilt: 50" x 50"
Wall Hanging: 24" x 34"

Materials*

Fabric I (pink-on-blue print)	1¾ yards
Fabric II (blue solid)	1 yard
Fabric III (blue-and-ivory check)	1 yard
Fabric IV (light pink print)	1¼ yards
Fabric V (bright pink solid)	1⅛ yards
Fabric VI (pink texture-look print)	¾ yard
Backing fabric for crib quilt	3 yards

Yardage includes enough fabric to make wall hanging from the same fabric. See instructions for making wall hanging separately and for additional yardage required for bumpers.

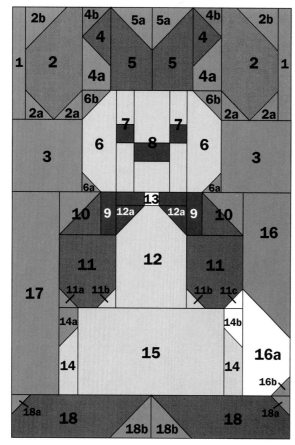

Block A—Make 9.

Cutting for Crib Quilt

Note: Cutting list below is for crib quilt only. Separate instructions follow for wall hanging.

From Fabric I, cut:

- One 11" x 42" strip.
  From this, cut:
  - One 9" x 11" for triangle-squares (A-10).
  - Two 2" x 33" strips.
    From these, cut:
    - Eighteen 1¼" x 2" (A-4a).
    - Twelve 2" squares (B-1b).
    - Seven 1" x 33" strips.
      From these, cut:
      - Four 1" x 16½" (21).
      - Nine 1" x 1½" (A-14a).
      - Fifty-four 1" squares (A-6a, A-11a, A-16b, A-18a).
      - Eighteen 1" x 3½" (A-1).
- Two 1¼" x 42" strips.
  From these, cut:
  - Fifty-four 1¼" squares (A-2a, A-6b).

- Six 1¾" x 42" strips.
  From these, cut:
  - Nine 1¾" x 6" (A-17).
  - Nine 1¾" x 4½" (A-16).
  - Fifty-four 1¾" squares (A-2b, A-5a, A-18b).
- Two 2½" x 42" strips.
  From these, cut:
  - Two 2½" x 8½" (20).
  - Eighteen 2½" x 2¾" (A-3).
- One 5½" x 42" strip.
  From this, cut:
  - Four 5½" x 6½" (19).
- Three 3½" x 42" strips.
  From this, cut:
  - Twelve 3½" squares (B-1a).
  - Eight 3½" x 6½" (22).
- Five 1½" x 42" strips.
  From this, cut:
  - Twelve 1½" x 12½" (23).
  - Twelve 1½" squares (B-1c).

From Fabric II, cut:

- One 1" x 42" strip for Strip Set 1 (A-7, A-8).
- Two 1¼" x 42" strips for Strip Set 2 (A-13).

- One 1" x 42" strip.
  From this, cut:
  - Eighteen 1" x 1¾" (A-9).
- One 1¼" x 42" strip.
  From this, cut:
  - Eighteen 1¼" squares (A-12a).
- Three 2" x 42" strips for Strip Set 3 (B-1).
- Two 2½" x 42" strips for checkerboard borders.
- Three 3½" x 42" strips for checkerboard corner blocks.

From Fabric III, cut:

- One 1" x 42" strip.
  From this, cut:
  - Nine 1" squares (A-11c).
  - Nine 1" x 1½" (A-14b).
- One 1" x 42" strip for Strip Set 2 (A-13).
- One 1¾" x 42" strip.
  From this, cut:
  - Nine 1¾" x 3¼" (A-16a).
- Three 2" x 42" strips for Strip Set 3 (B-1).
- Two 2½" x 42" strips for checkerboard borders.
- Three 3½" x 42" strips for checkerboard corner blocks.

From Fabric IV, cut:

- Twelve 1½" x 42" strips.
  From these, cut:
  - Twelve 1½" x 26" for quilt borders.
  - Eighteen 1½" x 3½" (A-6).
  - Eighteen 1" squares (A-11b).
  - Eighteen 1" x 2¼" (A-14).
- One 2" x 42" strip for Strip Set 1 (A-7, A-8).
- One 1½" x 42" strip for Strip Set 1 (A-7, A-8).
- One 2½" x 42" strip.
  From this, cut:
  - Nine 2½" x 3¼" (A-12).
- One 5" x 42" strip.
  From this, cut:
  - Nine 2¾" x 5" (A-15).

From Fabric V, cut:

- Five 3" x 42" strips for binding.
- Two 2" x 42" strips.
  From these, cut:
  - Eighteen 2" x 3½" (A-2).

♦ One 1¼" x 42" strip.
From this, cut:
  • Eighteen 1¼" squares (A-4b).

From Fabric VI, cut:
♦ One 2" x 42" strip.
From this, cut:
  • Eighteen 1¼" x 2" (A-4).
♦ One 2½" x 42" strip.
From this, cut:
  • Eighteen 2¼" x 2½" (A-11).
♦ One 11" x 42" strip.
From this, cut:
  • One 9" x 11" for triangle-squares (A-10).
  • Six 1¾" x 33" strips.
From these, cut:
    • Eighteen 1¾" x 2¾" (A-5).
    • Eighteen 1¾" x 4½" (A-18).

Piecing the Bunny Blocks

1. Using diagonal-corner technique, make one of Unit 12 and two each of units 2, 5, 6, and 18. Note that in each case, the second unit is a mirror image. Refer to Block A Assembly diagram carefully to position pieces correctly.

2. Using diagonal-corner technique, make one of Unit 11 with diagonal corners 11a and 11b as shown in Assembly diagram. Make another Unit 11, using diagonal corners 11b and 11c.

3. Using diagonal-end technique, make one of Unit 14 with diagonal end 14a. Then make a mirror-image unit, using diagonal end 14b as shown in Assembly diagram.

4. Use diagonal-end technique to add piece 4a to piece 4. Complete Unit 4 by adding diagonal corner 4b as shown in Assembly diagram. Make a mirror-image unit for second Unit 4.

5. To make Unit 16, use diagonal-end technique to add piece 16a to piece 16. Complete unit by adding diagonal corner 16b as shown.

6. Assemble strips designated for units 7 and 8 as shown in diagram for Strip Set 1, joining 1½" and 2" strips of Fabric IV to 1" strip of Fabric II. For Unit 7, cut eighteen 1"-wide segments. For Unit 8, cut nine 1½"-wide segments.

7. Assemble strips designated for Unit 13 as shown in diagram for Strip Set 2, joining 1¼" strips of Fabric II to both sides of 1" strip of Fabric III. Cut nine 1"-wide segments for Unit 13.

8. To make Unit 10, see page 17 for instructions on half-square triangles. On wrong side of 9" x 11" piece of Fabric I, draw a 3 x 4-square grid of 2⅛" squares. With right sides facing, match marked fabric with 9" x 11" piece of Fabric VI. Stitch grid as directed on page 17. Cut 24 triangle-squares from grid—this includes two for each block for both quilt and wall hanging, plus two extras.

9. To assemble Section A, begin by joining one of Unit 1 to one side of each Unit 2 as shown in Assembly diagram. Add Unit 3 to bottom of joined units. Join units 4 and 5 in a row as shown, being careful to position mirror-image units correctly on right and left sides of center. Join units 6, 7, and 8 in a row as shown. Join the two rows; then add combined 1-2-3 units to sides to complete Section A.

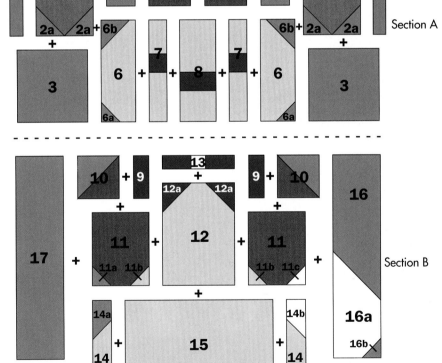

Block A Assembly

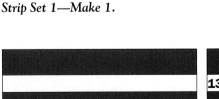

Strip Set 1—Make 1.

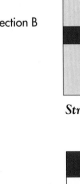

Strip Set 2—Make 1.

10. To assemble Section B, begin by joining one of Unit 9 to Fabric VI side of each Unit 10 as shown in Assembly diagram. Join combined 9-10 units to top of each Unit 11. Join Unit 13 to top of Unit 12; then join all combined units in a row as shown. Join one of Unit 14 to each side of Unit 15, referring to diagram to position mirror-image units correctly. Join combined 14-15 units to bottom of first combined unit. Join units 16 and 17 to sides as shown to complete Section B.

11. To assemble Section C, join two of Unit 18 as shown.

12. Join sections A, B, and C to complete one bunny block. Make nine bunny blocks for crib quilt.

Piecing the Heart Blocks

1. Referring to diagram of Strip Set 3, join 2" strips of fabrics II and III. Make three strip sets. From these, cut fifty-six 2"-wide segments. Join segments in rows of four as shown in Heart Unit 1 diagram. Make 12 of Unit 1.

2. Positioning Unit 1 with a Fabric II square in the upper left corner, join diagonal corners 1a, 1b, and 1c to make left half of one block as shown in Block B Assembly diagram.

3. Positioning Unit 1 in the same manner, join diagonal corners as shown to make a mirror-image unit for right half of block.

4. Join halves to complete one block. Make six heart blocks.

Piecing the Checkerboard Borders

Referring to diagram of Strip Set 3, join 2½" strips of fabrics II and III. Make two strip sets. From these, cut twenty-two 2½"-wide segments (set aside remainder for wall hanging). Referring to Quilt Assembly diagram, join segments in two rows of 11 segments each.

Piecing the Corner Blocks

Referring to diagram of Strip Set 3, join 3½" strips of fabrics II and III. Make three strip sets. From these, cut thirty-two 3½"-wide segments. Join segments in eight rows of four segments each, in the same manner as for Heart Unit 1. Referring to Quilt Assembly diagram, join these rows in pairs to make each checkerboard corner block.

Crib Quilt Assembly

1. Join a Unit 19 to top and bottom edges of two heart blocks. Join a Unit 20 to top and bottom edges of one bunny block. Referring to Quilt Assembly diagram, assemble center section by joining these units with four of Unit 21 as shown.

2. Join checkerboard borders to top and bottom of center section as shown.

3. Join Fabric IV border strips to sides of center section. Press seam allowances towards borders; then trim excess border fabric. Add borders to top and bottom edges in the same manner.

4. Join a Unit 22 to top and bottom edges of four heart blocks. Add bunny blocks to both sides of two of these heart units; then join a Unit 23 to bunny block sides to complete two outer sections.

5. Referring to Quilt Assembly diagram, join one completed outer section to top and bottom edges of center section.

6. Join a Unit 23 to both sides of two remaining heart units. Add bunny blocks and Unit 23 strips as shown to complete side sections.

7. Join corner blocks to both sides of each side section. Join these sections to quilt sides.

8. Join remaining Fabric IV strips in pairs end-to-end to make four borders.

9. Mark center of each quilt side. Matching centers, join border strips to sides of quilt. Press seam allowances toward borders; then trim excess fabric from both ends of borders. Add borders to top and bottom in the same manner.

Quilting and Finishing

Outline-quilt patchwork in blocks and checkerboard borders. Quilt background as desired.

Make 210" of straight-grain binding for crib quilt. See page 23 for directions on making and applying binding.

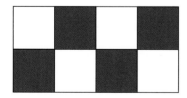

Heart Unit 1

Strip Set 3

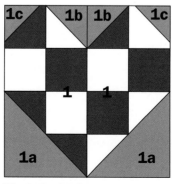

Block B—Make 6.

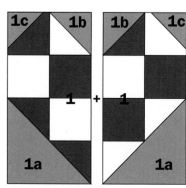

Block B Assembly

58

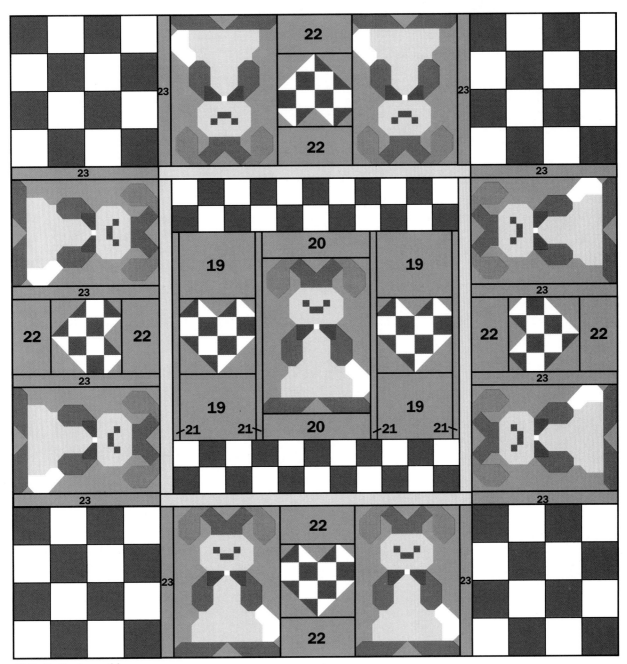

Crib Quilt Assembly

Wall Hanging Cutting

To make wall hanging from same fabrics as crib quilt, the only additional yardage needed is ¾ yard for backing. Use fabrics left over from quilt to cut pieces listed below (except for Unit 10, which was sewn during preparation for crib quilt). To make wall hanging separately, you need ¼ yard each of fabrics I, II, III, and VI, ½ yard each of fabrics IV and V, and ¾ yard backing fabric.

From Fabric I, cut:

♦ One 3½" x 42" strip.
   From this, cut:
   • Two 3½" x 6½" (22).
   • Four 1" x 3½" (A-1).
   • Two 3½" squares (B-1a).
   • One 3½" x 6½" for triangle-squares (A-10).
   • Four 2½" x 2¾" (A-3).

♦ One 2" x 42" strip.
   From this, cut:
   • Two 2" squares (B-1b).
   • Four 1¼" x 2" (A-4a).
   • Two 1½" squares (B-1c).
   • Twelve 1¼" squares (A-2a, A-6b).
   • Twelve 1" squares (A-6a, A-11a, A-16b, A-18a).
   • Two 1" x 1½" (A-14a).

♦ One 1¾" x 42" strip.
   From this, cut:
   • Twelve 1¾" squares (A-2b, A-5a, A-18b).
   • Two 1¾" x 4½" (A-16).
   • Two 1¾" x 6" (A-17).

From Fabric II, cut:

◆ Three 2½" x 42" strips.
  From these, cut:
  - Two 2½" x 42" and one 2½" x 10" for checkerboard borders.
  - One 2" x 16" (B-1).
  - Two 1¼" x 2" (A-13).
  - Four 1¼" squares (A-12a).
  - One 1" x 7" (A-7, A-8).
  - Four 1" x 1¾" (A-9).

From Fabric III, cut:

◆ Three 2½" x 42" strips.
  From these, cut:
  - Two 2½" x 42" and one 2½" x 10" for checkerboard borders.
  - One 2" x 16" (B-1).
  - Two 1¾" x 3¼" (A-16a).
  - One 1" x 2" (A-13).
  - Two 1" x 1½" (A-14b).
  - Two 1" squares (A-11c).

From Fabric IV, cut:

◆ Six 1½" x 42" strips.
  From these, cut:
  - Two 1½" x 33" and two 1½" x 24½" for outer border.
  - Two 1½" x 10½" and two 1½" x 14½" for inner border.
  - Four 1½" x 3½" (A-6).
  - Four 1" x 2¼" (A-14).
  - Four 1" squares (A-11b).
◆ One 2¾" x 42" strip.
  From this, cut:
  - Two 2¾" x 5" (A-15).
  - Two 2½" x 3¼" (A-12).
  - One 2" x 7" and one 1" x 7" (A-7, A-8).

From Fabric V, cut:

◆ Three 3" x 42" strips for binding.
◆ One 4" x 42" strips.
  From this, cut:
  - Seven 4" x 6" for hanging loops.
◆ One 2" x 42" strip.
  From this, cut:
  - Four 2" x 3½" (A-2).
  - Four 1¼" squares (A-4b).

From Fabric VI, cut:

◆ One 4½" x 42" strip.
  From this, cut:
  - Four 4½" squares (24).
  - Four 1¾" x 4½" (A-18).
  - One 3½" x 6½" for triangle-squares (A-10).
  - Four 2¼" x 2½" (A-11).
◆ One 1¾" x 42" strip.
  From this, cut:
  - Four 1¾" x 2¾" (A-5).
  - Four 1¼" x 2" (A-4).

Wall Hanging Assembly

1. To make two bunny blocks, begin by following steps 1-5 under Piecing the Bunny Blocks on page 57.

2. To make units 7 and 8, join designated strips of Fabric IV to 1" x 7" strip of Fabric II. For Unit 7, cut four 1"-wide segments. For Unit 8, cut two 1½"-wide segments.

3. To make Unit 13, join 1¼" x 2" pieces of Fabric II to both sides of 1" x 2" piece of Fabric III. Cut two 1"-wide segments for Unit 13.

4. If you've made the crib quilt, you already have eight triangle-squares left over for the wall hanging's Unit 10. If making the wall hanging separately, see page 17 for instructions on half-square triangles to make Unit 10. On wrong side of 3½" x 6½" piece of Fabric I, draw a 1 x 2-square grid of 2⅛" squares. With right sides facing, match marked fabric with 3½" x 6½" piece of Fabric VI. Stitch grid as directed on page 17. Cut four triangle-squares from grid, two for each block.

5. Follow steps 9-12 under Piecing the Bunny Blocks to complete two blocks.

6. Referring to diagram of Strip Set 3, join 2" x 16" strips of fabrics II and III. Cut eight 2"-wide segments. Join segments in rows of four as shown in Heart Unit 1 diagram. Make two of Unit 1. Follow steps 2-4 under Piecing the Heart Blocks to make one heart block.

7. Join a Unit 22 to top and bottom of remaining heart block. Join bunny blocks to both sides of heart unit.

8. Join 20½" strips of Fabric IV to top and bottom edges of center section; then join 14½" strips to side edges.

9. For checkerboard borders, join 2½" x 42" strips of fabrics II and III as shown in diagram of Strip Set 3. Join 2½" x 10" strips in the same manner. From these, cut thirty-eight 2½"-wide segments.

10. Referring to Wall Hanging Assembly diagram, join checkerboard segments to make two rows of 12 segments each. Join checkerboard borders to top and bottom edges of center section.

11. Join remaining segments to make two rows of seven segments each. Join Unit 24 corner squares to both ends of each row. Join rows to quilt sides.

12. Join 33" border strips to top and bottom edges of wall hanging; then join 24½" strips to quilt sides.

13. Outline-quilt patchwork or quilt as desired.

14. To make hanging loops, press under ¼" on short sides of each loop piece. With right sides facing, fold each piece in half lengthwise. Stitch ¼" from raw edge. Turn right side out and press seam to center back of each strip.

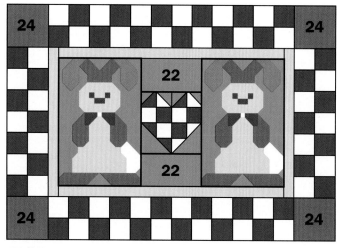

Wall Hanging Assembly

15. Fold each loop piece in half. Matching raw edges, pin a loop to backing at each top corner. Pin remaining loops to top edge in the same manner, spacing them approximately 3⅝" apart. Topstitch loop ends to backing.

16. Make 120" of straight-grain binding. See page 23 for directions on making and applying binding. Binding will cover raw ends of hanging loops.

Crib Bumpers

These instructions are for two 6" x 26" bumpers and two 6" x 50" bumpers. Adjust yardage and instructions as necessary to make different sizes.

To make bumpers that coordinate with crib quilt, you will need an additional 1¾ yards of Fabric II (includes backing) and ⅝ yard of Fabric III. Additional materials needed are ¾ yard of muslin, 10⅛ yards of ⅛"-diameter pink cording, ⅝ yard of 60"-wide low-loft batting for quilting, and 1⅛ yards of 60"-wide high-loft batting for padding.

1. From Fabric II, cut and set aside four 6½" x 42" strips for backing and eight 1½" x 42" strips for ties.

2. Cut eight 2½" x 42" strips from each of fabrics II and III. Cut two strips of each fabric in half.

3. Referring to Strip Set 4 diagram, join full-length strips to make two strip sets and half-strips to make third strip set. Use remaining strips to assemble Strip Set 5 in the same manner. Cut thirty-eight 2½"-wide segments each from strip sets 4 and 5.

4. For each short bumper, join 13 segments in a row, alternating segments. For each long bumper, join 25 segments in the same manner.

5. For quilting, cut four 6½" x 42" strips of muslin. From two strips, cut 6½" x 28" pieces for short bumpers. Piece remaining muslin to make two 6½" x 55" backings for long bumpers. Cut and piece Fabric II backing in the same manner; then cut two matching pieces of batting for each bumper.

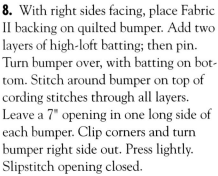

Strip Set 4—Make 3.

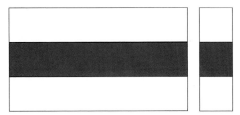

Strip Set 5—Make 3.

6. Sandwich a layer of low-loft batting between checkerboard (faceup) and muslin for each bumper. Outline-quilt patchwork. Trim batting and muslin to edge of patchwork.

7. Matching raw edges and beginning at center on one long side, pin cording around each bumper on right side. Clip corners and overlap cording ends. Using zipper or cording foot, stitch close to cording.

8. With right sides facing, place Fabric II backing on quilted bumper. Add two layers of high-loft batting; then pin. Turn bumper over, with batting on bottom. Stitch around bumper on top of cording stitches through all layers. Leave a 7" opening in one long side of each bumper. Clip corners and turn bumper right side out. Press lightly. Slipstitch opening closed.

9. From tie fabric, cut sixteen 1½" x 20" strips. Press under ¼" on short ends of each strip; then press under ¼" on each long edge. With wrong sides facing, press each strip in half lengthwise. Topstitch all pressed edges. Fold ties in half. Pin fold of one tie to back of each bumper corner and topstitch to secure.

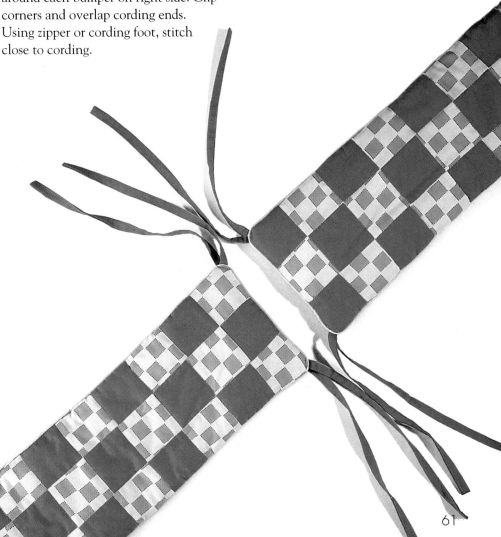

Stars & Stripes

Strip-pieced stripes and stars of half-square triangles create an All-American wall hanging or table cover. In red, white, and blue, it makes a patriotic statement, but this design works just as well in other color combinations.

Quick-Piecing Techniques:

Finished Size
Blocks: 40 blocks, 6" square   Wall Hanging: 60" x 60"

Materials

	Fabric I (navy solid)	1½ yards
	Fabric II (muslin)	2⅛ yards
	Fabric III (black-on-red textured-look print)	1¾ yards
	Fabric IV (barn red solid)	1⅛ yards
	Backing fabric	3¾ yards

Cutting
Refer to diagrams on page 64 to identify blocks and units designated in cutting list.

From Fabric I, cut:
♦ Two 14" x 42" strips.
  From these, cut:
  • Four 14" x 21" for triangle-squares (1).
♦ Eight 2" x 42" strips.
  From these, cut:
  • 156 2" squares (3).

♦ One 2½" x 42" strip.
  From this, cut:
  • Four 2½" x 9½" (4).

From Fabric II, cut:
♦ Two 14" x 42" strips.
  From these, cut:
  • Four 14" x 21" for triangle-squares (1).
♦ Four 3½" x 42" strips.
  From these, cut:
  • Forty 3½" squares (2).
♦ Eighteen 1⅜" x 42" strips for strip sets.

From Fabric III, cut:
♦ Eight 2½" x 42" strips for borders.
♦ Six 3" x 42" strips for binding.
♦ One 4½" x 42" strip.
  From this, cut:
  • Eight 4½" squares (7).
♦ Two 6½" x 42" strips.
  From these, cut:
  • Eight 6½" squares (8).
  • Two 2½" x 29" strips.
    From these, cut:
    • Four 2½" x 4" (6).
    • Four 2" x 2½" (5).
    • Four 2" squares (3a).

From Fabric IV, cut:
♦ Twenty-six 1⅜" x 42" strips for strip sets.

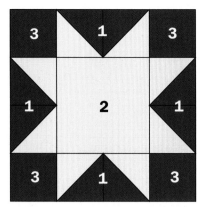

Block A—Make 36.

Piecing the Star Blocks

1. See page 17 for instructions on half-square triangles. On wrong side of each 14" x 21" piece of Fabric II, draw a 5 x 8-square grid of 2⅜" squares. With right sides facing, match each marked fabric with 14" x 21" piece of Fabric I. Stitch each grid as directed on page 17. Cut 80 triangle-squares from each grid (320 total).

2. To make Unit 1, join all triangle-squares in pairs, positioning the dark triangles in the center of each pair.

3. Referring to Block A Assembly diagram, add a Unit 1 to opposite sides of Unit 2. Press seam allowances toward Unit 2.

4. Join a Unit 3 square to both ends of each remaining Unit 1. Press seam allowances toward Unit 3. Join units to top and bottom of center section.

5. Make Block B in the same manner as Block A, substituting a red Unit 3a in one corner as shown in Block B diagram.

Center Section Assembly

1. Referring to Center Section Assembly diagram, join four of Block B, positioning red corners as shown.

2. Join a Unit 5 to each end of two Unit 4 strips. Press seam allowances toward Unit 4. Join units to top and bottom of 4-star center section.

3. Join Units 4 and 6 as shown. Press seam allowances toward Unit 4. Join units to sides of center section.

Strip Piecing

Referring to strip set diagrams, join 1⅜"-wide strips of Fabrics II and IV as shown to make Strip Set 1 and Strip Set 2. Use a generous ¼" seam so that Strip Set 1 measures 4½" wide and Strip Set 2 measures 6½" wide. Adjust seams as necessary to achieve desired widths.

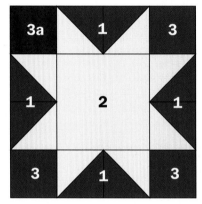

Block B—Make 4.

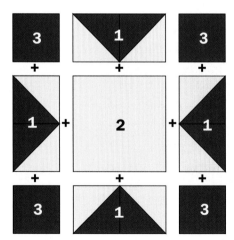

Block A Assembly

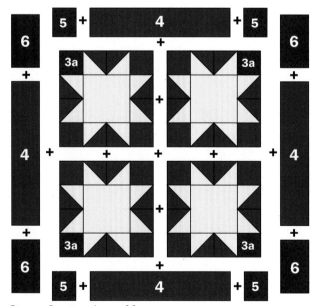

Center Section Assembly

Strip Set 1—Make 6.

Strip Set 2—Make 2.

Quilt Assembly

Quilt Assembly

Refer to Quilt Assembly diagram throughout assembly.

1. Determine length of one side of center section. From two of Strip Set 1, cut four pieces equal to that length. If all four sides are not equal, cut these strip set pieces equal to the measurement of the *shortest* side.

2. Join trimmed strip sets to top and bottom edges of center section, referring to page 15 for tips on easing.

3. Join a Unit 7 to each end of two remaining trimmed strip-set pieces. Join these units to sides of center section.

4. Join remaining star blocks in rows, making four rows of four blocks each and four rows of five blocks each.

5. Join four-star rows to top and bottom edges of quilt.

6. Join a Unit 8 to each end of remaining four-star rows. Join these rows to quilt sides.

7. Measure quilt sides as in Step 1. From remaining Strip Set 1 units, cut four strips to needed length. Join trimmed strip sets to top and bottom edges of quilt. Add a Unit 7 to each end of remaining strips. Join these strips to quilt sides.

8. Cut each Strip Set 2 in half. Join each segment to one end of a five-star row. Compare rows to sides of quilt and trim strip-set end to match quilt. Join trimmed strips to top and bottom edges of quilt.

9. Add a Unit 8 to each end of remaining rows. Join rows to quilt sides.

10. Join border strips in pairs end-to-end. Measuring from center of each strip, cut two 2½" x 58" borders and two 2½" x 62" borders. Matching centers of borders and quilt, join shorter borders to top and bottom edges; then trim ends of border to match quilt sides. Add remaining borders to quilt sides in the same manner.

Quilting and Finishing

Outline-quilt patchwork or quilt as desired. Purchased stencils were used to mark 4" stars in Units 7 and 8.

Make 250" of binding. See page 23 for directions on making and applying straight-grain binding.

Water *Lily*

Strip piecing makes fast work of the corners in each of these pretty lily blocks. This quilt features light and dark lilies alternating in a lavender sea. What other color schemes might be effective? Try pink and white lilies framed in green, or use bright-colored scraps to make a variety of lilies set in a sea of dark blue. You'll find instructions for the coordinating pillow sham on page 71.

Quick-Piecing Techniques:

Finished Size

Blocks: 42 blocks, 7¾" square   Quilt: 78¼" x 101"

Materials

▮	Fabric I (dark purple print)	4½ yards
▨	Fabric II (lavender print)	3 yards
▮	Fabric III (purple solid)	1¼ yards
▨	Fabric IV (purple print)	⅜ yard
▨	Fabric V (purple print)	1¾ yards
▮	Fabric VI (dark purple print)	⅛ yard
▢	Fabric VII (lavender print)	⅛ yard
	Backing fabric	6¼ yards

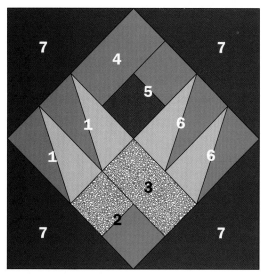

Block A—Make 24.

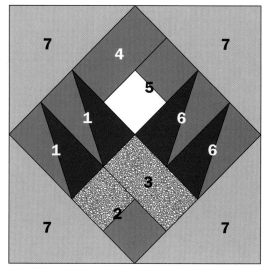

Block B—Make 18.

Cutting

From Fabric I, cut:
- Nine 3" x 42" strips for binding.
- Six 4¾" x 42" strips.
  From these, cut:
  - Forty-eight 4¾" squares. Cut each square in half diagonally to get 96 A-7.
- Twelve 5¼" x 42" strips.
  From these, cut:
  - Forty-five 5¼" x 10¼" (8, 9). Cut these rectangles as shown in Cutting diagram to get eight triangles from each piece for a total of 360 triangles.*
- Two 4" x 42" strips.
  From these, cut:
  - Nine 4" x 8" (B-1, B-6). Cut these rectangles as shown in Cutting diagram to get eight triangles from each piece for a total of 72 triangles.*
- Nine 3" x 42" strips for outer border. From three of these strips, cut:
  - Two 3" x 21".
  - Four 3" x 18".

From Fabric II, cut:
- Five 4¾" x 42" strips.
  From these, cut:
  - Thirty-six 4¾" squares. Cut each square in half diagonally to get 72 B-7.

- Twelve 5¼" x 42" strips.
  From these, cut:
  - Forty-five 5¼" x 10¼" (8, 9). Cut these rectangles as shown in Cutting diagram to get eight triangles from each piece for a total of 360 triangles.*
- Three 4" x 42" strips.
  From these, cut:
  - Twelve 4" x 8" (A-1, A-6). Cut these rectangles as shown in Cutting diagram to get eight triangles from each piece for a total of 96 triangles.*

From Fabric III, cut:
- Five 4" x 42" strips.
  From these, cut:
  - Twenty-one 4" x 8" (A-1, A-6, B-1, B-6). Cut these rectangles as shown in Cutting diagram to get eight triangles from each piece for a total of 168 triangles.*
- Two 3¼" x 42" strips.
  From these, cut:
  - Forty-two 1⅞" x 3¼" (A-4, B-4).
- Five 1⅞" x 42" strips (A-2, A-5, B-2, B-5).

From Fabric IV, cut:
- Two 3¼" x 42" strips.
  From these, cut:
  - Forty-two 1⅞" x 3¼" (A-3, B-3).
- Two 1⅞" x 42" strips (A-2, B-2).

From Fabric V, cut:
- Nine 4¼" x 42" strips.
  From these, cut:
  - Forty-two 4¼" x 8¼" (10).
- Nine 2" x 42" strips for inner border. From three of these strips, cut:
  - Six 2" x 16".

From Fabric VI, cut:
- Two 1⅞" x 42" strips (A-5).

From Fabric VII, cut:
- One 1⅞" x 42" strip (B-5).

* *Note:* Each rectangle yields eight triangles, four of which point to the right and four to the left. Store "righties" and "lefties" separately. Trim ¾" from narrow tip of all these triangles.

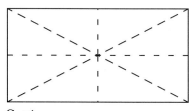

Cutting

Piecing the Blocks

1. To make Unit A-1, join small triangles of fabrics II and III, using righties. The resulting rectangle will measure 1⅞" x 3¼". Make two of Unit 1. Make two of Unit A-6 in the same manner, using lefties.

2. Join 1⅞" strips of fabrics III and IV to make two of Strip Set 1. From these, cut forty-two 1⅞"-wide segments for units A-2 and B-2. (*Note:* Save all strip-set remnants for optional pillow sham.)

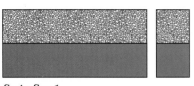

Strip Set 1

Strip Set 2

Strip Set 3

3. Join 1⅞" strips of fabrics III and VI to make two of Strip Set 2. From these strip sets, cut twenty-four 1⅞"-wide segments for Unit A-5.

4. Join 1⅞" strips of fabrics III and VII to make one of Strip Set 3. From this strip set, cut eighteen 1⅞"-wide segments for Unit B-5.

5. To assemble Block A, begin by joining two of Unit 1 as shown in Block Assembly diagram. Join units 2 and 3; then add this combined unit to Unit 1 pair. To assemble top half of block, join units 4 and 5 and two of Unit 6 in a row as shown. Join halves to complete lily section. Join A-7 triangles to opposite sides of lily section; press seam allowances toward triangles. Add A-7 triangles to remaining sides to complete block. Make 24 of Block A.

6. Make 18 of Block B in the same manner, referring to block diagram for color and placement of each unit.

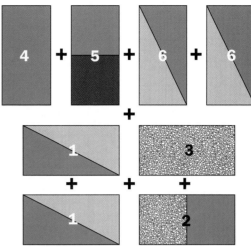

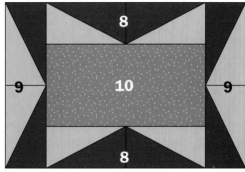

Block Assembly

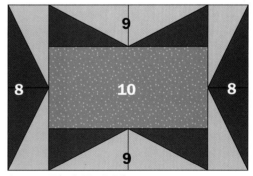

Setting Block X—Make 24.

Setting Block Y—Make 18.

Piecing Setting Blocks

1. Using a scant ¼" seam allowance, join 360 pairs of large triangles of fabrics I and II, making 180 lefty pairs and 180 righty pairs. Each resulting rectangle will be 2½" x 4⅜".

2. Paying careful attention to color placement as shown in setting block diagrams, join one lefty rectangle and one righty rectangle to form Unit 8.

Make 96 of Unit 8. Join remaining rectangles as shown to make 84 of Unit 9.

3. Positioning fabrics as shown in Setting Block X diagram, join one of Unit 8 to each long side of Unit 10. Add one of Unit 9 to each side as shown. Make 24 of Setting Block X.

4. Make 18 of Setting Block Y in the same manner, changing positions of units 8 and 9 as shown.

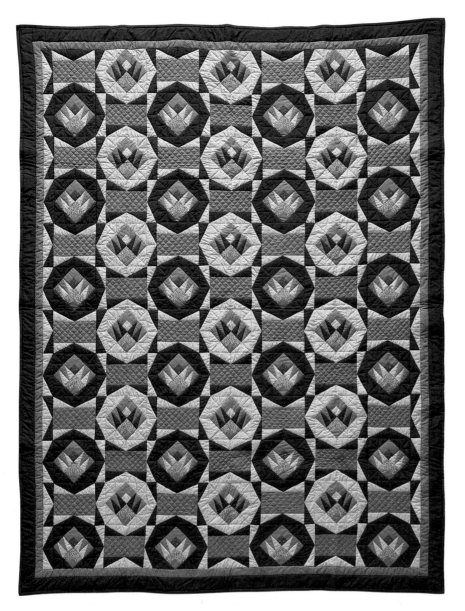

join border to top edge of quilt top. Press seam allowances and trim border fabric at ends. Repeat for bottom edge.

5. To piece inner side borders, join a 42" strip of Fabric V to both ends of each remaining 16" strip to make a 99"-long border strip. Join borders to quilt sides in the same manner.

6. To piece top and bottom outer borders, join an 18" strip of Fabric I to both ends of a 42" strip to make two 77"-long borders. For sides, join a 42" strip to both ends of a 21" strip to make two 104"-long borders. Join outer borders to quilt top in the same manner as inner borders.

Quilting and Finishing

Quilt in-the-ditch around all patchwork. Quilt an X from corner to corner of all A and B blocks. Quilt a diagonal grid of 1" squares in all Unit 10 pieces.

Make 380" of binding. See page 23 for directions on making and applying straight-grain binding.

Quilt Assembly

1. Referring to Row Assembly diagram, join three of Block B and four of Setting Block X to make Row 1, alternating blocks as shown. Make six of Row 1.

2. Join four of Block A and three of Setting Block Y to make Row 2, positioning blocks as shown. Complete Row 2 with a Unit 8 on each end of the row, positioning fabrics as shown. Make six of Row 2.

3. Starting with a Row 1 and alternating row types, join all rows.

4. To piece inner border for top edge, join a 16" strip of Fabric V to both ends of a 42" strip to make a 73"-long border. Matching centers of quilt and border,

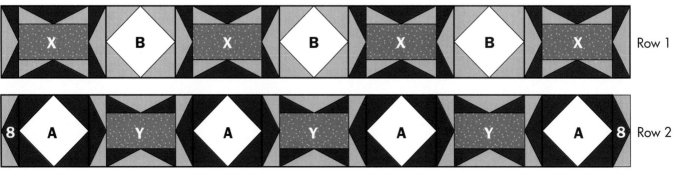

Row Assembly

Water *Lily* Pillow Sham

Finished Size

Blocks: 3 blocks, 7¾" square   Sham: 26¾" x 61¼" (Queen size)

Use the same fabrics, instructions, and diagrams that you used to make the Water Lily quilt for this coordinating pillow sham. Unit numbers correspond to quilt units unless otherwise indicated.

Materials

	Fabric I (dark purple print)	2¼ yards
	Fabric II (lavender print)	⅜ yard
	Fabric III (purple solid)	⅜ yard
	Fabric IV (purple print)	¼ yard
	Fabric V (purple print)	¼ yard
	Muslin for quilting lining	1¾ yards
	4"-wide Battenberg lace	4⅞ yards

Cutting

From Fabric I, cut:

♦ One 5¼" x 42" strip.
  From this, cut:
  • Three 5¼" x 10¼" (9).
    Cut these rectangles as shown in Cutting diagram on page 68 to get 24 triangles.*
♦ One 2½" x 42" strip.
  From this, cut:
  • Four 2½" x 10" (Sham-2).
♦ One 5¼" x 42" strip.
  From this, cut:
  • Two 5¼" x 18" for outer border.
  • Four 2½" squares (Sham-1).
♦ Two 5¼" x 62" lengthwise strips for outer border.
♦ Two 27¼" x 33" for backing.
♦ Two 4" x 8" (B-1, B-6).
  Cut these rectangles as shown in Cutting diagram on page 68 to get 16 triangles. (Only 12 are needed; discard four extras.)*

From Fabric II, cut:

♦ One 5¼" x 42" strip.
  From this, cut:
  • Three 5¼" x 10¼" (9).
    Cut these rectangles as shown in Cutting diagram on page 68 to get 24 triangles.*
♦ One 4¾" x 42" strip.
  From this, cut:
  • Six 4¾" squares.
    Cut each square in half diagonally to get 12 B-7.

From Fabric III, cut:

♦ Four 2½" x 42" strips.
  From these, cut:
  • Four 2½" x 26" and two 2½" x 12½" for inner border.
  • Three 1⅞" squares (B-2).

♦ Three 1⅞" x 3¼" (B-4).
♦ Two 4" x 8" (B-1, B-6).
  Cut these rectangles as shown in Cutting diagram on page 68 to get 16 triangles. (Only 12 are needed; discard four extras.)*

From Fabric IV, cut:

♦ One 1⅞" x 42" strip.
  From this, cut:
  • Three 1⅞" squares (B-2).
  • Three 1⅞" x 3¼" (B-3).
♦ Five 1¼" x 42" strips.
  From these, cut:
  • Four 1¼" x 27" and two 1¼" x 17" for middle border.

From Fabric V, cut:

♦ Two 6" x 8¼" (Sham-3).

Note: Each rectangle yields eight triangles, four of which point to the right and four to the left. Store "righties" and "lefties" separately. Trim ¾" from narrow tip of all these triangles.

Piecing the Blocks and Sashing

1. Referring to block diagrams and instructions for Water Lily blocks on pages 68 and 69, make three of Block B. Use three segments of Strip Set 3 left over from the quilt for Unit 5.
2. Referring to diagrams and instructions on page 69, make 12 of Unit 9.
3. Join one of Unit 9 to top and bottom edges of each Water Lily block.
4. Join one of Unit 9 to each long side of Sham Unit 3. Join Sham Unit 2 to top and bottom edges of assembled units.
5. Join Sham Unit 1 squares to ends of two remaining Unit 9.

6. Referring to Pillow Sham Assembly diagram, join assembled units in a row.

Adding Borders

1. Join 12½" strips of Fabric III to short sides of sham top. Piece pairs of 26" strips end-to-end to make two 51½"-long border strips for top and bottom edges. Matching centers of sham and border strip, join borders to top and bottom edges. Press seam allowances toward borders and trim excess border fabric at ends.
2. Join middle borders to sham in the same manner, adding short strips to sides first and then piecing pairs of long strips to make borders for top and bottom edges.
3. Join outer borders to pillow sham.
4. Cut four pieces of lace to fit along seam lines between middle and outer borders. Pin or baste in place, butting ends of adjacent pieces at corners.

Quilting and Finishing

1. Cut muslin and batting slightly larger than sham. Quilt in-the-ditch around patchwork. Quilt a diagonal grid of 1" squares in Unit 3 and inner border. Topstitch lace edges to secure it, quilting into sham at the same time.
2. Press under ¼" on one short end of each backing piece. Press under an additional ¼" and topstitch in place to hem.
3. With right sides facing and corners matching, place backing pieces on sham front, overlapping hemmed edges of backing pieces in center. Stitch ¼" seam around sham. Trim excess batting and lining from seam allowances and clip corners. Turn sham right side out.

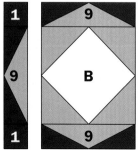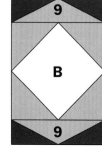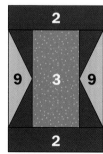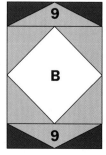

Pillow Sham Assembly

Pillow Talk

Add style to your decor with a batch of pretty pillows. The pillows and shams in this book have envelope-style backs that are fast to assemble and easy to remove for cleaning. Use the following instructions to finish any pillow top.

Materials

For each pillow back, you need two fabric rectangles. The *width* of each rectangle must be the same as the width of the front. The *height* of each rectangle should be half the height of the front plus 3". For example, if your pillow patchwork is 12½" square, then backing rectangles should be 12½" x 9½".

Make or purchase a pillow form that is the desired finished size of the pillow. If you want to buy a form but the patchwork is not a standard size, add borders around the block to make it big enough to accommodate an available form.

Instructions

1. On one widthwise edge of each rectangle, turn under ¼" and then ⅝". Press fold. Topstitch ½" from folded edge and then edgestitch.

2. With wrong side up, lay one rectangle on table. Referring to diagram, position second rectangle (also wrong side up) so that hemmed edges overlap and both pieces form a square or rectangle that matches pillow front. Pin layers together at envelope opening. Machine-baste overlapped edges at sides.

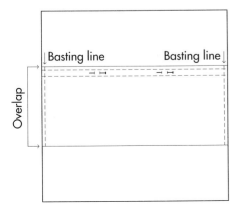

3. With right sides facing and raw edges aligned, stitch back to front around all edges, taking a ½" seam. Backstitch at overlap points.

4. Remove pins. Clip corners; then turn pillow right side out through envelope opening. Insert pillow form.

Adding a Ruffle

1. Measure around sides of pillow front and multiply the total by 2 to determine length of ruffle strip needed.

2. Cut or piece fabric strips that are twice as wide as the desired finished ruffle plus 1". (Example: Cut strips 7" wide to make a finished ruffle 3" wide.) Join strips end-to-end to make a continuous strip equal to needed length. Join ends.

3. With wrong sides facing and raw edges aligned, fold strip in half lengthwise and press. Measure four equal sections and mark each with a pin.

4. Stitch a line of loose basting ⅜" from raw edge of first ruffle section, leaving 2" of thread at each end. Repeat for remaining ruffle sections.

5. On pillow front, mark center of each side with a pin. With right sides facing, pin end of one ruffle section at one center point on pillow front. Gather ruffle, distributing fullness evenly, until section fits between pins. Aligning raw edges, pin gathered section to pillow front. Repeat for remaining sections.

6. Stitch back to pillow front as described above, with ruffle sandwiched in between.

Stained Glass Floral

A beautiful scalloped border provides the finishing touch for this intricate design. The joined blocks create a fascinating pattern of interweaving lattice that carries through to the scallops. Make a complete bedroom ensemble with these instructions for a matching flanged pillow, table cover, and embellished linens. We recommend this project for experienced quiltmakers.

Quick-Piecing Techniques:

Finished Size

Blocks: 30 blocks, 17" square
      17 scallops, 6½" x 17"

Quilt: 98" x 109½"

Materials*

	Fabric I (tan-on-ivory print)	5¼ yards
	Fabric II (tan solid)	1 yard
	Fabric III (slate blue solid)	5¾ yards
	Fabric IV (dark blue print)	3 yards
	Fabric V (navy solid)	3¼ yards
	Backing fabric	9 yards

* See instructions for matching pillow, table topper, and embellished linens for additional yardage needed.

Cutting

Note: In the following cutting list and throughout these instructions where pieces are used in all four scallops (Blocks B, C, D, and E), designation is Scallops plus a unit number. Pieces designated as A-, B-, C-, D-, and E- are used only in individual blocks.

From Fabric I, cut:

- Twenty-seven 2" x 42" strips. From these, cut:
  - 120 2" x 4" (A-2).
  - 240 2" squares (A-11).
  - 120 1" x 2" (A-8).
- Fifty-four 1½" x 42" strips. From these, cut:
  - 1,148 1½" squares (A-1a, A-3, A-10a, A-14a, Scallops-3a, Scallops-10a).
  - 154 1½" x 2" (A-5, Scallops-4).
  - Thirty-four 1½" x 6" (Scallops-2).
  - Thirty-four 1" x 1½" (Scallops-8).
- Twelve 1" x 42" strips. From these, cut:
  - 480 1" squares (A-7a, A-9b, A-12a).
- Eight 2½" x 42" strips. From these, cut:
  - 120 2½" squares (A-6).
- Three 3½" x 42" strips. From these, cut:
  - Thirty 3½" squares (A-15).

From Fabric II, cut:

- Two 15" x 42" strips. From these, cut:
  - Three 15" x 21" for triangle-squares (A-13, Scallops-11).

From Fabric III, cut:

- Three 15" x 42" strips. From these, cut:
  - Six 15" x 21" for triangle-squares (A-13, Scallops-11).
- Twenty-three 2" x 42" strips. From these, cut:
  - 120 2" x 3" (A-1).
  - 120 1½" x 2" (A-4).
  - 120 2" squares (A-7).
  - 164 1" x 2" (A-18a, Scallops-4a, C-1a, D-1a, E-1a).

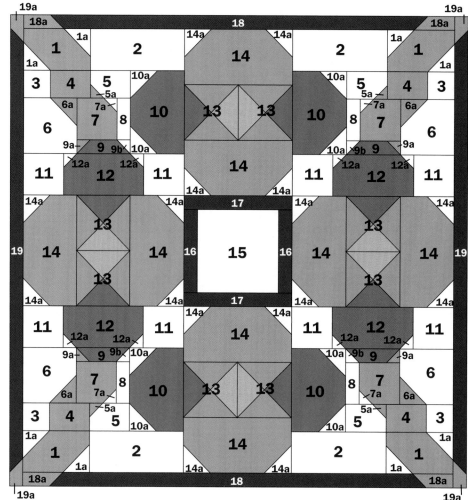

Block A—Make 30.

- Six 1" x 42" strips. From these, cut:
  - 240 1" squares (A-5a, A-9a).
- Nineteen 4½" x 42" strips. From these, cut:
  - 274 2½" x 4½" (A-14, Scallops-10).
  - Thirty-four 2" x 4½" (Scallops-3).
- Twelve 1½" x 42" strips. From these, cut:
  - Sixty-eight 1½" x 2½" (Scallops-2a, Scallops-5).
  - 120 1½" squares (A-6a).
  - 144 1" x 1½" (A-19a, B-1a).
- From scraps, cut:
  - One 2½" square. Cut this square in half diagonally to get two triangles (D-13, E-13).
  - One 2" square. Cut this square in half diagonally to get two triangles (D-12, E-12).

From Fabric IV, cut:

- Thirteen 2½" x 42" strips. From these, cut:
  - 120 1" x 2½" (A-9).
  - 120 2½" x 3½" (A-10).
- Six 1½" x 42" strips. From these, cut:
  - Sixty-eight 1½" squares (Scallops-4b, Scallops-6).
  - Thirty-four 1½" x 3½" (Scallops-9).
- Eleven 2" x 42" strips. From these, cut:
  - 120 2" x 3½" (A-12).
  - Seventeen 2" squares. Cut each square in half diagonally to get 34 triangles (Scallops-7).
- Two 15" x 42" strips. From these, cut:
  - Three 15" x 21" for triangle-squares (A-13, Scallops-11).

From Fabric V, cut:

◆ One 34" square for bias binding.
◆ Sixty-nine 1" x 42" strips.
 From these, cut:
 • Seventy-two 1" x 16½" (A-19, B-1).
 • Five 1" x 15½" (C-1, D-1, E-1).
 • Sixty 1" x 14½" (A-18).
 • Sixty 1" x 4½" (A-17).
 • Sixty 1" x 3½" (A-16).
◆ Three 1½" x 42" strips for top border.

Piecing the Blocks

1. To make units A-13 and Scallops-11, see pages 17 and 18 for instructions on *quarter-square* triangles. On wrong side of each 15" x 21" piece of Fabric III, draw a 4 x 6-square grid of 3¼" squares. With right sides facing, match three marked pieces with 15" x 21" pieces of Fabric II. Match remaining three marked pieces with 15" x 21" pieces of Fabric IV. Stitch each grid as directed for *half-square* triangles on page 17. Cut 48 triangle-squares from each grid (288 total). Press seam allowances on all triangle-squares toward Fabric III.

2. Referring to instructions on page 18, draw a diagonal line on wrong side of each Fabric II/III triangle-square. With right sides facing and seams aligned, match marked triangle-squares with Fabric III/IV triangle-squares so that Fabric III in each square is on top of different fabric in opposite square. Stitch these pairs as directed on page 18. Make 282 quarter-triangle squares. Designate 240 as Unit A-13, 34 as Scallops-11, and eight for matching pillow. Use six remaining triangle-squares for coordinating tablecloth or embellished linens or discard.

3. Using diagonal-corner technique, make one each of units 1, 5, 6, 7, 9, 10, and 12 as shown in Section A of Section Assembly diagram.

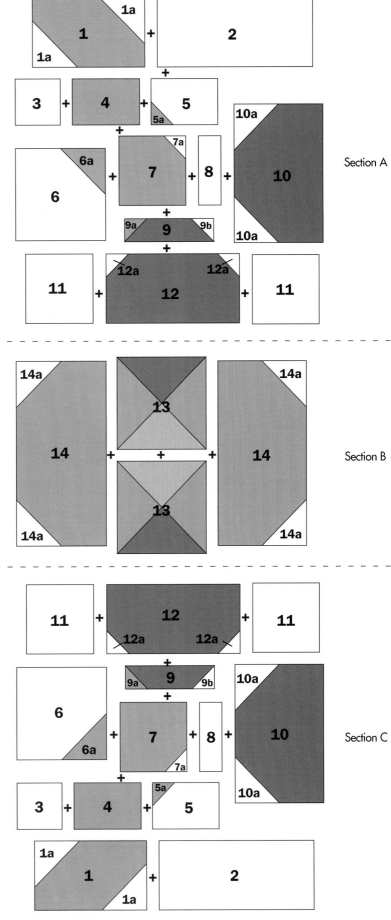

Section A

Section B

Section C

Section Assembly

4. To assemble Section A, begin by joining units 7 and 8. Add Unit 9 to bottom of combined units as shown. Join Unit 6 to left side of units 7 and 9. Join units 3, 4, and 5 in a row; then add row to top of combined 6-7-8-9 unit. Join Unit 10 to right side. Join units 1 and 2; then add this row to top. Join units 11 and 12 in a row as shown and add row to bottom of combined units to complete Section A. Make two of Section A for each block.

5. Using diagonal-corner technique, make two of Unit 14 for each Section B.

6. To assemble Section B, join two of Unit 13, positioning fabrics as shown in Section Assembly diagram. Join one of Unit 14 to each side of Unit 13 pair as shown to complete Section B. Make four of Section B for each block.

7. Section C is a mirror image of Section A. Using diagonal-corner technique, make one each of units 1, 5, 6, 7, 9, 10, and 12, being careful to position each corner as shown in Section Assembly diagram. Following diagram, assemble units for Section C in the same sequence as for Section A. Make two of Section C for each block.

8. Referring to color diagram of Block A to make center square, join a Unit 16 to opposite sides of Unit 15. Add Unit 17 to top and bottom to complete center square.

9. Referring to Block A Assembly diagram, join sections A, B, and C as shown for left side of block. Join one of each section in the same manner for

right side of block (this section is turned upside down when sections are joined). For middle section, join one of Section B to top and bottom of center square. Join three parts of block as shown in Assembly diagram.

10. Using diagonal-end technique, make two each of units 18 and 19, being careful to change angle of opposite ends on each unit as shown in Block A diagram. Add Unit 18 to top and bottom of block. Complete block by joining Unit 19 to sides. Make 30 Stained Glass Floral blocks.

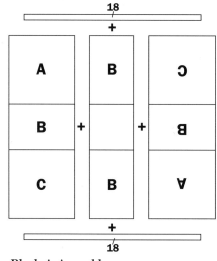

Block A Assembly

Piecing the Scallops

1. To begin Block B, use diagonal-end technique to make one of Unit B-1 as shown in Scallop Assembly diagram.

2. Make one of Unit 2; then change angle of diagonal end to make a mirror image of Unit 2 as shown.

3. To prepare Unit 3, measure and mark a 1¾" square on wrong side of fabric at *bottom left corner* of half of the pieces. Draw a diagonal line through this square from lower right corner to upper left corner. On wrong side of remaining pieces, draw a 1¾" square at *bottom right corner*. Draw a diagonal line from lower left corner to upper right corner. Cut on these diagonal lines and discard trimmed triangle.

4. Using diagonal-corner technique, add 3a to each Unit 3 piece as shown in Scallop Assembly diagram, being careful to position corners correctly. For each Block B, make one of Unit 3 and one mirror image Unit 3.

5. To make Unit 4, join pieces 4 and 4a to make a square. Add diagonal corner 4b as shown, making two mirror-image units for each Block B.

6. Set two of Unit 5 aside for blocks D and E. On remaining Unit 5 pieces, mark a 1¼" square on one end. Draw diagonal lines through each square as described in Step 3. Trim Unit 5 pieces.

7. In the same manner, mark 1¼" squares on *two opposite corners* of 17 Unit 10 pieces as shown in Scallop Assembly diagram and trim. Add diagonal corners to remaining 17 Unit 10 pieces as shown.

8. Join a Unit 11 pair, positioning fabrics as shown. Add a trimmed Unit 10 to bottom of joined Unit 11 pair; then add a Unit 10 with corners to top.

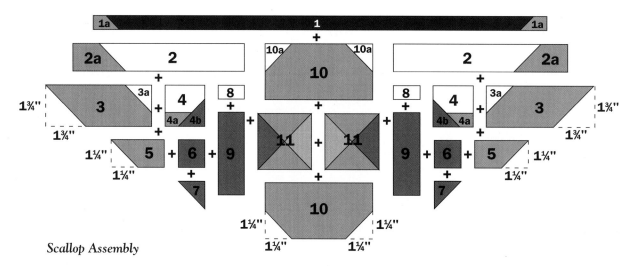

Scallop Assembly

9. To assemble left side of Block B, refer to Scallop Assembly diagram. Begin by joining square end of Unit 5 to Unit 6. Add Unit 7 to bottom of Unit 6. Join Unit 4 to square end of Unit 3 as shown; then join this to top of 5-6-7 unit as shown. Join Unit 8 to top of Unit 9 and add this to right side of combined units. Add Unit 2 to top.

10. Make right side of block in the same manner, using mirror-image units.

11. Join left and right sides of scallop to center section as shown. Add Unit B-1 to top to complete scallop. Make 12 of Block B.

12. For Block C, use diagonal-end technique to make Unit C-1 as shown. Repeat steps 2–11 to assemble Block C in the same manner as Block B, substituting Unit C-1. Make three of Block C.

13. To make one Block D scallop, assemble right side and center as for blocks B and C. For left side, add Unit 12 to an untrimmed Unit 5 as shown in Block D diagram; then continue to assemble left side as before. Join Unit 13 to left corner as shown to complete Block D.

14. Block E is a mirror image of Block D. Assemble center and left sections as for blocks B and C. For right side, add units 12 and 13 as described in Step 13. Make one Block E as shown.

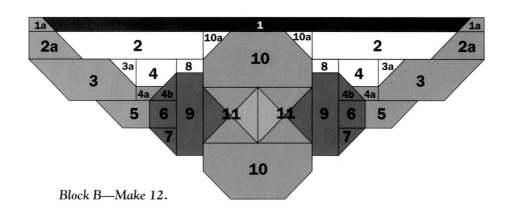

Block B—Make 12.

Block C, Unit 1

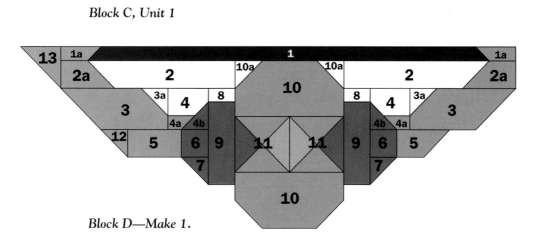

Block D—Make 1.

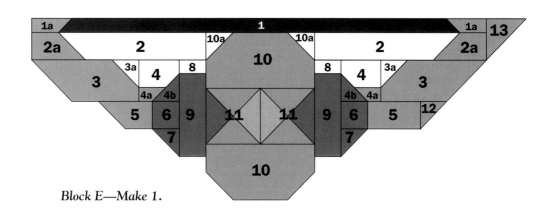

Block E—Make 1.

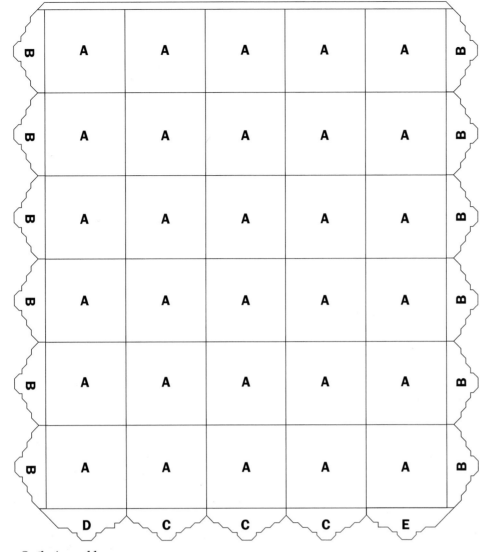

Quilt Assembly

Quilt Assembly

1. Join A blocks in six horizontal rows of five blocks each. Join rows.

2. Referring to Quilt Assembly diagram, join six of Block B end-to-end to make a row for each quilt side. Join one row to each quilt side, matching corners at top and bottom.

3. Join three of Block C in the same manner for quilt bottom. Add Block D to left end of row and Block E to right end. Join row to bottom of quilt, matching corners.

4. Join three 1½"-wide strips of Fabric V end-to-end for top border. Trim 10" from each end. Matching centers of border and quilt top, join border to quilt. Referring to Quilt Assembly diagram, trim corners at same angle to match adjacent scallops.

Quilting and Finishing

Outline-quilt patchwork or quilt as desired.

For bias binding, cut 34" square of Fabric V in half diagonally. Starting from cut edges, cut 2"-wide diagonal strips. Join strips end-to-end to make a continuous strip 14 yards long. Press strip in half with wrong sides facing, being careful not to stretch bias. Follow directions on page 23 for applying binding. Take special care to miter corners and angles around scalloped edge.

Flanged Pillow

To make one pillow, you need additional yardage in the following quantities: ¼ yard of Fabric I, ⅛ yard each of fabrics III and IV, ¾ yard of Fabric V, and one 18" square each of muslin and batting.

1. From Fabric V, cut four 2¼" x 21" pieces for flange and two 12½" x 21" pieces for pillow back. Set these aside.

2. Cut pieces for one of Block A. Follow instructions given for quilt to assemble one block, using eight of Unit 13 left over from quilt top.

3. Sandwich batting between block (faceup) and muslin. Quilt pillow as desired; then trim batting and muslin even with block.

4. Join flange strips to top and bottom edges. Trim excess fabric even with sides of block. Join remaining strips to pillow sides.

5. See page 73 for instructions on making a lap-back finish with 12½" x 21" backing pieces. When backing is complete, topstitch in seam lines between block and flange strips through both layers.

6. Insert a custom-made or purchased 18"-square pillow form.

Table Topper

To make one 38"-square table topper, you need additional yardage in the following quantities: ¾ yard each of fabrics I and III, ⅜ yard of Fabric IV, 2 yards of Fabric V (includes backing and binding), and a 42" square of batting.

1. For backing, cut a 42" square of Fabric V. For binding and borders, cut eight 2½" x 42" strips.

2. Cut two 15" x 21" pieces of Fabric III for quarter-square triangles. Using matching pieces of fabrics II and IV left over from quilt, mark and stitch grids as directed in Step 1 under Piecing the Blocks. Following instructions in Step 2, make 48 triangle-squares. Use 32 triangle-squares for table topper and set remaining squares aside for linens.

3. Cut pieces for four of Block A. Follow instructions given for quilt to assemble four blocks.

4. Join blocks in two rows of two blocks each; then join rows.

5. Add Fabric V border strips to opposite sides of assembled blocks. Press seam allowances toward borders and trim excess border fabric. Add borders to remaining sides in the same manner.

6. Quilt table topper as desired; then trim batting and backing even with block.

7. Join four remaining strips end-to-end to make 155" of binding. See page 23 for directions on making and applying straight-grain binding.

Embellished Linens

To embellish one queen-size sheet and two standard pillowcases, you need additional yardage in the following quantities: ¼ yard each of fabrics I and IV, ½ yard of Fabric III, ⅛ yard of Fabric V. If you have not already made quarter-square triangles as described in Table Topper Step 2, add ½ yard each of fabrics II, III, and IV.

1. If you have not already made the table topper, refer to Step 2 of those instructions to make quarter-square triangles. You need 16 triangle-squares.

2. For sheet, cut pieces for six of Block B. For each pillowcase, you will make one scallop that is a hybrid of blocks D and E—that is, the center section remains the same, but you will make the left side of Block D and the right side of Block E. Cut pieces for two of Block D/E hybrid for pillowcases.

3. For sheet, follow instructions given for quilt to assemble six B blocks.

4. Join blocks end-to-end in a row. Press under ¼" around scallop edge, clipping corners to seam line. Turn under ¼" along top edge and press.

5. Fold scallop border in half to find center. Find center of sheet in the same manner. Matching centers, pin border to top edge of sheet.

6. If border is longer than sheet, trim border to within ¼" of sheet sides. Press under ¼" on border ends and pin even with sheet sides.

7. Appliqué or topstitch border edges to sheet. Quilt in-the-ditch through border and sheet for extra stability.

8. For pillowcases, assemble left side and center of block, referring to diagram of Block D. For right side, refer to diagram of Block E. Make two blocks.

9. Turn and press raw edges of blocks as directed for sheet border. Appliqué or topstitch one block to side edge of each pillowcase. Quilt as above if desired.

Which Came First?

The chicken or the egg? Each gets equal credit in this charming picnic cloth, complete with napkins tucked into corner pockets. Strip-pieced borders frame eight whimsical hens and their eggs.

Quick-Piecing Techniques:

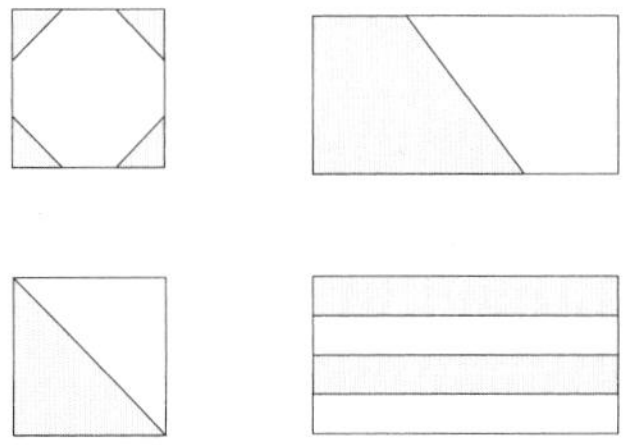

Finished Size
Blocks: 8 chicken blocks, 9" x 18"
             43 egg blocks, 2¼" x 3"

Cloth: 67½" x 68½" with
            four 14"-square
            napkins

Materials

	Fabric I (blue solid)	4⅜ yards
	Fabric II (gold-on-yellow print)	2 yards
	Fabric III (black-on-red print)	1¾ yards
	Fabric IV (white-on-white print)	1⅜ yards
	Fabric V (brown-on-gold print)	¼ yard
	Fabric VI (gold solid)	⅛ yard
	Fabric VII (black solid)	⅛ yard
	Backing fabric	4¼ yards

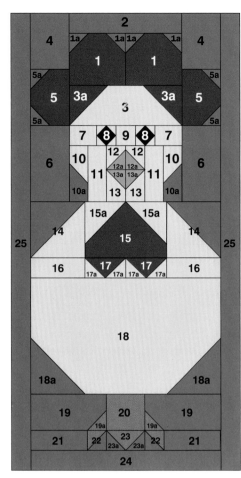

Chicken Block—Make 8.

Cutting
From Fabric I, cut:
◆ One 15" x 42" strip.
  From this, cut:
  • One 15" x 29"; then cut this piece into twelve 1¼" x 29" strips (egg border sashing).
  • One 8" x 15" for triangle-squares (14).
  • One 5" x 8" for triangle-squares (22).
◆ Twenty-five 1¼" x 42" strips.
  From these, cut:
  • Eight 1¼" x 23" (egg border sashing).
  • Sixteen 1¼" x 18½" (25).
  • Eight 1¼" x 5" (2).
  • Eight 1¼" x 8" (24).
  • 252 1¼" squares (1a, 5a, 23a, 26a).
  • Sixteen 1¼" x 2" (10a).
  • Twenty-four 1¼" x 2¾" (21, 28).
◆ Three 2" x 42" strips.
  From these, cut:
  • Thirty-two 2" x 3½" (6, 19).

◆ Six 2¾" x 42" strips.
  From these, cut:
  • Sixteen 2" x 2¾" (4).
  • Sixteen 2¾" squares (18a).
  • Thirty-six 2¾" x 3½" (27).
  • Six 2⅜" x 2¾" (29).
◆ Eight 4½" x 35" strips for outer borders.
◆ Four 11" squares for corner pockets.
◆ Four 14" squares and four 9½" squares for napkins.

From Fabric II, cut:
◆ Seven 4" x 42" strips for binding.
◆ Three 2¾" x 42" strips.
  From these, cut:
  • Forty 2¾" squares for sashing squares and napkin corners.
◆ Two 5" x 42" strips.
  From these, cut:
  • Eight 2" x 5" (3).
  • Eight 5" x 8" (18).
◆ Seven 1¼" x 42" strips.
  From these, cut:
  • Sixteen 1¼" x 1⅝" (7).
  • Forty 1¼" squares (9, 17a).
  • Sixteen 1¼" x 2" (10).
  • Thirty-two 1¼" x 2" (11, 16).
  • Sixteen 1¼" x 1½" (12).
  • Sixteen 1¼" x 1¾" (13).
◆ Two ⅞" x 42" strips.
  From these, cut:
  • Sixty-four ⅞" squares (8a).
◆ One 2" x 42" strip.
  From this, cut:
  • Sixteen 2" squares (15a).
◆ One 8" x 15" for triangle-squares (14).

From Fabric III, cut:
◆ Two 3" x 42" strips for pocket binding.
◆ Thirty-one 1¼" x 42" strips for strip-pieced sashing.
◆ Two 2¾" x 42" strips.
  From these, cut:
  • Sixteen 2¾" squares (1).
  • Eight 2¾" x 3½" (15).
◆ Three 2" x 42" strips.
  From these, cut:
  • Sixteen 2" squares (3a).
  • Sixteen 2" x 2¾" (5).
  • Sixteen 1¼" x 2" (17).

From Fabric IV, cut:
◆ Twenty-six 1¼" x 42" strips for strip-pieced sashing.
◆ Three 3½" x 42" strips.
  From these, cut:
  • Forty-three 2¾" x 3½" (26).

From Fabric V, cut:
◆ One 5" x 8" for triangle-squares (22).
◆ One 1¼" x 34" strip.
  From this, cut:
  • Sixteen 1¼" squares (19a).
◆ One 2" x 34" strip.
  From this, cut:
  • Eight 1¼" x 2" (23).
  • Eight 2" squares (20).

From Fabric VI, cut:
◆ One 1¼" x 42" strip.
  From this, cut:
  • Thirty-two 1¼" squares (12a, 13a).

From Fabric VII, cut:
◆ One 1¼" x 42" strip.
  From this, cut:
  • Sixteen 1¼" squares (8).

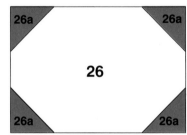

Egg Block—Make 43.

Piecing the Blocks

1. Referring to Chicken Block Assembly diagram, use diagonal-corner technique to make two each of units 1, 5, 8, 12, 13, 17, and 19; then make one each of units 3, 15, 18, and 23. Use diagonal-end technique to make two of Unit 10.

2. To make Unit 14, see page 17 for instructions on half-square triangles. On wrong side of 8" x 15" piece of Fabric I, draw a 2 x 4-square grid of 3⅛" squares. With right sides facing, match marked fabric with 8" x 15" piece of Fabric II. Stitch grid as directed on page 17. Cut 16 triangle-squares from the grid, two for each block.

3. To make Unit 22, mark a 2 x 4-square grid of 1⅝" squares on wrong side of 5" x 8" piece of Fabric I. With right sides facing, match marked fabric with 5" x 8" piece of Fabric V. Stitch grid as directed on page 17. Cut 16 triangle-squares from the grid, two for each block.

4. To assemble Section A, begin by joining two of Unit 1 as shown in Block Assembly diagram. Join Unit 2 to top of Unit 1 as shown; then join Unit 3 to bottom. Join Unit 4 to Unit 5, positioning Unit 5 as shown, for each side of Section A. Join combined 4-5 units to sides to complete Section A.

5. To assemble Section B, begin by joining units 7, 8, and 9 in a row as shown. Join units 12 and 13; then add units 10 and 11 in a row. Join both rows. Complete Section B by adding one of Unit 6 to each side as shown.

6. To assemble Section C, join one of Unit 14 to each side of Unit 15. Join units 16 and 17 in a row as shown. Join rows to complete Section C.

7. To assemble Section E, join one of Unit 19 to each side of Unit 20 as shown. Join units 21, 22, and 23 in a row as shown. Join rows; then add Unit 24 at bottom.

8. Join sections A-E in order as shown in assembly diagram. Complete chicken block by adding a Unit 25 to each side.

9. Using diagonal-corner technique, make 43 egg blocks as shown.

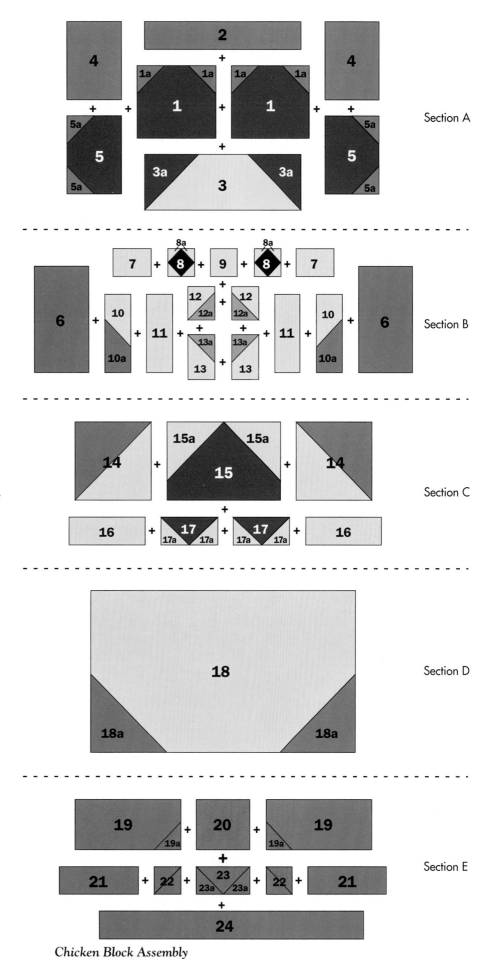

Chicken Block Assembly

85

Strip-Pieced Sashing

See page 18 for general instructions on strip piecing. Save strip set remnants for napkin trim.

1. Referring to diagrams of strip sets A and B, join 1¼" x 42" strips of fabrics III and IV as shown. Press all seam allowances toward Fabric III.

2. Cut thirty-two 3½"-wide segments of Strip Set A and sixteen 3½"-wide segments of Strip Set B. Join segments as shown to make 16 of Sashing Unit 1.

3. Cut twenty 6½"-wide segments of Strip Set A and ten 6½"-wide segments of Strip Set B. Join segments as shown to make 10 of Unit 2, adding yellow sashing squares to both ends of each unit.

4. Stitch one of Sashing Unit 1 to top and bottom edges of each chicken block.

5. Referring to quilt photograph, join four chicken blocks in a row with Unit 2 sashing strips between them and at both ends of row. Repeat to make second row of chicken blocks.

6. Cut sixteen 4¼"-wide segments of Strip Set A and fourteen 4¼"-wide segments of Strip Set B. Join segments as shown to make two of Sashing Unit 3.

7. Cut ten 5" segments and two 5⅜" segments from each strip set. Join segments as shown to make two of Sashing Unit 4, adding yellow corner squares to ends of each unit. Set aside sashing units 3 and 4 until egg border is added.

Egg Borders

1. Referring to border diagram, join four egg blocks and three of Unit 27 as shown. Add a Unit 28 at both ends of row. Make four rows. Press seam allowances away from egg blocks.

2. Add 1¼" x 23" Fabric I sashing strips to long sides of each egg row.

3. For long egg borders, join nine egg blocks and eight of Unit 27 in a row in the same manner. Add Unit 29 pieces to ends of each row. Assemble three rows. Piece two 29" Fabric I sashing strips end-to-end to make sashing for long sides of each row. Matching centers, join sashing strips to egg rows. Trim excess sashing fabric from ends.

4. Join shorter egg rows to ends of chicken rows. Adjust border seams as necessary to make border ends align with ends of chicken blocks.

5. Join a long egg border to top of each chicken row, aligning ends. Add remaining border to bottom of one row.

6. Position rows as shown in photograph and join.

Quilt Assembly

1. Join Sashing Unit 3 to opposite sides of cloth. Then join Sashing Unit 4 to remaining edges.

2. Join pairs of outer border strips end-to-end to make four border strips.

3. Mark center of each quilt side. Matching centers, join borders to top and bottom edges of quilt. Press seam allowances toward borders; then trim excess fabric from both ends of borders. Add side borders in the same manner.

Quilting

Outline-quilt patchwork and borders or quilt as desired. Trim batting and backing even with quilt top.

Corner Pockets

1. With wrong sides facing, fold each 11" square in half diagonally. Baste raw edges together.

2. With wrong sides facing, press Fabric III binding strips in half lengthwise. Cut 17" of binding for each pocket.

3. With right sides facing and raw edges aligned, stitch binding to each triangle's diagonal edge. Turn binding over to wrong side of triangle and topstitch. Trim excess binding at ends.

4. Matching raw edges at corners, baste triangles to quilt top.

Finishing

Make 280" of straight-grain binding. See page 23 for directions on making and applying binding.

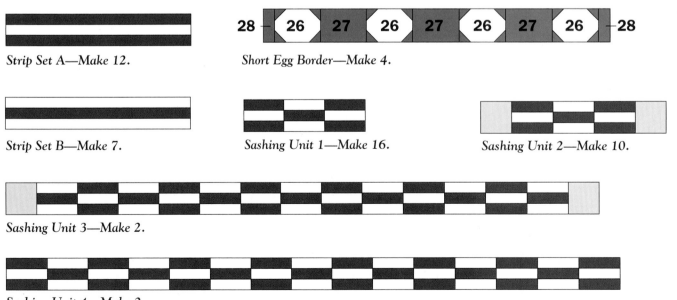

Strip Set A—Make 12.

28 — **26** **27** **26** **27** **26** **27** **26** — **28**

Short Egg Border—Make 4.

Strip Set B—Make 7.

Sashing Unit 1—Make 16.

Sashing Unit 2—Make 10.

Sashing Unit 3—Make 2.

Sashing Unit 4—Make 2.

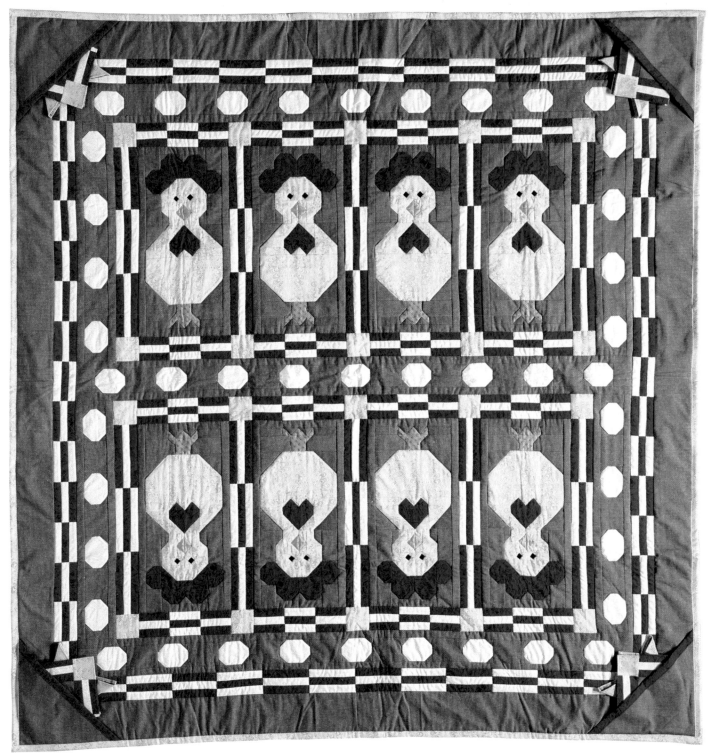

Napkins

1. Cut thirty-two 2¾"-wide segments from remainder of Strip Set A and sixteen 2¾"-wide segments from Strip Set B.
2. Join segments in rows of three, placing one B segment between two A segments. Make 16 rows. Add a yellow corner square to both ends of eight rows.
3. With right sides facing, join short sashing rows to opposite sides of each

9½" napkin square. Add long sashing rows to remaining sides.
4. With right sides facing, match each pieced napkin to a 14" napkin square. Stitch around all sides, leaving a 4" opening in one side for turning. Turn napkin right side out; slipstitch opening closed.
5. By hand or machine, quilt in-the-ditch on patchwork seam lines.

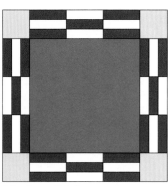

Napkin—Make 4.

Friends

This charming quilt gives your little girl 23 dolls to sleep with, and she'll love naming each new friend. The diagonal-corner technique makes the dolls quick to sew. You'll enjoy creating individual outfits for each doll with scraps of fabric, ribbon, and lace. The hair is made from knotted strips of torn muslin—it's easy and it's fun! The quilt pictured has buttons for added whimsy, but parents should consider safety when choosing embellishments. To make one more friend, see page 94 for patterns and instructions for the Best Friend Doll.

Quick-Piecing Techniques:

Finished Size

Blocks: 18 doll blocks, 12" x 18"
       5 doll blocks, 12" x 24"
       4 heart blocks, 9½" square

Quilt: 65" x 101"

Materials

	Fabric I (muslin or other flesh color)	¾ yard
	Fabric II (pink-and-blue marbled-look print)	2 yards
	Fabric III (solid dark pink)	1½ yards
	Fabric IV (solid medium pink)	1½ yards
	Fabric V (burgundy print)	2 yards
	Fabric VI (scraps of 30 assorted pink and blue fabrics)	¼ yard each
	Heavy unbleached muslin for hair bows	¾ yard
	Backing fabric	6 yards
	Assorted buttons	
	Assorted scraps of lace and ribbon trims	
	Brown, red, and black fine-tipped fabric markers	

Cutting

From Fabric I, cut:

- Three 5" x 42" strips.
  From these, cut:
  - Twenty-three 4½" x 5" (A-1, B-1, C-1).
- Two 1⅞" x 42" strips.
  From these, cut:
  - Forty-six 1⅝" x 1⅞" (A-7, B-7, C-7).
- One 2½" x 42" strip.
  From this, cut:
  - Twenty-three 1¾" x 2½" (A-12, B-12, C-12).
    Note: Leg color is optional. To make tights for some dolls, substitute ticking scraps for some of these pieces.

From Fabric II, cut:

- Eight 1" x 42" strips for middle borders.
  From four of these, cut:
  - Four 1" x 32¾".
  - Four 1" x 9".
- Two 13" x 42" strips.
  From these, cut:
  - Four 13" squares. Cut each square in half diagonally to get eight triangles for quilt corners.
  - Five 4⅞" squares. Cut each square in half diagonally to get 10 triangles (A-9).
  - Five 3⅞" squares. Cut each square in half diagonally to get 10 triangles (A-10).
- One 12½" x 42" strip.
  From this, cut:
  - Five 4¼" x 12½" (A-19).
  - Five 2¾" x 12½" (A-20).
- Two 1¾" x 42" strips.
  From these, cut:
  - Forty 1¾" squares (A-1a, A-11a).
  - Ten 1" x 1¾" (A-13).
- One 4½" x 42½" strip.
  From this, cut:
  - Ten 4¼" x 4½" (A-2).
- Three 2½" x 42" strips.
  From these, cut:
  - Ten 2½" x 9½" (A-18).
  - Ten 1½" x 2" (A-17).
  - Ten ⅞" x 1⅞" (A-8).

- From strip scraps, cut:
  - Ten 3" x 3¼" (A-15).
  - Thirty 1" squares (A-16a).

From Fabric III, cut:

- Three 1¾" x 42" strips.
  From these, cut:
  - Seventy-two 1¾" squares (B-1a, B-11a).

- Two 4⅞" x 42" strips.
  From these, cut:
  - Nine 4⅞" squares. Cut each square in half diagonally to get 18 triangles (B-9).
  - Nine 3⅞" squares. Cut each square in half diagonally to get 18 triangles (B-10).

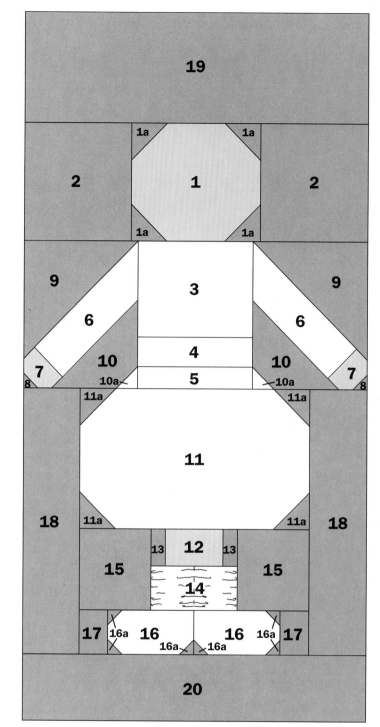

Block A—Make 5.

- Two 4½" x 42" strips.
  From these, cut:
  - Eighteen 4¼" x 4½" (B-2).
- Three 1" x 42" strips.
  From these, cut:
  - Eighteen 1" x 1¾" (B-13).
  - Eighteen 1" squares (B-16a).
  - Eighteen 1" x 1½" (B-17a).
- Two 3" x 42" strips.
  From these, cut:
  - Eighteen 3" x 3¼" (B-15).
  - Eighteen ⅞" x 1⅞" (B-8).
- Four 2½" x 42½" strips.
  From these, cut:
  - Eighteen 2½" x 8½" (B-18a).

From Fabric IV, cut:

- Three 1¾" x 42" strips.
  From these, cut:
  - Seventy-two 1¾" squares (C-1a, C-11a).
- Two 4½" x 42" strips.
  From these, cut:
  - Eighteen 4¼" x 4½" (C-2).
- Two 4⅞" x 42" strips.
  From these, cut:
  - Nine 4⅞" squares. Cut each square in half diagonally to get 18 triangles (C-9).
  - Nine 3⅞" squares. Cut each square in half diagonally to get 18 triangles (C-10).
- Three 1" x 42" strips.
  From these, cut:
  - Eighteen 1" x 1¾" (C-13).
  - Eighteen 1" squares (C-16a).
  - Eighteen 1" x 1½" (C-17a).
- Two 3" x 42" strips.
  From these, cut:
  - Eighteen 3" x 3¼" (C-15).
  - Eighteen ⅞" x 1⅞" (C-8).
- Four 2½" x 42½" strips.
  From these, cut:
  - Eighteen 2½" x 8½" (C-18a).

From Fabric V, cut:

- Two 6¼" x 42" strips.
  From these, cut:
  - Four 6¼" squares (21).
  - Eight 4¼" x 6¼" (22).
- Eight 3" x 42" strips for binding.

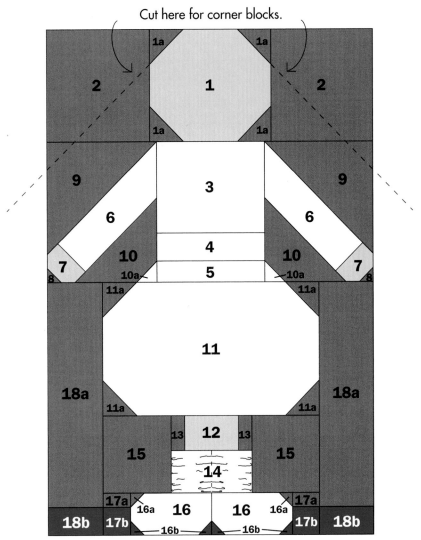

Cut here for corner blocks.

Block B—Make 9 with background Fabric III.
Block C—Make 9 with background Fabric IV.

- From strip scraps, cut:
  - Seventy-two 1" squares (B-16b, C-16b).
- Twenty 1½" x 42" strips.
  From 14 of these, cut:
  - Two 1½" x 27" and four 1½" x 31½" for inner border.
  - Two 1½" x 18" and four 1½" x 13½" for outer border.
  - Eight 1½" x 14½" for corner borders.
  - Thirty-six 1½" x 2½" (B-18b, C-18b).
  - Thirty-six 1½" squares (B-17b, C-17b).

From assorted Fabric VI scraps, cut the following pieces for each doll block:

- One 5¼" x 8½" (11-skirt).*
- One 1¼" x 4½" (5-skirt top).*
- Two 1¼" squares (10a-skirt top sides).*
- One 1½" x 4½" (4-belt).
- One 3¾" x 4½" (3-blouse).
- Two 1⅞" x 5½" (6-sleeves).
- One 3½" square (14-socks).
- Two 2" x 3½" (16-shoes).

*Note: Cut units 5, 10a, and 11 from same fabric to give uniform appearance to skirt. Mix and match other fabrics as desired.

Piecing the Doll Blocks

1. Center face pieces (Unit 1) over full-size face pattern on page 96, leaving ¼" seam allowance extending on all sides. Using pen color indicated on pattern, trace face details onto each piece. Add red dots for freckles if desired. Let ink dry before piecing Unit 1.

2. Referring to Block A Assembly diagram, use diagonal-corner technique to make one each of units 1, 11, and 16.

3. For each arm, join units 6, 7, and 8 in a row as shown in Block A Assembly diagram.

4. Referring to Arm Assembly diagram, add Unit 9 to left side of one arm, placing triangle at top of arm so that tip overlaps arm top ¼" as shown. Press triangle open. Aligning ruler with top edge of triangle, trim arm top at a 45° angle as shown. Next, align ruler with left edge of triangle to trim bottom of unit. Join Unit 10 to right side of arm with tip overlapping arm top ¼" as before. Press triangle open; then align ruler with triangle edge to trim bottom of hand as shown. Trim triangle tips from seam allowances. Add diagonal corner 10a as shown in Block A Assembly diagram to complete arm unit.

5. Make right arm unit in the same manner, reversing triangle positions to make a mirror-image unit.

6. Run a gathering stitch down sides of each Unit 14 piece. Gather sides to reduce height to 2". Topstitch sides and center to secure gathers.

7. To assemble Section A, join one of Unit 2 to opposite sides of each Unit 1 as shown in Block A Assembly diagram.

8. To assemble Section B, begin by joining units 3, 4, and 5 in a row as shown. Join arm units to sides, making sure that arm tops match at blouse shoulders.

9. To assemble Section C, begin by joining one of Unit 13 to both sides of Unit 12. Add Unit 14 to bottom of this unit as shown. Join one of Unit 15 to each side of combined unit. Join two of Unit 16 as shown; then add one of Unit 17 to each end of row. Join this row to bottom of assembled units 14 and 15. Join Unit 11 to top; then add one of Unit 18 to each side as shown.

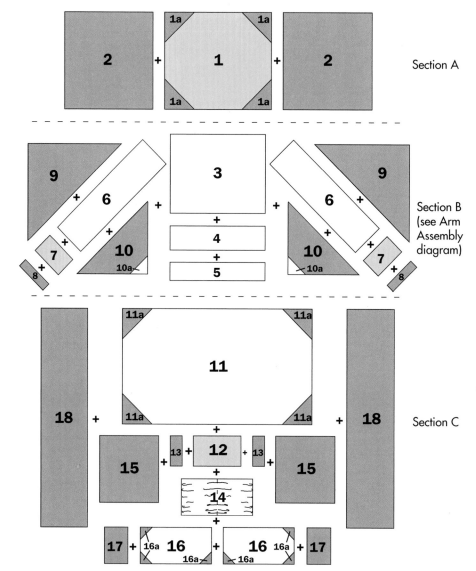

Block A Assembly

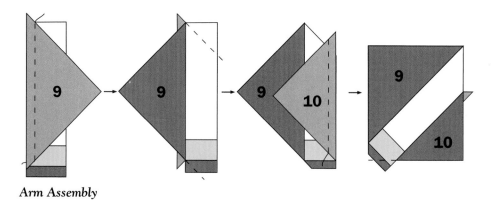

Arm Assembly

10. Join sections A, B, and C. Complete Block A by adding Unit 19 to top and Unit 20 to bottom. Make five of Block A.

11. To make blocks B and C, follow steps 1 through 8 above. Note that Unit 16 has two colors of diagonal corners in these blocks. For units 17 and 18, join a and b parts to make a complete unit; then follow Step 9 above to assemble Section C. Join sections. In this manner, make nine of Block B and nine of Block C.

Piecing the Corner Heart Blocks

1. Referring to Block D diagram, join one of Unit 22 to adjacent sides of each Unit 21 as shown, stopping stitching ¼" from inner corner of heart.

2. On wrong side of each Unit 22 piece, measure and mark 2" on both sides of each corner. Draw a diagonal line connecting these points. Trim each corner on diagonal line as shown.

Quilt Assembly

1. Referring to quilt photograph, join five A blocks in a row, turning blocks 2 and 4 upside down as shown. Match seams carefully so dolls' hands align.

2. Join two 1½" x 31½" strips of Fabric V end-to-end for each side border. Matching centers of block row and borders, sew border to each long side of center section. Press seam allowances toward borders. Join 1½" x 27" strips of Fabric V to each short side to complete center section.

3. Referring to photo, join six doll blocks for each long side of quilt, alternating B and C blocks and matching Fabric V at feet. Join three blocks for each short side in the same manner.

4. Blocks at both ends of each row must be mitered for corners. Referring to Block B/C diagram, pick out stitching to remove top 1a triangle from head on appropriate outside edge. Press exposed seam allowance flat; then align ruler with raw edge. Trim units 2 and 9 on that side as shown.

5. Join 1½" x 14½" strips of Fabric V to one straight leg of each 13" corner triangle of Fabric II. Strips are longer than triangle sides. Referring to Corner Assembly diagram, join one triangle to each mitered block, aligning Fabric V strip at bottom. Align ruler with mitered edge of block to trim triangle and Fabric V strip as shown.

6. Join three-block rows to short sides of quilt, beginning and ending stitching ¼" from row ends. Join six-block rows to long sides of quilt in the same manner.

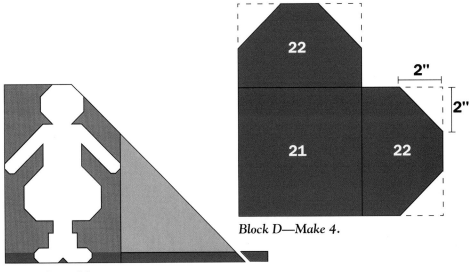

Block D—Make 4.

Corner Assembly

7. With right sides facing, pin corners together, matching triangles and borders. Beginning at corner of inner border, stitch each mitered seam. Press seam allowances to one side.

8. Turn under ¼" on all edges of each heart block and press. Center a heart on each corner so that top of heart meets dolls' hands. Heart cleft and bottom point should align with mitered seam. Hand-appliqué hearts in place.

9. For Fabric II borders, join two 42"-long strips end-to-end; then add a 9" strip to both ends to make a 101"-long border for each side. Join two 1" x 32¾" strips to make a 65" border for each end. Matching centers, join long borders to quilt sides. Press seam allowances toward border and trim excess border fabric. Join short borders to remaining sides in the same manner.

10. For outer border, join a 1½" x 42" strip of Fabric V to both ends of an 18"-long strip to make a 101" border for each quilt side. Join these to long sides of quilt as before. Next, join 13½" strips to both ends of a 42" strip to make a 68"-long border for each end. Join these to remaining quilt sides.

Quilting and Finishing

1. Mark quilting designs on quilt top as desired, using homemade or purchased stencils. The quilt shown has small hearts quilted at block corners and large hearts quilted in heart blocks.

2. Quilt a line down center of legs and socks. Quilt marked designs. Outline-quilt patchwork and corner hearts.

3. Make 336" of binding. See page 23 for directions on making and applying straight-grain binding.

4. Tear heavy muslin into twenty-three 1" x 42" strips; then tear each strip into 4½" pieces. Tear 4½" pieces of scrap dress fabrics. Tie a tight knot in center of each piece. Trim excess threads. Scatter bows on each doll's head as desired and hand-tack securely in place.

5. Embellish dresses with scraps of ribbon and lace. Add buttons as desired. Buttons should not be used on quilts intended for very young children.

Best Friend Doll

This best friend will go everywhere with the little girl who loves her and chooses her special name. This easy-to-make doll is the finishing touch to the Friends quilt or an ideal gift for any occasion. You can make her from scrap fabrics, but you'll find yardage for purchased materials below.

Finished Size
Approximately 21" tall

Materials

Fabric I (muslin or other flesh color)	⅜ yard
Fabric II (dark slate blue)	⅛ yard
Fabric III (light cranberry print)	⅜ yard
Fabric IV (slate blue mini-dot)	¼ yard
Fabric V (blue-on-ivory stripe or ticking)	⅛ yard
Fabric VI (white solid)	¼ yard
¼"-wide ecru lace trim	2 yards
2"-wide lace trim with fabric center strip	⅜ yard
Two ⅞"-diameter decorative buttons	
One ⅝"-diameter ribbon rose	
Brown, red, and black fine-tipped fabric markers	
Template material	
Polyester filling	

Cutting

For head/body, hands, and shoes, make templates from patterns on page 96 and 97.

From Fabric I, cut:
♦ Two head/bodies.
♦ Four hands.
♦ Four 3" x 5" for arms.

From Fabric II, cut:
♦ Four shoes.

From Fabric III, cut:
♦ One 6½" x 16" for skirt.
♦ Two 6" x 9" for blouse.
♦ Two 6" x 7½" for socks.

From Fabric IV, cut:
♦ Two 5¼" x 9" for sleeves.
♦ One 5" x 8" for apron.

From Fabric V, cut:
♦ Four 3" x 6" for tights.
(For natural-colored legs, cut these pieces from Fabric I.)

From Fabric VI, cut:
♦ One 7" x 16" for petticoat.

Doll Body Assembly

1. Center one head piece over full-size pattern on page 96. Using pen color indicated on pattern, trace face details onto muslin. Let ink dry.
2. With right sides facing, join heads by stitching from dot to dot around shoulders and head. Backstitch.
3. On each side of body, begin stitching again 3" below shoulder dot and stitch to bottom edge. Backstitch at beginning and end of each seam.

4. Clip curves and corners to seam line; then trim seam allowance to ⅛". Turn head/body right side out.
5. Turn under ¼" around each armhole and at bottom edge. Press hems and topstitch.
6. With right sides facing and straight edges aligned, join a hand to one end of each arm piece. With right sides facing, join two arms, leaving top open. Turn arm to right side; then stuff to within 2" of top. Baste arm top where stuffing stops to secure stuffing. Repeat to make second arm.
7. Slip arm seam allowances into body armholes. Topstitch arms in place.
8. Stuff head and body firmly to within ½" of bottom. Baste bottom edges together loosely to keep stuffing from falling out.
9. With right sides facing, join long edges of two leg pieces to make a tube. Repeat to make second leg. Do not turn tubes yet.
10. With right sides facing, join two shoe pieces, leaving top open. Turn shoe right side out. Repeat to make second shoe.
11. With right sides facing, fold one sock piece in half widthwise and join short edges to make a tube. Turn sock right side out. With wrong sides facing, fold sock in half so that raw edges align, making a tube of double thickness. Press folded edge. Repeat to make second sock.
12. Place a shoe inside one sock, with raw edges aligned and back seam of shoe matching sock seam. (Sock will be larger, so fold a few small pleats to make edges match.) With raw edges aligned and sock/shoe seam matching one leg seam, place sock/shoe inside one leg. Pin or baste all layers; then machine-stitch around raw edges. Turn leg right side out. Repeat to complete second leg.
13. Stuff legs to within 2" of top. Baste leg tops to secure stuffing.
14. Loosen body basting enough to insert legs. Pin or baste legs in place. Topstitch across body bottom through all layers, securing legs.

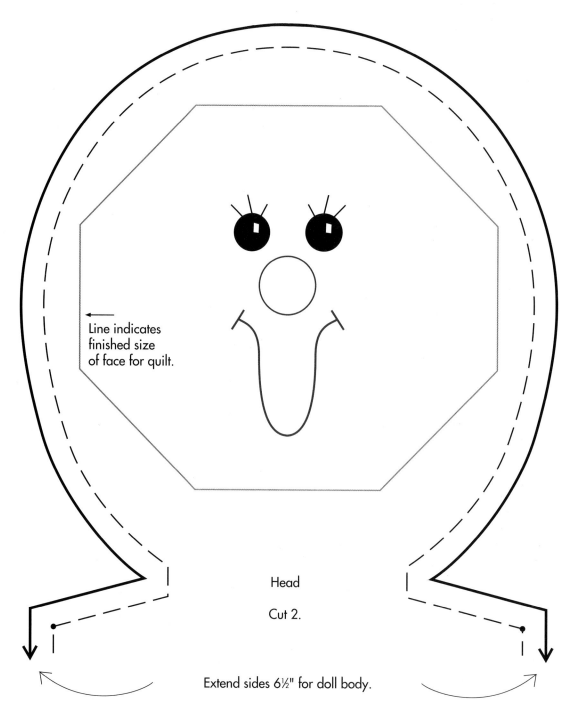

Line indicates finished size of face for quilt.

Head

Cut 2.

Extend sides 6½" for doll body.

15. Pull socks down a little to cover leg/shoe seam lines, giving socks a rumpled look. Sew buttons to top front of shoes. Remove any visible basting stitches.

Making Doll Hair

Tear scraps of fabrics I, III, and IV into 1"-wide strips. Tear strips into 5"-long pieces. Tie knots in center of each piece. Clip raveled threads. Tack bows to doll's head, mixing colored bows with muslin bows evenly. Cover head back, top, and around face with bows.

Doll Dress Assembly

1. With right sides facing, join short sides of petticoat. Turn right side out. To hem, turn under ¼" on one long edge; then turn under ¼" again and press. Position ¼" lace trim on top of hem and topstitch, securing hem.

2. Turn under ¼" hem at top edge of petticoat and gather. Slip petticoat onto doll and pull gathers to fit waist. Secure gathers and hand-tack petticoat to body.

3. To make neck and back opening, fold one blouse piece in half lengthwise and then crosswise, creasing to mark

center. On wrong side of fabric, align a ruler with crosswise crease and draw a 2¾"-long line (1⅜" on each side of center point) as shown in Blouse Facing diagram. Next, draw a line on lengthwise crease from center point to bottom edge as shown. Put both blouse pieces together with right sides facing and stitch ¼" from drawn lines. Cut through both layers on marked lines and clip corners as indicated in red.

4. Turn blouse right side out and press. Hand-sew ¼" lace trim around neck edge and down one side of back opening.

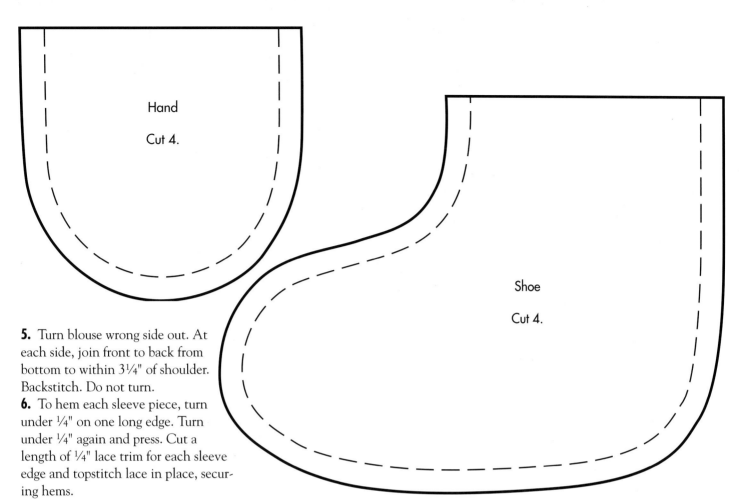

Hand

Cut 4.

Shoe

Cut 4.

5. Turn blouse wrong side out. At each side, join front to back from bottom to within 3¼" of shoulder. Backstitch. Do not turn.

6. To hem each sleeve piece, turn under ¼" on one long edge. Turn under ¼" again and press. Cut a length of ¼" lace trim for each sleeve edge and topstitch lace in place, securing hems.

7. With right sides facing, fold each sleeve in half and join short ends to make a tube. Turn right side out. Gather top edge to measure 6¼". With right sides facing, insert gathered end of each sleeve into blouse armhole, adjusting gathers to fit. Stitch sleeves to blouse.

8. Turn blouse right side out. Tack ribbon rose to center front at neckline.

9. To make skirt, join short sides of skirt piece with right sides facing, starting at one edge and stopping 3" from opposite edge. Backstitch. Press under seam allowance on both sides of 3" opening. Topstitch edges of opening.

10. Turn under ¼" at skirt bottom; then turn under ½" and press. Slipstitch hem. Gather skirt top to fit bottom of blouse. With right sides facing, join skirt to blouse, matching back openings.

11. Gather bottom of each sleeve ½" from top of lace trim. Put dress on doll. Pull sleeve gathers tight around arm and secure gathers. Slipstitch edges of dress back together, allowing back lace trim to cover stitches.

12. Turn under ¼" along one long edge of apron and both short sides. Press; then turn under another ¼" on all three sides. Topstitch side hems. Cut a length of ¼" lace trim to fit bottom edge, turning ends of lace over sides to back. Topstitch lace, securing bottom hem. Gather top edge of apron to 5½".

13. Cut a length of 2"-wide lace trim to fit around doll's waist, overlapping ½" in back. Center waistband on gathered apron top and topstitch. Turn under ¼" on one end of trim.

14. Put apron on doll, pinning waistband around waist.

15. To make apron shoulder straps, cut two 8" lengths of ¼" lace trim. Tack one end of each piece inside apron waistband at front about 2½" apart. Turn lace over shoulders and tack remaining ends inside waistband at back. Tack apron waistband to dress. Overlap waistband ends at back and tack to secure.

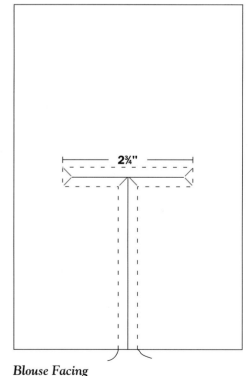

2¾"

Blouse Facing

Black-Eyed Susan

A humble flower becomes a masterpiece in this easy-to-sew design. The appliquéd leaves are an elegant touch to a quilt that assembles in no time with basic patchwork techniques and strip piecing. Use scraps to make accessory pillows for an ensemble that's bright as sunshine.

Quick-Piecing Techniques:

Finished Size
Blocks: 17 blocks, 12" square   Quilt: 83½" x 104½"
    4 corner blocks, 15½" square

Materials

	Fabric I (white-on-white print)	4 yards
	Fabric II (yellow-on-black print)	2¼ yards
	Fabric III (black mini-print)	1 yard
	Fabric IV (yellow solid)	3⅝ yards
	Fabric V (green mini-print)	1 yard
	Backing fabric	6 yards
	Tracing paper or template plastic	

Cutting

Refer to diagrams on pages 100 and 101 to identify blocks and units designated in cutting list.

From Fabric I, cut:
◆ Four 14½" x 42" strips.
   From these, cut:
- Thirty-four 4" x 14½" for pieced outer border.

◆ Ten 1½" x 42" strips.
   From these, cut:
- Thirty-six 1½" x 5" (4).
- 144 1½" squares (2a).

◆ Twelve 2⅞" x 42" strips for strip sets 1 and 2.

◆ Three 2½" x 42" strips.
   From these, cut:
- Thirty-six 2½" squares (1).

◆ One 13" x 42" strip.
   From this, cut:
- Three 13" squares.
    Cut squares in half diagonally to get six setting triangles.

From Fabric II, cut:
◆ One 30" square for bias binding.
◆ Eight 4" x 42½" strips.
   From these, cut:
- Seventy-two 2½" x 4" (2).
- Thirty-six 4" squares (3).

◆ Five 2½" x 42" for strip sets 3 and 4.

From Fabric III, cut:
◆ Ten 1¼" x 42½" strips for inner border.
   From eight of these, cut:
- Eight 1¼" x 26".
- Four 1¼" x 16½".

◆ Three 1½" x 42" strips.
   From these, cut:
- Fifty-four 1½" squares (3a, 5).
- Nine 1½" x 3½" (6).

◆ One 2½" x 42" strip.
   From this, cut:
- Four 2½" squares (9).

◆ Five 1¼" x 42" strips.
   From these and scraps from previous steps, cut:
- Eight 1¼" x 14½" (10).
- Eight 1¼" x 16" (11).

From Fabric IV, cut:
◆ Thirteen 2⅞" x 42" strips for strip sets 1 and 2.
◆ Four 2½" x 42" strips for strip sets 3 and 4.
◆ One 2⅞" x 42" strip.
   From this, cut:
- Eight 2⅞" squares (7).

◆ Four 16" x 42" strips.
   From these, cut:
- Thirty-eight 4" x 16" for pieced outer border.

From Fabric V, cut:
◆ One 6½" x 42" strip.
   From this, cut:
- Sixteen 2½" x 6½" (8).

◆ Two 8" x 42" strips.
   From these, cut:
- Twelve 5½" x 8" for leaves.

◆ Four 1¾" x 26" for inner border.

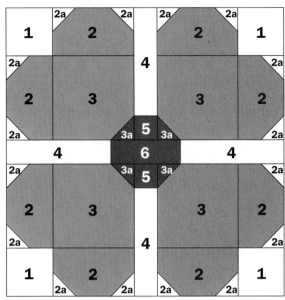

Block A—Make 9.

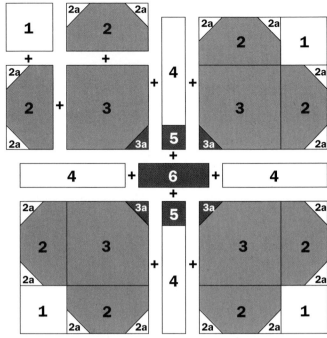

Block A Assembly

Piecing the Blocks

1. Using diagonal-corner technique, make eight of Unit 2 and four of Unit 3 as shown in Block A Assembly diagram.

2. Referring to upper left corner of Block A Assembly diagram, join Unit 1 to side of one Unit 2; then join another Unit 2 to top of one Unit 3. Press both seam allowances toward Unit 2. Join these combined units as shown to complete one petal section. Make three more petal sections in the same manner.

3. Join one Unit 5 to one end of two of Unit 4 as shown.

4. Turning petal sections as shown, join two sections to opposite sides of each 4-5 unit.

5. To make center bar, join two of Unit 4 to opposite ends of Unit 6.

6. Join petal sections to both sides of center bar as shown to complete block. Make nine of Block A.

7. Referring to diagrams of strip sets 1 and 2, use a scant seam allowance to join strips of fabrics I and IV as shown. Each finished strip set should measure 12½" wide. Press seam allowances toward Fabric IV.

8. For Block B, cut twenty-four 2⅞"-wide segments from Strip Set 1 and sixteen segments from Strip Set 2. Each segment is a horizontal row of the block.

9. Referring to Block B Assembly diagram, arrange three Strip Set 1 segments and two Strip Set 2 segments in rows as shown. Join rows to complete block. Make eight of Block B.

10. For Block C, cut sixteen 2⅞"-wide segments of Strip Set 1 and eight segments of Strip Set 2.

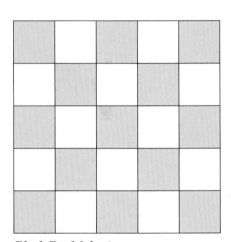

Block B—Make 8.

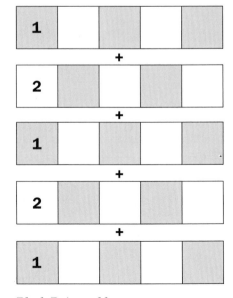

Block B Assembly

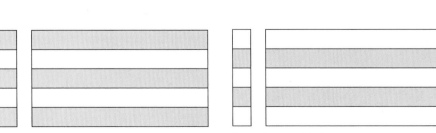

Strip Set 1—Make 3.   *Strip Set 2—Make 2.*

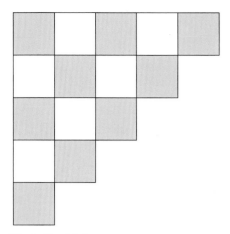

Block C—Make 8.

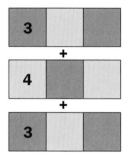

3
+
4
+
3

Nine-Patch Assembly

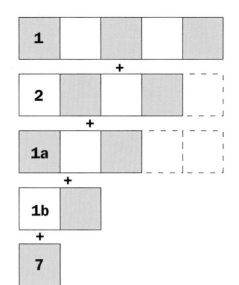

Block C Assembly

11. Arrange segments in horizontal rows as shown in Block C Assembly diagram. Row 1 is a segment from Strip Set 1. Row 2 is a Strip Set 2 segment with a Fabric I square removed. For next row, separate a Strip Set 1 segment between third and fourth squares as shown—the three-square unit becomes Row 1a and the two-square unit becomes Row 1b. The last row is a Unit 7 square. Join rows as shown to complete one block. Make eight of Block C.

12. Referring to diagrams of strip sets 3 and 4, join strips of fabrics II and IV as shown. Each finished strip set should measure 6½" wide. Press seam allowances toward Fabric II.

Strip Set 3—Make 2.

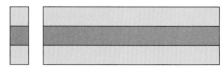

Strip Set 4—Make 1.

13. Cut thirty-two 2½"-wide segments from Strip Set 3 and 16 segments from Strip Set 4.

14. Referring to Nine-Patch Assembly diagram, arrange two Strip Set 3 segments and one Strip Set 4 segment in rows as shown. Join rows. Make four nine-patches for each Block D.

15. Referring to Block D Assembly diagram, join a nine-patch to opposite sides of two of Unit 8. Press seam allowances toward Unit 8.

16. To make Block D center bar, join a Unit 8 to opposite sides of each Unit 9. Press seam allowances toward Unit 8. Join nine-patch rows to opposite sides of center bar as shown.

17. Add a Unit 10 to top and bottom of block as shown in block diagram. Join Unit 11 to remaining sides to complete Block D. Make four of Block D.

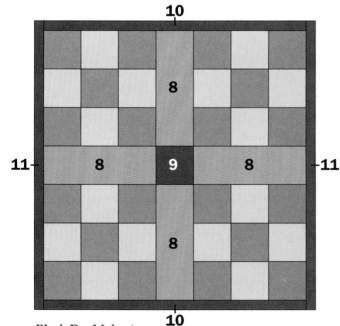

Block D—Make 4.

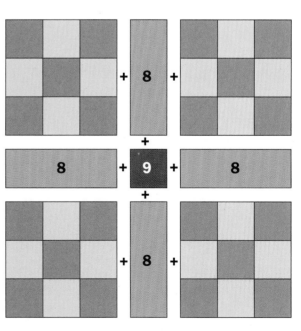

Block D Assembly

Appliqué

Trace leaf pattern onto tracing paper or template plastic. Cut out leaf template; then mark one side of template as right side. Trace template onto six 5½" x 8" pieces of Fabric V with right side up; then trace template on remaining pieces with right side down. For machine appliqué, cut out each leaf on drawn line. For hand appliqué, add ¼" seam allowance when cutting.

Referring to photograph, position two leaves on each setting triangle as shown, keeping leaves clear of seam allowances on triangle edges. Using method of your choice, appliqué leaves in place on all six triangles.

Quilt Assembly

1. Referring to Quilt Assembly diagram, join blocks A, B, C, and setting triangles in diagonal rows as shown. Then join rows.
2. Before adding borders, use a rotary cutter and acrylic ruler to trim excess fabric from edges of Block C.
3. For side borders, join a 15"-long strip of Fabric III to both ends of each 42½"-long strip. Matching centers of border and quilt side, join borders to quilt sides.
4. Join two 27½"-long strips of Fabric III to opposite sides of each 27½"-long strip of Fabric V, making four strip sets.

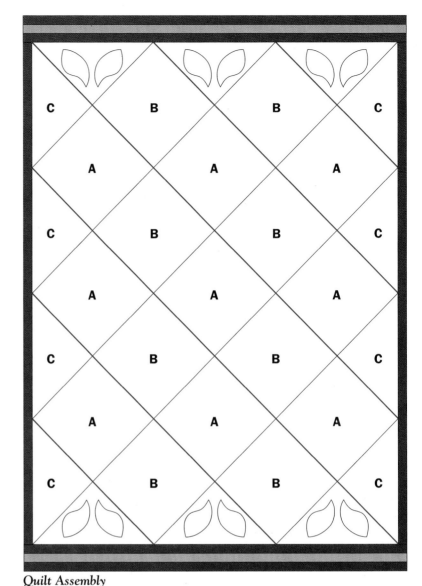

Quilt Assembly

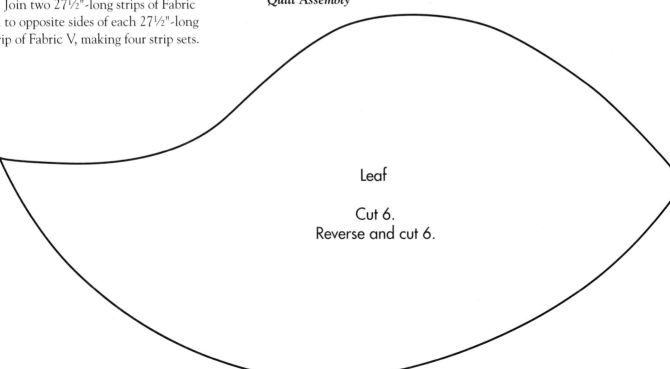

Leaf

Cut 6.
Reverse and cut 6.

5. Referring to Quilt Assembly diagram, join two strip sets end-to-end for top border. Matching center seam of border with center of top edge, join border to quilt top. Repeat for bottom border.

6. For each side outer border, join eleven 4" x 16" pieces of Fabric IV and ten 4" x 14½" pieces of Fabric I in a row as shown in photograph. Join borders to quilt sides, easing to fit as necessary. (See page 15 for tips on easing.)

7. For top border, join eight 4" x 16" pieces of Fabric IV and seven 4" x 14½"

pieces of Fabric I in a row as shown. Add one of Block D to each end of the row. Join row to top of quilt. Repeat for bottom border.

Quilting and Finishing

1. Outline-quilt blocks or quilt as desired. Quilt veins in leaves. Quilt straight lines in each piece of outer border, 1" from each seam line.

2. Before applying binding, decide whether to leave corners square on Fabric IV pieces in outer border or to trim

them as shown in photograph. To mark a curve at each corner, use bottom of a coffee mug or soda can as a template. Trim corners as desired.

3. Cut 30" square of Fabric II in half diagonally. Starting from each diagonal edge, cut 2"-wide strips. Join strips end-to-end to make a continuous strip of bias binding. With wrong sides facing, press strip in half, being careful not to stretch bias edges. See page 23 for directions on applying binding.

Mountain Greenery

Combine scraps with three quick-piecing techniques to create a wall hanging that celebrates our native land. The four blocks that comprise this design represent blue skies and purple-tinged mountains sheltering forests and wildlife. Strip piecing makes quick work of tree trunks and antlers. Dimensional ears and jute tails add charm to frolicking deer. The Christmas tree skirt on page 111 is made with the same blocks.

Quick-Piecing Techniques:

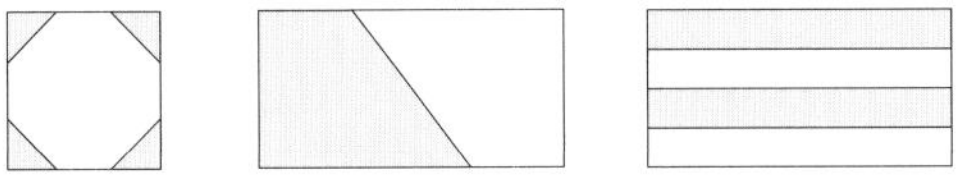

Finished Size

Blocks: 4 mountain blocks, 7" square
     10 pine tree blocks, 7" square
     4 deer blocks, 6¼" x 8¾"
     32 tree blocks, 4" x 4⅞"

Wall Hanging: 44" x 60"

Materials

	Fabric I (white solid)	⅛ yard
	Fabric II (six assorted lavender prints and solids)	scraps or ⅛ yard each
	Fabric III (32 assorted green prints and solids)	scraps or ⅛ yard each
	Fabric IV (dark brown solid)	¼ yard
	Fabric V (light tan print)	1½ yards
	Fabric VI (tan print)	¼ yard
	Fabric VII (pale blue solid)	⅜ yard
	Fabric VIII (medium blue solid)	⅜ yard
	Fabric IX (navy solid)	1⅜ yards
	Backing fabric	3¾ yards
	⅛"-wide jute trim	⅛ yard
	Template material or tracing paper	

Cutting

Before cutting, trace ear pattern onto template material or tracing paper.

From Fabric I, cut:
- Two 1½" x 42" strips.
  From these, cut:
  - Four 1½" x 7½" (A-9).
  - Four 1½" x 6½" (A-8).

From Fabric II scraps, cut:
- Four 3½" squares (A-1) from darkest lavender.
- Four 1½" x 3½" (A-2) from dark lavender.
- Eight 1½" x 4½" (A-3, A-4) from dark or medium lavenders.
- Four 1½" x 5½" (A-5) from light lavender.
- Four 1½" x 5½" (A-6) and four 1½" x 6½" (A-7) from lightest lavender.

From Fabric III scraps, cut:
- Thirty-two 4⅝" x 4⅞" (D-1).
- Forty 1½" x 3½" (B-3, B-6, B-9, B-12).
- Forty 1½" x 4½" (B-4, B-7, B-10, B-13).

From Fabric IV, cut:
- Three 1" x 42" strips for strip sets 1 and 2.
- Three ⅝" x 42" strips for strip sets 3 and 4.

From Fabric V, cut:
- Two 2¾" x 42" strips for Strip Set 1.
- Five 2¼" x 42" strips for strip sets 2 and 3.
- One 2½" x 42" strip for Strip Set 4.
- One 1½" x 42" strip for Strip Set 4.
- One 1⅜" x 42" strip for Strip Set 4.
- One 4¾" x 42" strip.
  From this, cut:
  - Four 2¼" x 4¾" (C-5).
  - Five 3⅞" squares. Cut each square in half diagonally to get 10 triangles (B-1).
  - Four 3" x 3¼" (C-1).
- One 1" x 42" strip.
  From this, cut:
  - One 1" x 31" (22).
  - Four 1" x 1¾" (C-9a).

- Five 1½" x 42" strips.
  From these, cut:
  - Twenty 1½" x 3½" (B-11).
  - Twenty 1½" x 2½" (B-8).
  - Twenty-four 1½" squares (B-5, C-13a).
  - Four 1½" x 3" (C-4).
  - Four 1½" x 2⅞" (C-14).
  - Four 1" x 1½" (C-7a).
  - Eight 1⅜" squares (C-15b, C-16b).
  - Four 1¼" squares (C-10b).
  - Four 1⅛" squares (C-12a).
  - Eight 1" squares (C-6a).

- One 7⅞" x 42" strip.
  From this, cut:
  - Three 7⅞" squares. Cut each square in half diagonally to get six triangles (20).
  - One 5⅞" square. Cut square in half diagonally to get two triangles (21).
  - Three 1¼" x 9¼" (24).
  - Two 1⅞" x 9¼" (23).

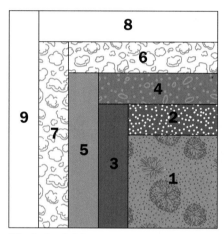

Block A—Make 4.

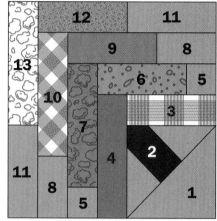

Block B—Make 10.

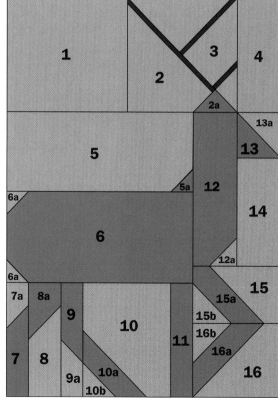

Block C—Make 4.

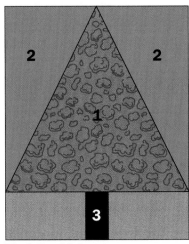

2 **2**

1

3

Block D—Make 32.

♦ One 2½" x 42" strip.
  From this, cut:
  • Four 2½" x 3" (C-10).
  • Four 2⅛" x 2½" (C-16).
  • Four 1¼" x 2½" (C-8).
  • Four 1¾" x 2⅛" (C-15).

From Fabric VI, cut:
♦ One 2½" x 42" strip.
  From this, cut:
  • Four 2½" x 4¾" (C-6).
  • Four 1" x 2½" (C-7).
  • Four 2⅛" squares (C-16a).
  • Four 2" squares (C-10a).
♦ One 1¾" x 42" strip.
  From this, cut:
  • Four 1¾" x 2⅛" (C-15a).
  • Four 1¼" x 1¾" (C-8a).
  • Four 1½" squares (C-13).
  • Four 1½" x 3⅞" (C-12).
  • Two 1½" squares. Cut each
    square in half diagonally to get
    four triangles (C-2a).
♦ One 1" x 42" strip.
  From this, cut:
  • Four 1" x 3" (C-11).
  • Four 1" x 2¼" (C-9).
  • Four 1" squares (C-5a).
♦ From scraps, cut:
  • Eight ears, cutting four with
    template faceup and four more
    with template facedown.

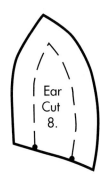

Ear
Cut
8.

From Fabric VII, cut:
♦ One 10⅞" x 42" strip.
  From this, cut:
  • One 10⅞" square. Cut square
    in half diagonally to get two
    triangles (19).
  • One 7⅞" square. Cut square in
    half diagonally to get two triangles
    (18). Discard one triangle.
  • One 7½" square (17).

From Fabric VIII, cut:
♦ Two 5⅜" x 42" strips.
  From these, cut:
  • Eight 5⅜" x 10½".
    Cut these as shown in Cutting
    diagram to get eight D-2 triangles
    from each piece, four of which
    point to the right and four to the
    left. Store "righties" and "lefties"
    separately. Trim ⅞" from narrow
    tip of all 64 of these triangles.

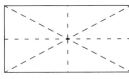

Cutting

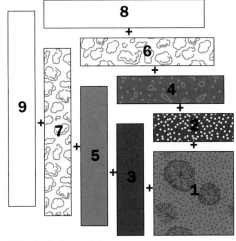

Block A Assembly

From Fabric IX, cut:
♦ Five 3" x 42" strips for binding.
♦ Six 2½" x 42" strips.
  From four of these, cut:
  • Four 2½" x 23" for outer border.
  • Two 2½" x 16" for outer border.
  • Three 1¼" x 19".
    From these, cut:
    • Fourteen 1¼" x 5⅜" (25).
♦ Six 1½" x 42" strips.
  From these, cut:
  • Two 1½" x 41" for inner border.
  • Four 1½" x 22¾" for inner border.
  • Four 1½" x 5⅜" (26).
♦ Two 1¾" x 42" strips.
  From these, cut:
  • Ten 1¾" x 5⅜" (27).

Piecing the Mountain Blocks
Referring to Block A Assembly diagram, join units in numerical order as shown. As strips are added, press seam allowances away from newest strip. Make four of Block A.

Piecing the Pine Tree Blocks
1. For Block B, refer to Strip Set 1 diagram and join two 2¾" x 42" strips of Fabric V to opposite sides of one 1" x 42" strip of Fabric IV. Cut strip set into ten 2¾"-wide segments.
2. Fold each segment in half to find center of long edge and mark. Referring to Diagram 1, cut from both bottom corners to center of top edge to make one tree trunk (Unit 2).

Strip Set 1—Make 1.

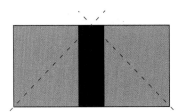

Diagram 1

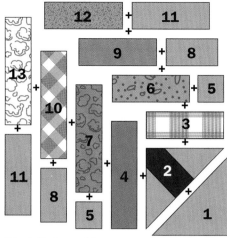

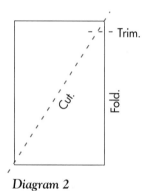

Block B Assembly

7. For border pine trees (Block D), begin by making two of Strip Set 2, joining two 2¼" x 42" strips of Fabric V to opposite sides of one 1" x 42" strip of Fabric IV for each strip set. Press seam allowances toward Fabric IV. From these strip sets, cut thirty-two 1½"-wide segments for tree trunks (Unit D-3).

8. With right sides facing, fold each 4⅝" x 4⅞" piece of Fabric III in half lengthwise as shown in Diagram 2. With fold at right, cut through both layers from bottom left to top right as shown. Discard trimmed corners. Trim ½" from tip of each remaining D-1 triangle.

Piecing the Deer Blocks

1. Referring to Strip Set 3 diagram, join 2¼" x 42" strip of Fabric V to ⅝" x 42" strip of Fabric IV. From this, cut four 4¾"-wide segments. Fold each segment in half to find center of one long edge and mark. Referring to Diagram 3, cut from both bottom corners of each segment to center of top edge to make one C-2 triangle. Next, trim 1" from left corner of triangle as shown in Diagram 4. Join triangle 2a to cut edge to complete Unit 2.

2. Referring to Strip Set 4 diagram, join three strips of Fabric V and two ⅝" x 42" strips of Fabric IV as shown, placing 2½"-wide strip on top, 1⅜"-wide strip in middle, and 1½"-wide strip at bottom. From this strip set, cut four 2⅜"-wide segments. Fold each segment in half to find center of one long edge and mark. Referring to Diagram 5, cut from both bottom corners of each segment to center of top edge to make one C-3 unit.

3. Join diagonal edges of units 1 and 2 as shown in Block B Assembly diagram, making a square. Press seam allowances toward Unit 1.

4. Join Unit 3 to top of square; then add Unit 4 to left side as shown.

5. Join Unit 5 to one end of Unit 6; then join 5-6 unit to top of block. Join another Unit 5 to one end of Unit 7; then join 5-7 unit to left side.

6. Join a Unit 8 to ends of units 9 and 10. Join a Unit 11 to ends of unit 12 and 13. Join combined units in order shown in Block B Assembly diagram. Make 10 of Block B.

Diagram 2

9. Referring to Block D Assembly diagram, join a righty Unit 2 to left side of Unit 1, aligning trimmed tip of Unit 2 with bottom edge of Unit 1. Join a lefty Unit 2 to opposite side of Unit 1 in the same manner.

10. Join Unit 3 to bottom of tree top to complete pine tree block. Make 32 of Block D.

Diagram 3

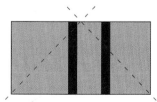

Diagram 4

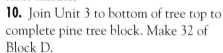

Strip Set 2—Make 2.

Strip Set 3—Make 1.

Strip Set 4—Make 1.

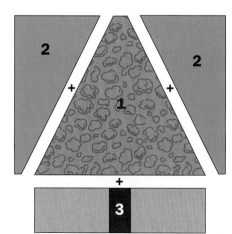

Block D Assembly

Diagram 5

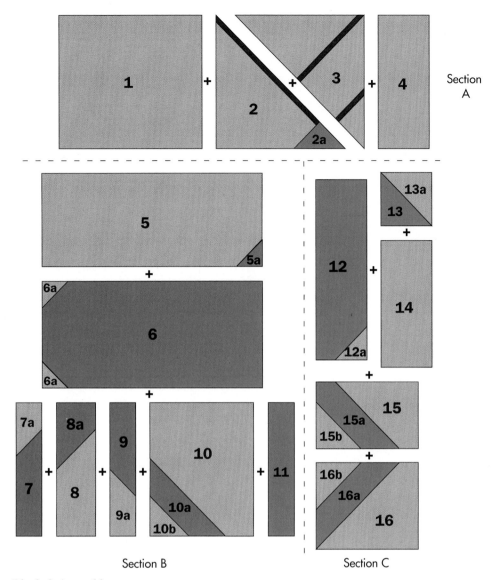

Section
A

Section B

Section C

Block C Assembly

3. Using diagonal-corner technique, make one each of units 5, 6, 12, and 13 as shown in Block C Assembly diagram.
4. Units 10 and 16 have double diagonal corners. For Unit 10, add 10a as a diagonal corner; then add 10b to the same corner in the same manner. Make Unit 16 in the same manner.
5. Using diagonal-end technique, make one each of units 7, 8, and 9.
6. Unit 15 is a combination of diagonal-end and diagonal-corner techniques. Add 15a to 15 as a diagonal end; then join diagonal corner 15b as shown.
7. To assemble Section A of block, join Unit 2 to Unit 3. Join units 1 and 4 to sides of 2-3 square as shown.

8. To assemble Section B, begin at bottom. Join units 7, 8, 9, 10, and 11 in a row as shown. Join Unit 6 to top of row. Cut a ¾"-long piece of jute for each block. Matching raw edges, pin one end of jute to top edge of Unit 6 where 6 and 6a meet. Join Unit 5 to top of Unit 6, catching jute in seam. Ravel jute end to fluff tail.
9. To assemble Section C, join units 13 and 14 as shown. Join Unit 12 to left side; then join units 15 and 16 to bottom.

10. With right sides facing, join two ear pieces, stitching from dot to dot and leaving straight edge open. Trim and clip seam allowance; then turn right side out. Fold bottom corners of ear in, overlapping at center as shown in Diagram 6. Matching raw edges and with fold faceup, pin ear to bottom of Unit 2 where 2 and 2a meet.

Diagram 6

11. To assemble block, join sections B and C. Join Section A to top, catching ear in seam. Make four of Block C.

Quilt Assembly

1. Referring to Quilt Assembly diagram, join A and B blocks in diagonal rows as indicated by red lines. Add units 17, 18, 20, and 21 to row ends as shown. Join rows; then join Unit 19 triangles to top corners. Complete center section by joining Unit 22 to bottom.

2. Join four deer blocks in a row as shown, sewing a Unit 24 between blocks. Join a Unit 23 to each row end. Join deer row to bottom of center section.

3. Join two 1½" x 22¾" strips of Fabric IX end-to-end to make a 45"-long border for each side. Join borders to quilt sides. Press seam allowances toward border and trim border ends.

4. Assemble two side rows of eight D blocks each, sewing a Unit 25 between blocks. Join a row to each quilt side, easing as necessary. (See page 15 for tips on easing.)

5. Join 1½" x 41" strips of Fabric IX to top and bottom. Press seam allowances toward border and trim border ends.

6. For top and bottom rows, begin by joining six D blocks for each row, sewing a Unit 27 between blocks. Join a Unit 26 to both ends of each row; then add one more block at each end. Join rows to top and bottom of quilt, aligning each Unit 26 with inner side borders.

7. Join a 2½" x 16" strip of Fabric IX to end of a 42"-long strip for each outer side border. Join borders to quilt sides. Press seam allowances toward border and trim ends.

8. For each top and bottom outer border, join two 2½" x 23" strips of Fabric IX end-to-end. Join borders to top and bottom edges. Press and trim as before.

Quilting and Finishing

Outline quilt patchwork or quilt as desired.

Make 210" of binding. See page 23 for directions on making and applying straight-grain binding.

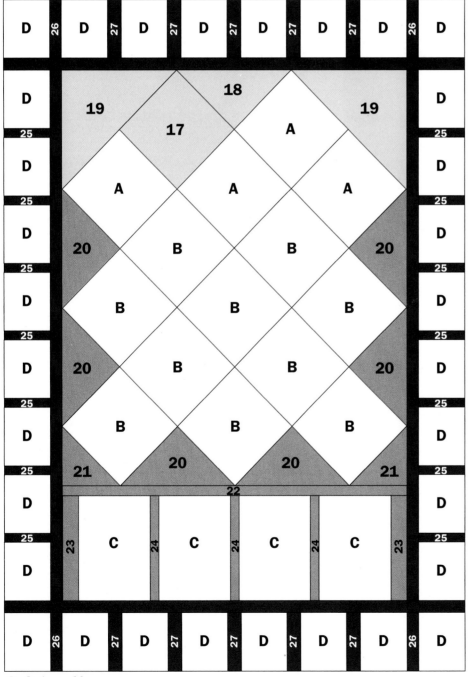

Quilt Assembly

Mountain Greenery Tree Skirt

Dress your tree in homespun holiday style with patchwork pine trees, pinwheels, and prancing reindeer. This fast and easy project is an excellent introduction to four quick-piecing techniques, so it's ideal for beginners.

Quick-Piecing Techniques:

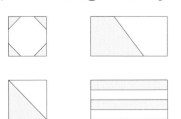

Finished Size

Blocks: 8 pinwheel blocks, 7" square
       8 pine tree blocks, 7" square
       4 deer blocks, 7" x 8¾"
       4 striped blocks, 5¼" x 7"

Tree Skirt: 41" square

Materials

	Fabric I (white-on-red pinstripe)	⅝ yard
	Fabric II (brick red plaid)	⅝ yard
	Fabric III (five assorted green prints and checks)	scraps or ⅛ yard each
	Fabric IV (dark brown print or solid)	scraps or ⅛ yard
	Fabric V (red-on-tan mini-print)	⅜ yard
	Fabric VI (brown mini-dot)	¼ yard
	Fabric VII (red-and-green homespun plaid)	⅝ yard
	Fabric VIII (dark cranberry plaid)	1⅛ yards
	Fabric IX (dark green check or print)	⅜ yard
	Backing fabric	1¼ yards
	⅛"-wide jute trim	⅛ yard

Cutting

Before cutting, make a template of ear pattern (page 107).

From Fabric I, cut:

♦ One 20" square for triangle-squares (A-1).
♦ One 7½" square for skirt center.

From Fabric II, cut:

♦ One 20" square for triangle-squares (A-1).

From Fabric III scraps, cut:

♦ Eight 1½" x 3½" (B-3) and eight 1½" x 4½" (B-4).

♦ Eight 1½" x 3½" (B-6) and eight 1½" x 4½" (B-7).
♦ Eight 1½" x 3½" (B-9) and eight 1½" x 4½" (B-10).
♦ Eight 1½" x 3½" (B-12) and eight 1½" x 4½" (B-13).
♦ Four 3⅞" squares. Cut each square in half diagonally to get eight triangles (B-1).

From Fabric IV, cut:

♦ One 1" x 42" strip for Strip Set 1.
♦ Three ⅝" x 42" strips for strip sets 3 and 4.

From Fabric V, cut:

♦ Two 2¾" x 42" strips for Strip Set 1.
♦ Three 1½" x 42" strips.
  From these, cut:
  • Sixteen 1½" x 3½" (B-11).
  • Sixteen 1½" x 2½" (B-8).
  • Sixteen 1½" squares (B-5).

From Fabric VI, cut:

♦ One 2½" x 42" strip.
  From this, cut:
  • Four 2½" x 4¾" (C-6).
  • Four 1" x 2½" (C-7).
  • Four 2⅛" squares (C-16a).
  • Four 2" squares (C-10a).
♦ One 1¾" x 42" strip.
  From this, cut:
  • Four 1¾" x 2⅛" (C-15a).
  • Four 1¼" x 1¾" (C-8a).
  • Four 1½" squares (C-13).
  • Four 1½" x 3⅞" (C-12).
  • Two 1½" squares. Cut each square in half diagonally to get four triangles (C-2a).
♦ One 1" x 42" strip.
  From this, cut:
  • Four 1" x 3" (C-11).
  • Four 1" x 2¼" (C-9).
  • Four 1" squares (C-5a).
♦ From scraps, cut:
  • Eight ears, cutting four with template faceup and four more with template facedown.

From Fabric VII, cut:

♦ One 2¼" x 42" strip for Strip Set 3.
♦ One 2½" x 42" strip for Strip Set 4.
♦ One 1½" x 42" strip for Strip Set 4.
♦ One 1⅜" x 42" strip for Strip Set 4.
♦ One 1½" x 42" strip.
  From this, cut:
  • Four 1½" squares (C-13a).
  • Four 1" x 1½" (C-7a).
  • Eight 1⅜" squares (C-15b, C-16b).
  • Four 1¼" squares (C-10b).
  • Four 1⅛" squares (C-12a).
  • Eight 1" squares (C-6a).
♦ One 3" x 42" strip.
  From this, cut:
  • Four 3" x 3¼" (C-1).
  • Four 1½" x 3" (C-4).
  • Four 2½" x 3" (C-10).
  • Four 1½" x 2⅞" (C-14).
  • Four 1" x 1¾" (C-9a).

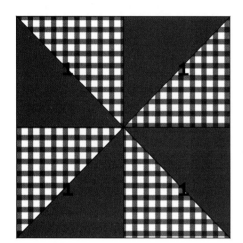

Block A —Make 8.

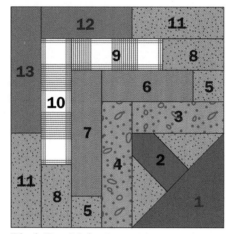

Block B —Make 8.

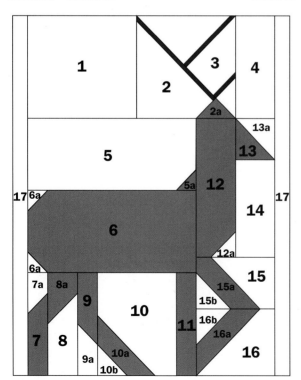

Block C —Make 4.

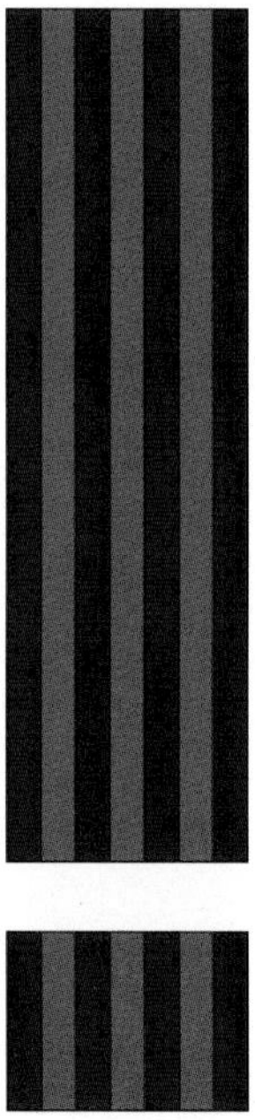

Strip Set 5—Make 1.

- One 2½" x 42" strip.
  From this, cut:
  - Four 1¼" x 2½" (C-8).
  - Four 2⅛" x 2½" (C-16).
  - Four 2¼" x 4¾" (C-5).
  - Four 1¾" x 2⅛" (C-15).
- Two ⅞" x 42" strips.
  From these, cut:
  - Eight ⅞" x 9¼" (C-17).

From Fabric VIII, cut:

- One 18" square for bias binding.
- Four 1½" x 42" strips for Strip Set 5.
- Four 2½" x 42" strips for outer border.

From Fabric IX, cut:

- Three 1½" x 42" strips for Strip Set 5.
- Four 1½" x 38" for inner border.

Piecing the Blocks

1. See page 17 for instructions on half-square triangles. On wrong side of 20" square of Fabric I, draw a 4 x 4-square grid of 4⅜" squares. With right sides facing, match marked fabric with 20" square of Fabric II. Stitch grid as directed on page 17. Cut 32 triangle-squares from grid.

2. Referring to Block A Assembly diagram, join four triangle-squares in two rows of two squares each. Join rows to complete Block A. Make 8 of Block A.

3. For Block B, follow steps 1–6 of Piecing the Pine Tree Blocks for wall hanging (page 107). Referring to Block B diagram at left for fabric placement, make eight of Block B for tree skirt.

4. For Block C, follow Piecing the Deer Blocks instructions given for wall hanging (page 108). Referring to Block C diagram at left, make four of Block C. Complete blocks by joining one of Unit 17 to both sides as shown here.

5. For striped blocks, refer to Strip Set 5 diagram to join 1½" x 42" strips of fabrics VIII and IX as shown. Cut strip set into four 5¾" segments.

Tree Skirt Assembly

1. Referring to Tree Skirt Assembly diagram, join two A blocks and two B blocks as shown to make each corner section. Green triangles in diagram indicate position of each B-1 for correct placement of pine trees.

2. For center sections, join a striped block to top of each C block.

3. For top row, join two corner sections with a center section between them as shown in diagram. Repeat for bottom row, positioning fabrics as shown. Assemble middle row by joining center sections to opposite sides of 7½" square of Fabric I. Join rows.

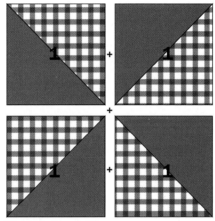

Block A Assembly

4. Join Fabric IX border strips to top and bottom edges of tree skirt. Press seam allowances toward borders; then trim excess border fabric at ends. Join borders to remaining sides in the same manner.

5. Join Fabric VIII borders to tree skirt in the same manner as inner border.

Quilting and Finishing

1. Mark a 1½"-wide cable in border. Outline-quilt patchwork or quilt as desired. Quilt border design.

2. Draw a 6" circle in center square. To make skirt opening, cut out circle and down one seam as indicated by dashed line in Tree Skirt Assembly diagram.

3. For bias binding, cut 18" square of Fabric VIII in half diagonally. Starting from cut edges, cut 2"-wide diagonal strips. Join strips end-to-end to make a continuous strip 5 yards long. Press strip in half with wrong sides facing, being careful not to stretch bias. Follow directions on page 23 for applying binding to skirt opening and around borders.

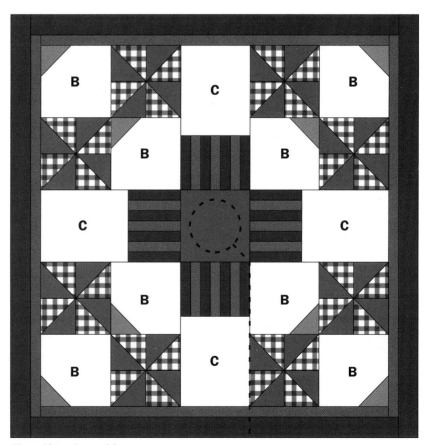

Tree Skirt Assembly

Mountain Greenery Stockings

There's nothing like plaid to evoke the cozy atmosphere of a country Christmas. Mix up scraps of plaids, checks, and little prints in tan, cranberry, and forest green to make this pair of holiday stockings. Hung by the mantel with care, they will delight and impress your family and guests—and only you will know how fun and easy they are to make!

Quick-Piecing Techniques:

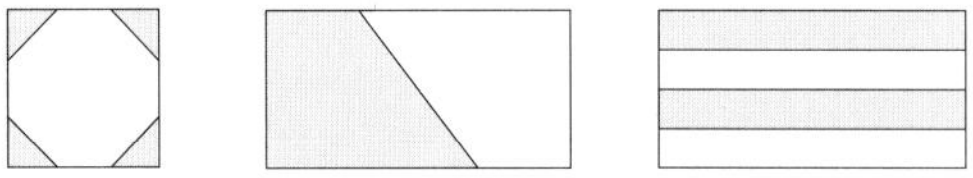

Finished Size

Blocks: 1 pine tree block, 7" square
1 deer block, 6¾" x 8¾"

Stockings: 9¾" x 18"

Materials (for both stockings)

Fabric I (green-on-tan check)	½ yard
Fabric II (red-on-tan plaid)	¼ yard
Fabric III (four green plaids and checks)	scraps
Fabric IV (red-on-tan mini-print)	½ yard
Fabric V (dark brown print)	¼ yard
Fabric VI (dark brown print or solid)	scraps
Fabric VII (cranberry plaid)	10" square
Lining fabric	¾ yard
Fleece or low-loft batting	¾ yard
⅛"-wide jute trim	1"
⅛"-diameter cording	2½ yards
Template material or tracing paper	
Tear-away stabilizer (optional for machine embroidery only)	

Cutting

Before cutting, trace deer ear pattern (page 107) and stocking toe pattern (page 116) onto template material or tracing paper.

From Fabric I, cut:
♦ One 11" x 42" strip.
  From this, cut:
  • One 11" x 20" for deer stocking back.
  • One 8" x 11" for deer stocking toe (Stocking-1).
  • One 2½" x 7¼" (Stocking-2).
  • Two ¾" x 9¼" (C-17).
  • One 2¼" x 5" for Strip Set 3.
  • One 1" x 1½" (C-7a).
  • One 1" x 1¾" (C-9a).
  • Two 1" squares (C-6a).
♦ One 3" x 42" strip.
  From this, cut:
  • One 3" x 3¼" (C-1).
  • One 2½" x 3" for Strip Set 4.
  • One 1½" x 3" for Strip Set 4.
  • One 1⅜" x 3" for Strip Set 4.
  • One 1½" x 3" (C-4).
  • One 2½" x 3" (C-10).
  • One 1½" x 2⅞" (C-14).
  • One 1¼" x 2½" (C-8).
  • One 2⅛" x 2½" (C-16).
  • One 2¼" x 4¾" (C-5).
  • One 1¾" x 2⅛" (C-15).
  • One 1½" square (C-13a).
  • One 1¼" square (C-10b).
  • Two 1⅜" squares (C-15b, C-16b).
  • One 1⅛" square (C-12a).

From Fabric II, cut:

- Two 7" x 14½" for cuffs.
- Two 1¼" x 4" for hangers.

From Fabric III, cut:

- One 1½" x 3½" (B-3) and one 1½" x 4½" (B-4).
- One 1½" x 3½" (B-6) and one 1½" x 4½" (B-7).
- One 1½" x 3½" (B-9) and one 1½" x 4½" (B-10).
- One 1½" x 3½" (B-12) and one 1½" x 4½"(B-13).

From Fabric IV, cut:

- One 11" x 42" strip. From this, cut:
  - One 11" x 20" for tree stocking back.
  - One 8" x 11" for tree stocking toe (Stocking-1).
  - One 3½" x 11". From this, cut:
    - Two 1½" x 3½" (B-11).
    - Two 1½" x 2½" (B-8).
    - Two 1½" squares (B-5).
    - One 3½" x 7¼" (Stocking-5).
    - Two 2⅜" x 2¾" for Strip Set 1.
    - One 4¼" square. Cut this square in half diagonally to get two triangles (Stocking-4).
    - One 2⅛" square. Cut this square in half diagonally to get two triangles (Stocking-3).

From Fabric V, cut:

- One 2½" x 42" strip. From this, cut:
  - One 2½" x 4¾" (C-6).
  - One 1" x 2½" (C-7).
  - One 2⅛" square (C-16a).
  - One 1¾" x 2⅛" (C-15a).
  - One 1" x 2¼" (C-9).
  - One 2" square (C-10a).
  - One 1½" square (C-13).
  - One 1½" x 3⅞" (C-12).
  - One 1½" square. Cut square in half diagonally to get two triangles (C-2a). Discard one triangle.
  - One 1¼" x 1¾" (C-8a).
  - One 1" x 3" (C-11).
  - One 1" square (C-5a).

- From scraps, cut:
  - Two ears, cutting one with template faceup and one with template facedown.

From Fabric VI, cut:

- One 1" x 2⅜" for Strip Set 1.
- Three ⅝" x 5" for strip sets 3 and 4.

From Fabric VII, cut:

- One 10" square for piping.

From each of lining and fleece, cut:

- Two 11" x 20" pieces for each stocking.

Piecing the Blocks

1. To make pine tree (Block B), begin with Step 1 of Piecing the Pine Tree Blocks instructions given for wall hanging (page 107). To make Strip Set 1, join designated pieces of fabrics V and VI to make a miniature strip set that is 2¾" wide. Follow steps 2–6 to make one Block B, omitting piece B-1.

2. To make deer (Block C), follow Piecing the Deer Blocks instructions given for wall hanging (page 108). Use designated strips to make strip sets 3 and 4. Make one of Block C. Complete block by joining one of Unit 17 to both sides.

Stocking Assembly

1. For pine tree stocking, turn Block B on point. Join Stocking-3 triangles to bottom and Stocking-4 triangles to top edge. Aligning your ruler with triangle sides, trim block corners as shown in Pine Tree Stocking Assembly diagram. Join Stocking-1 to bottom edge of pine tree block and Stocking-5 to top edge.

2. For deer stocking, join Stocking-1 to bottom edge of Block C and Stocking-2 to top edge.

3. Sandwich one piece of fleece between stocking front (faceup) and lining (facedown). Outline-quilt patchwork on each stocking front; then add random quilting lines to stocking as desired. Trim fleece and lining to edge of stocking fronts. If desired, add decorative machine stitching ½" from stocking edges.

4. With right sides facing, place stocking front on 11" x 20" piece of backing fabric. Using front as a pattern, cut stocking back. Repeat for back lining and fleece.

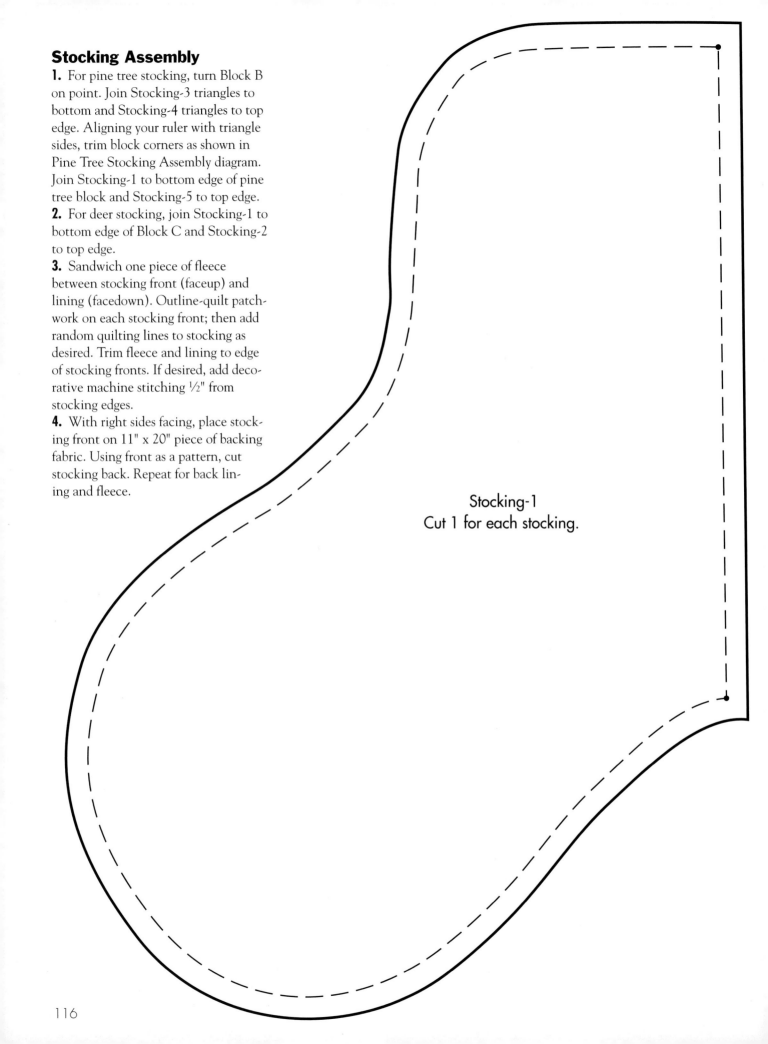

Stocking-1
Cut 1 for each stocking.

5. Layer back, fleece, and lining. Machine-quilt backs with randomly curving lines or as desired.

6. Cut 10" square of Fabric VII in half diagonally. Starting from cut edges, cut 1"-wide diagonal strips. Join strips end-to-end to make a continuous bias strip approximately 45" long for each stocking. Use bias to cover cording to make piping. Use a zipper foot on your sewing machine to stitch piping to each stocking front. (It's all right if piping doesn't reach top of stocking since cuff will cover top.)

7. With right sides facing, join backs to fronts, leaving tops open. Trim and clip seam allowances. Turn stockings right side out.

8. Press under ¼" on both long sides of each hanger strip. With wrong sides facing, fold each pressed strip in half lengthwise, bringing folded edges together. Topstitch through all layers close to edge. Matching raw edges, stitch hanger ends to lining back at seam on left side of stocking.

9. With wrong sides facing, fold each cuff piece in half lengthwise and press to crease. Unfold cuff. By hand or by machine, satin-stitch a name or initials in center of strip, positioning bottom of letters ⅜" from crease. Letters should be approximately 1½" high.

10. With right sides facing, join ends of each cuff. Press seam allowances open. Turn tubes right side out. Press under ¼" at bottom edge of each cuff (edge farthest from embroidery).

11. Use pins to mark center back on each stocking. With raw edges aligned, place one unfolded cuff inside each stocking top, with right side of cuff against lining. Align cuff seam with center back of stocking. Stitch cuff to stocking top, catching hanger end in stitching.

12. Pull each cuff out. With wrong sides facing, refold cuff on crease (embroidery will be upside down and facing in). Pin hemmed edge over seam allowance at stocking top and topstitch or slipstitch by hand. Fold each cuff down over stocking top and pull each hanger up.

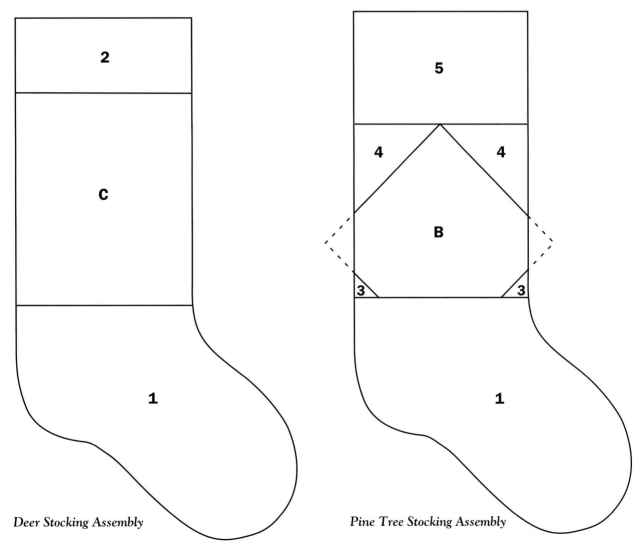

Deer Stocking Assembly   *Pine Tree Stocking Assembly*

Trellis

A *variety of quick-piecing techniques creates blossoms of luscious grape and teal climbing a patchwork trellis. When the flower blocks and leaf blocks are joined, the block outlines seem to disappear amid a garden of pretty posies. Even the flowers at the border corners blend so well into the design that they seem to have grown there. We recommend this quilt for experienced quiltmakers.*

Quick-Piecing Techniques:

Finished Size
Blocks: 10 leaf blocks, 18" square
       10 flower blocks, 18" square
       4 corner flower blocks, 20" triangle

Quilt: 90" x 106"

Materials

	Fabric I (light mauve-and-teal mottled-look print)	4¼ yards
	Fabric II (white-on-white print)	2⅜ yards
	Fabric III (dark teal solid)	½ yard
	Fabric IV (dark teal texture-look print)	⅝ yard
	Fabric V (dark mauve solid)	⅝ yard
	Fabric VI (burgundy print)	½ yard
	Fabric VII (dark mauve-and-teal texture-look print)	2¼ yards
	Fabric VIII (light mauve solid)	¾ yard
	Fabric IX (dark teal print)	2 yards

Cutting
Refer to diagrams on pages 120 and 124 to identify blocks and units designated in cutting list.

From Fabric I, cut:
◆ One 9⅞" x 42" strip.
  From this, cut:
    ● Two 9⅞" squares. Cut both squares in half diagonally to get four triangles (17).
    ● Ten 1¼" x 9" (A-7).
◆ Ten 9¼" x 42" strips.
  From these, cut:
    ● Thirty-eight 9¼" squares. Cut each square in quarters diagonally to get 152 triangles (15).
    ● Five 4⅞" squares. Cut each square in half diagonally to get 10 triangles (B-9).
◆ Five 1¼" x 42" strips.
  From these, cut:
    ● Ninety 1¼" squares (A-2a, A-3a, A-8b).
    ● Ten 1¼" x 8⅜" (A-6).
◆ Five 2" x 42" strips.
  From these, cut:
    ● Forty 2" x 4" (A-4).
    ● Ten 2" x 3½" (B-8).

- Five 1¼" x 42" strips for Strip Set 1 (A-8).
- Three 5¼" x 42" strips.
  From these, cut:
  - Twenty 5¼" squares. Cut each square in half diagonally to get 40 triangles (B-1).
  - Ten 2" x 5" (B-6).
- One 4" x 42" strip.
  From this, cut:
  - One 4" x 12½" for triangle-squares (B-5a).
  - Five 3⅞" squares. Cut each square in half diagonally to get 10 triangles (B-3).
- From scraps, cut:
  - Five 1⅞" squares. Cut each square in half diagonally to get 10 triangles (B-5b).
  - Ten 1½" squares (B-4a).

From Fabric II, cut:
- Thirty-four 1⅞" x 42" strips.
  From these, cut:
  - Twenty 1⅞" x 10½" (B-12).
  - Thirty 1⅞" x 13¼" (A-9, B-14).
  - Ten 1⅞" x 11⅞" (B-13).
  - Seventy-six 1⅞" x 7" (16).
  - Ten 1⅞" x 5½" (B-10).
  - Ten 1⅞" x 5" (B-2).
  - Ten 1⅞" x 2" (B-7).
  - Ten 1⅞" squares (B-13b).
- One 4" x 42" strip.
  From this, cut:
  - One 4" x 12½" for triangle-squares (B-5a).
  - Five 2¼" squares. Cut each square in half diagonally to get 10 triangles (B-9a).
  - Four 2" squares (C-5).

- Five 1⅞" x 42" strips for Strip Set 1 (A-8).

From Fabric III, cut:
- Two 1⅞" x 42" strips.
  From these, cut:
  - Ten 1⅞" squares (A-9a).
  - Ten 1¼" x 1⅞" (A-6a).
  - Ten 1⅞" x 3¼" (B-13a).
- Five 1½" x 42" strips.
  From these, cut:
  - Ten 1½" x 15" (B-11).
  - Ten 1¼" squares (A-8c).
- One 2⅝" x 42" strips.
  From this, cut:
  - Ten 2⅝" squares (A-8a).

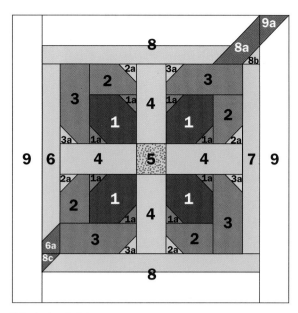

Block A—Make 10.

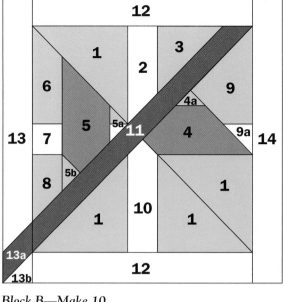

Block B—Make 10.

From Fabric IV, cut:

♦ Two 4⅞" x 42" strips.
  From these, cut:
  • Ten 4⅞" squares. Cut each square in half diagonally to get 20 triangles (B-4, B-5).
  • Two 1½" x 28½" for Border 1.
♦ Six 1½" x 42" strips for Border 1.

From Fabric V, cut:

♦ Three 1¼" x 42" strips.
  From these, cut:
  • Eighty 1¼" squares (A-1a).
♦ Four 1⅞" x 42" strips.
  From these, cut:
  • Forty 1⅞" x 4" (A-3).
♦ Three 2⅝" x 42" strips.
  From these, cut:
  • Sixteen 2⅝" squares (C-1).
  • Forty 1⅞" x 2⅝" (A-2).

From Fabric VI, cut:

♦ Three 2⅝" x 42" strips.
  From these, cut:
  • Forty 2⅝" squares (A-1).
♦ One 1¼" x 42" strip.
  From this, cut:
  • Thirty-two 1¼" squares (C-1a).
♦ Two 1⅞" x 42" strips.
  From these, cut:
  • Sixteen 1⅞" x 4" (C-3).
♦ From scraps, cut:
  • Sixteen 1⅞" x 2⅝" (C-2).

From Fabric VII, cut:

♦ Eight 6½" x 42" strips for Border 4.
  From four of these, cut:
  • Four 6½" x 36".
♦ One 9⅜" x 42" strip.
  From this, cut:
  • Four 9⅜" squares. Cut each square in half diagonally to get eight triangles (C-7).
♦ One 6⅞" x 42" strip.
  From this, cut:
  • Two 6⅞" squares. Cut each square in half diagonally to get four triangles (C-8).
  • Three 2" x 28" strips.
  From these, cut:
  • Twelve 2" x 4" (C-4).
  • Ten 2" squares (A-5).
♦ Four 1½" x 42" strips.
  From these, cut:
  • Four 1½" x 20" (C-9).
  • Four 1½" x 21" (C-10).
♦ From scraps, cut:
  • Twenty-four 1¼" squares (C-2a, C-3a).

From Fabric VIII, cut:

♦ Ten 2½" x 42" strips for Border 2.
  From these, cut:
  • Six 2½" x 29".
  • Four 2½" x 36".
♦ From scraps, cut:
  • Four 2" x 4" (C-6).
  • Eight 1¼" squares (C-2b, C-3b).

From Fabric IX, cut:

♦ Ten 3" x 42" strips for binding.
♦ Eight 2½" x 42" strips for Border 3.
  From four of these, cut:
  • Four 2½" x 36" for Border 3.
  • Eight 2" squares (C-7a).
♦ Ten 1½" x 42" strips for Border 5.
  From two of these, cut:
  • Two 1½" x 25".
  • Two 1½" x 10".

Piecing the Flower Blocks

1. Referring to Block A Assembly diagram, use diagonal-corner technique to make one of Unit 9 and four each of units 1, 2, and 3.

2. Using diagonal-end technique, make one of Unit 6.

3. Referring to Strip Set 1 diagram, join designated strips of fabrics I and II as shown. Make five strip sets. Cut four 10½"-wide segments from each strip set to get 20 of Unit 8.

4. Referring to top of Block A Assembly diagram, use diagonal-corner technique to add 8a to one of Unit 8. Press 8a; then add 8b in the same manner.

5. Referring to bottom of Block A Assembly diagram, use diagonal-corner technique to add 8c to one of Unit 8.

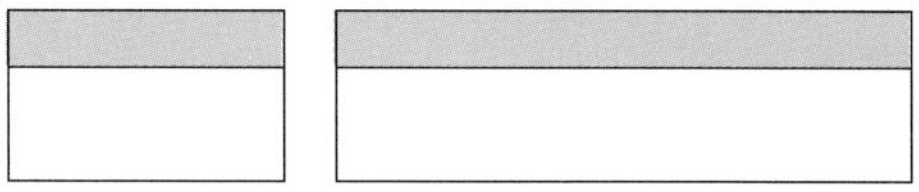

Strip Set 1—Make 5.

6. Referring to upper left corner of assembly diagram, join Unit 2 to top of Unit 1 as shown. Join Unit 3 to left side of 1-2 unit. Make three more 1-2-3 units in the same manner for petal sections.

7. Join two petal sections with one of Unit 4 between them. Press seam allowances toward Unit 4. Repeat with second pair of petal sections.

8. Join one of Unit 4 to opposite sides of Unit 5.

9. Positioning petal sections as shown, join both sections to opposite sides of combined 4-5-4 unit.

10. Join Unit 6 to left side of block as shown; then add Unit 7 to right side.

11. Positioning 8a and 8c as shown, join Unit 8 strips to top and bottom.

12. Positioning 9a as shown, join a Unit 9 to each side to complete block. Make 10 of Block A in this manner.

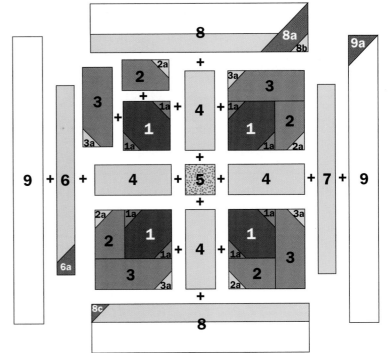

Block A Assembly

Piecing the Leaf Blocks

Note: Before constructing blocks, see page 13 for tips on stabilizing triangles to prevent stretching bias edges.

This block is made by assembling the units into four large triangles, which are then joined into pairs and sewn to opposite sides of the center stem piece.

1. To make triangle 1-2-3, begin by joining Unit 1 to Unit 2 as shown in Block B Assembly diagram, aligning short leg of triangle with side and end of Unit 2. Join Unit 3 to opposite side of Unit 2 in the same manner. Referring to Diagram 1, align ruler with triangle edges and trim Unit 2 as shown.

2. To make Unit 5a, see page 17 for instructions on half-square triangles. On wrong side of 4" x 12½" piece of Fabric II, draw a 1 x 5-square grid of 1⅞" squares. With right sides facing,

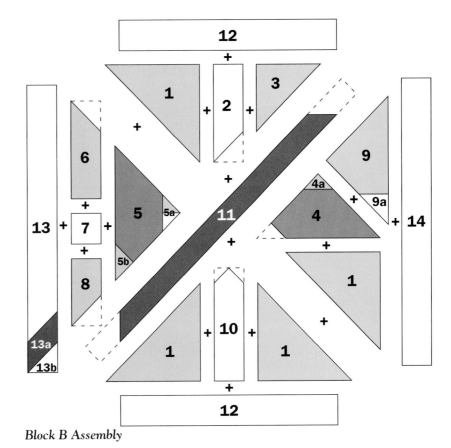

Block B Assembly

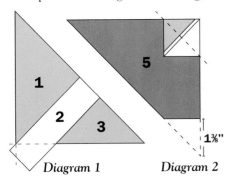

Diagram 1   *Diagram 2*

match marked fabric with 4" x 12½" piece of Fabric I. Stitch grid as directed on page 17. Cut 10 triangle-squares from grid.

3. With right sides facing, place one triangle-square at corner of one Unit 5 triangle, positioning triangle-square fabrics and seam as shown in Diagram 2. Using diagonal-corner technique, stitch diagonally across square, perpendicular to triangle-square seam. Trim and press diagonal corner.

121

4. Trim 1⅜" from tip of Unit 5 as shown in Diagram 2. Join 5b to Unit 5 at cut edge.

5. To make triangle 5-6-7-8, begin by joining units 6, 7, and 8 in a row as shown in Block B Assembly diagram. Press seam allowances away from Unit 7. With right sides facing, join this to Unit 5, carefully aligning 5b seam line with 7-8 seam line. Press joining seam allowance away from Unit 5. Referring to Diagram 3, align ruler with triangle edges and trim units 6 and 8 as shown.

6. On one end of each Unit 9 triangle, measure a right angle with 2½"-long legs as shown in Diagram 4. Draw a diagonal line from right-angle corner to triangle edge as shown in red. Cut off triangle tip on drawn line. Join 9a to Unit 9 at cut edge.

7. Using diagonal-corner technique, make one of Unit 4.

8. To make triangle 1-4-9, join units 4 and 9, matching edges as shown in Block B Assembly diagram. Join Unit 1 to long edge of Unit 4, aligning edges of units 1 and 9. Referring to Diagram 5, align ruler with edge of Unit 1 and trim tip of Unit 4 as shown.

9. To make triangle 1-10-1, join a Unit 1 to long sides of Unit 10 as shown in Block B Assembly diagram, aligning bottom edges of all three pieces. Referring to Diagram 6, align ruler with triangle edges and trim Unit 10 as shown.

10. Referring to assembly diagram, join triangle 1-2-3 to triangle 5-6-7-8. In the same manner, join triangle 1-4-9 to triangle 1-10-1.

11. Join block halves to opposite sides of stem (Unit 11), matching seam lines carefully. Trim ends of Unit 11 even with triangle edges.

12. Join one of Unit 12 to top and bottom of block.

13. Using diagonal-end technique, join 13a to Unit 13. Then add diagonal corner 13b. Join assembled Unit 13 to left edge of block. Join Unit 14 to right edge to complete block. Make 10 of Block B in this manner.

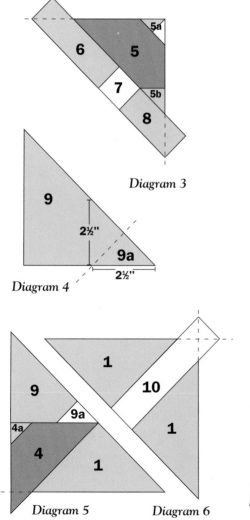

Diagram 3

Diagram 4

Diagram 5   Diagram 6

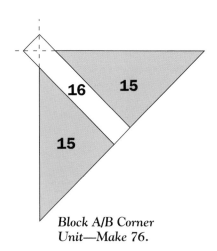

Block A/B Corner Unit—Make 76.

Adding Block Corners

Each block is set on point and squared off with triangular corners. All corners are the same except the four that fall at the corners of the assembled quilt.

1. Referring to Block A/B Corner Unit diagram, join Unit 15 triangles to sides of Unit 16. Align ruler with triangle edges and trim Unit 16 as shown. Make 76 corner units.

2. With right sides facing, align a corner unit on one side of a flower block so that Unit 16 is centered over one Unit 4 of the block. Join corner to block. Referring to diagram of Block A1, add corner units to remaining sides. Make eight of Block A1 in this manner.

3. Referring to diagram of Block A2, add one Unit 17 triangle to top right corner of one flower block. Join corner units to remaining sides to complete Block A2.

4. Referring to diagram of Block A3, add one Unit 17 triangle to bottom right corner of remaining flower block. Join corner units to remaining sides to complete Block A3.

5. Using leaf blocks, repeat step 2 to make eight of Block B1. To make blocks B2 and B3, position Unit 17 triangles as shown in diagrams; then add corner units to remaining sides.

Block A1—Make 8.

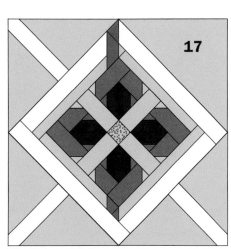

Block A2—Make 1.

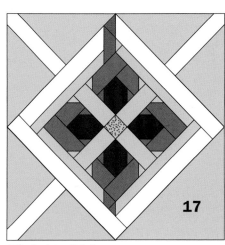

Block A3—Make 1.

Block B1—Make 8.

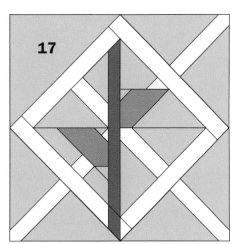

Block B2—Make 1.

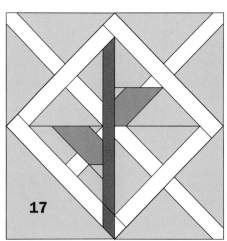

Block B3—Make 1.

Piecing the Corner Flower Blocks

1. Referring to Block C diagram, assemble units 1-6 in the same manner as for Block A. Be careful to note position of contrasting fabrics in units 2b, 3b, and 6.

2. Using diagonal-corner technique, join C-7a to corners of C-7 triangles.

3. Referring to Block C diagram, join one of Unit 7 to opposite sides of each Block C. Add Unit 8 as shown, making combined units into a large triangle.

4. Join Unit 9 and then Unit 10 as shown. Align ruler with Unit 7 triangles and trim ends of units 9 and 10.

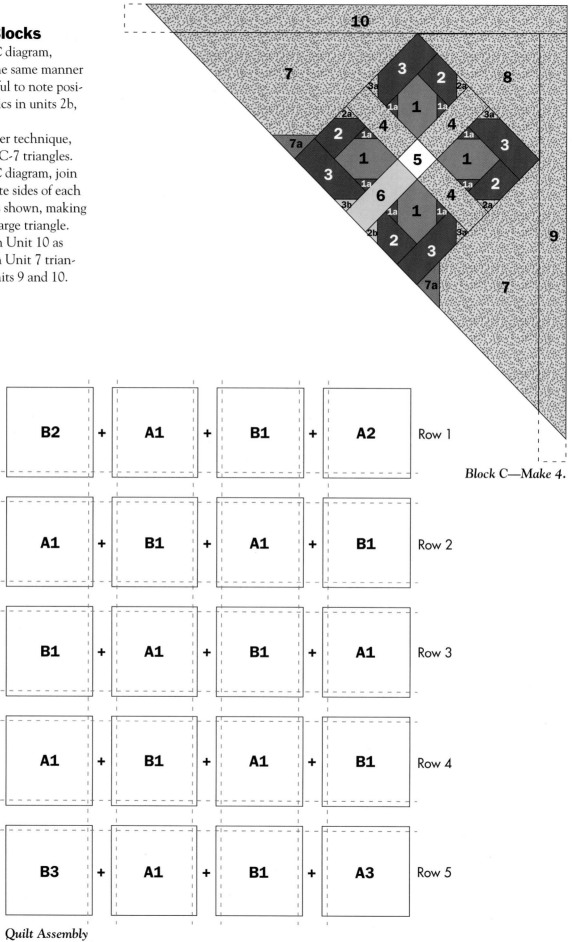

Block C—Make 4.

B2	+	**A1**	+	**B1**	+	**A2**	Row 1
A1	+	**B1**	+	**A1**	+	**B1**	Row 2
B1	+	**A1**	+	**B1**	+	**A1**	Row 3
A1	+	**B1**	+	**A1**	+	**B1**	Row 4
B3	+	**A1**	+	**B1**	+	**A3**	Row 5

Quilt Assembly

Quilt Assembly

Each block must be trimmed on two or more edges before it can be joined to its neighbor. Only the edges on the outside of the assembled quilt are not trimmed. Lay out blocks in rows as shown in Quilt Assembly diagram before you begin.

1. To make Row 1, trim 1" from bottom and both sides of one Block A1 and one Block B1. Trim 1" from bottom and right side of Block B2. Trim 1" from bottom and left side of Block A2. Join trimmed blocks in a row as shown.

2. Continue trimming and joining blocks in this manner to assemble rows 2-5, carefully noting block positions and trim lines indicated in Quilt Assembly diagram. Join rows.

3. For Border 1, join two 1½" x 42" strips of Fabric IV end-to-end for each side. Join a 28½"-long strip and a 42" strip for top and bottom borders.

4. Measure length of quilt top, measuring through middle rather than along sides. Trim Border 1 side borders to this length, cutting equal amounts from both ends of border strip. Sew borders to quilt sides, easing as necessary.

5. Measure quilt width through middle of quilt top. Trim remaining borders accordingly; then join borders to top and bottom edges of quilt.

6. For Border 2, join three 2½" x 29" strips of Fabric VIII end-to-end for each side. Matching centers of border strips and quilt, join borders to quilt sides. Join two 36"-long strips for top and bottom borders and join to quilt in the same manner.

7. For Border 3, join two 2½" x 42" strips of Fabric IX for each side and two 36"-long strips for top and bottom borders. For Border 4, join 6½"-wide strips of Fabric VII in the same manner. Aligning center seams, join matching strips of borders 3 and 4. Matching centers of combined border strips to center of each quilt side, join borders to quilt as before. Note that these borders do not meet at corners, but the ends will be covered by corner blocks.

8. Referring to Border Assembly diagram, baste corner flower blocks to quilt, aligning seams of borders and corners. Straight edges of corner blocks should align with edge of Border 4. Stitch corners in place and check for seam alignment. Trim borders underneath corners to ¼" seam allowance.

9. For Border 5, join a 1½" x 42" strip of Fabric IX to both ends of a 25"-long strip for each side. Join borders to quilt sides. Press seam allowances toward borders and trim excess fabric from ends. Join a 42" strip to both ends of a 10"-long strip for bottom and top borders and join to quilt.

Quilting and Finishing

Mark a 3"-wide cable or feather quilting design over borders 2 and 3 and widely spaced cross-hatching in Border 4. Outline-quilt patchwork; then stitch meandering lines of stipple quilting in background fabric to enhance trellis. Quilt border motifs.

Make 400" of binding. See page 23 for directions on making and applying straight-grain binding.

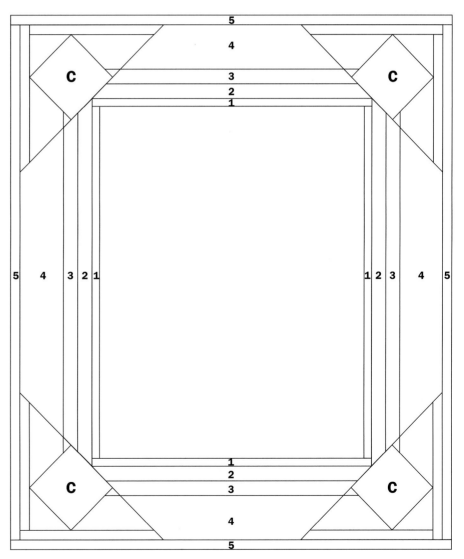

Border Assembly

Till the Cows Come Home

Round and round the cattle go, through patchwork fields and forests that surround the homes at the heart of this whimsical quilt. You can make all 36 bovine beauties from the same fabrics or with scraps for a more diverse herd. Strip piecing makes quick work of all the fences, tree trunks, and checkerboard borders. Because there is so much piecing in this quilt, we recommend it for experienced quiltmakers.

Quick-Piecing Techniques: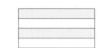

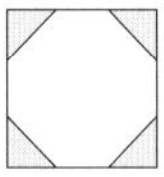

Finished Size

Blocks: 36 cow blocks, 6" x 10"
      12 large tree blocks, 4" x 6"
      80 small tree blocks, 2½" x 3½"
      8 long-stemmed tree blocks, 2½" x 5"
      4 corner tree blocks, 7½" square
      2 house blocks, 8" x 16"

Quilt: 90½" x 110½"

Materials

	Fabric I (black-on-burgundy check)	1 yard
	Fabric II (brick red print)	⅛ yard or scraps
	Fabric III (dark salmon print)	⅛ yard or scraps
	Fabric IV (salmon-pink solid)	1⅞ yards
	Fabric V (brown solid or print)	1 yard
	Fabric VI (light green solid)	1⅜ yards
	Fabric VII (green print)	1⅜ yards or scraps
	Fabric VIII (ivory miniprint)	4 yards
	Fabric IX (dark brown or black print)	⅜ yard or scraps
	Fabric X (black-on-brown print)	1 yard or scraps
	Fabric XI (burgundy solid)	3⅛ yards
	Backing fabric	8⅜ yards
	Black or brown embroidery floss	1 skein or scraps

Cutting

Refer to diagrams on page 128 to identify blocks and units designated in cutting list.

From Fabric I, cut:
- Ten 3" x 42" strips for binding.
- One 2½" x 42" strip.
  From this, cut:
  - Four 2½" squares (A-1a, A-2a).
  - Two 1½" squares (A-4).

From Fabric II, cut:
- Two 2½" x 8½" (A-2).

From Fabric III, cut:
- One 1¾" x 42" strip.
  From this, cut:
  - Four 1¾" x 6" (A-15).
  - Two 1½" x 2" (A-14).
  - Four 1¼" x 2" (A-12).

From Fabric IV, cut:
- One 14¾" x 42" strip.
  From this, cut:
  - One 7¼" x 14¾" (G-1).
    Cut this rectangle as shown in Cutting diagram to get eight G-1 triangles. Trim ¾" from narrow tip of each triangle.
  - Two 4½" x 34".
    From these, cut:
    - Twelve 4½" squares (19).
    - Two 2¼" x 6" for Strip Set 3a (G-3).

♦ Fifteen 3" x 42" strips for strip sets 5 and 6 (checkerboard borders).
♦ From scraps, cut:
  • Two 1½" x 3½" (A-11).
  • Four 1¼" x 3½" (A-9).

From Fabric V, cut:

♦ Eighteen ⅞" x 42" strips for Strip Set 1.
♦ Three 1" x 42" for strip sets 2 and 3 (B-3, C-3, D-3).
♦ Four 2½" x 42" strips.
  From these, cut:
  • 116 1¼" x 2½" (A-7, 21).
  • One 1" x 6" for Strip Set 3a (G-3).

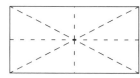

Cutting

From Fabric VI, cut:

♦ Sixteen 1½" x 42" strips for sashing.
♦ Eighteen 1" x 42" strips for tree/fence sashing.
♦ One 3" x 42" strip.
  From this, cut:
  • Eight 1¼" x 3" (C-4).
  • Two 2⅞" squares. Cut each square in half diagonally to get four G-4 triangles.
  • Two 1½" x 16½" (A-18).

From Fabric VII*, cut:

♦ Nine 3¼" x 42" strips.
  From these, cut:
  • Eighty-eight 3¼" x 3⅞" (B-2, C-2).
*Note: You can use a different green scrap for each tree or cut yardage as stated.

♦ One 4⅞" x 42" strip.
  From this, cut:
  • Four 4⅞" x 7⅜" (G-2).
♦ Two 4¾" x 42" strips.
  From these, cut:
  • Twelve 4¾" x 6¼" (D-2).

From Fabric VIII, cut:

♦ Eighteen ⅞" x 42" strips for Strip Set 1 (fences).
♦ Nine 1" x 42" strips for Strip Set 1 (fences).
♦ Four 1½" x 42" strips for Strip Set 2 (B-3).
♦ Two 2¼" x 42" strips for Strip Set 3 (C-3, D-3).
♦ Two 3¼" x 42" strips for Strip Set 4 (E-2, F-2).

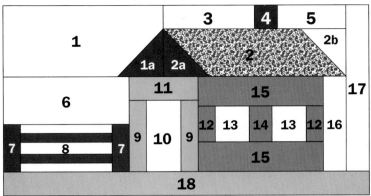

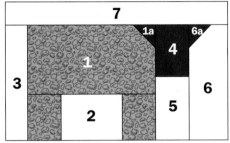

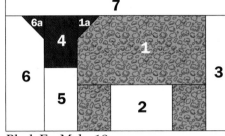

Block A—Make 2.

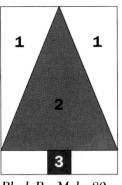

Block B—Make 80.
Block D—Make 12.

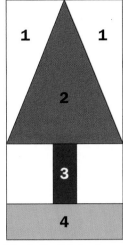

Block C—Make 8.

Block E—Make 18.

Block F—Make 18.

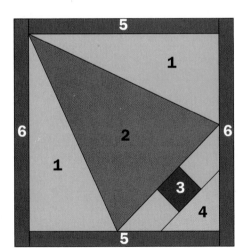

Block G—Make 4.

♦ Fourteen 2" x 42" strips.
  From these, cut:
  • Two 2" x 25" (27).
  • Four 2" x 15½" (26).
  • Sixteen 2" x 9¼" (25).
  • Eight 2" x 12" (23).
  • Four 2" x 11½" (22).
  • Two 2" x 3½" (A-10).
  • Four 2" squares (A-13).
  • Thirty-six 2" x 3¼" (E-5, F-5).
♦ One 2½" x 42" strip.
  From this, cut:
  • Two 2½" squares (A-2b).
  • Two 2½" x 6" (A-6).
  • Four 2¼" x 4" (28).

♦ Seventeen 1½" x 42" strips.
  From these, cut:
  • Thirty-six 1½" x 10½" (E-7, F-7).
  • Thirty-six 1½" x 5½" (E-3, F-3).
  • Two 1½" x 3½" (A-5).
  • Four 1½" x 4½" (A-3, A-16).
  • Two 1½" x 7½" (A-17).
  • Eight 1½" x 6½" (24).
♦ Two 8⅞" x 42" strips.
  From these, cut:
  • Twenty-two 3¾" x 8⅞" (B-1, C-1).
    Cut these as shown in Cutting diagram to get eight triangles from each piece (a total of 176). Trim ⅞" from narrow tip of each triangle. Each rectangle yields four triangles that point to the right and four that point left. Store righties and lefties separately.
♦ One 5¼" x 42½" strip.
  From this, cut:
  • Three 5¼" x 13¾" (D-1).
    Cut these as shown in Cutting diagram to get eight triangles from each piece (a total of 24). Trim 1⅛" from narrow tip of each triangle. Each rectangle yields four triangles that point to the right and four that point left. Store righties and lefties separately.

♦ Two 5½" x 42" strips.
  From these, cut:
  • Thirty-six 2¼" x 5½" (E-6, F-6).
♦ From scraps, cut:
  • Two 3½" x 7½" (A-1).

From Fabric IX, cut:
♦ Two 2¾" x 42" strips.
  From these, cut:
  • Thirty-six 2" x 2¾" (E-4, F-4).
♦ Three 1½" x 42" strips.
  From these, cut:
  • Seventy-two 1½" squares (E-1a, E-6a, F-1a, F-6a).

From Fabric X, cut:
♦ Three 6¼" x 42" strips.
  From these, cut:
  • Thirty-six 3½" x 6¼" (E-1, F-1).
♦ Four 2" x 42" strips for Strip Set 4 (E-2, F-2). *Note:* If you want scrap cows in your herd, cut shorter strips from fabrics to match E-1 and F-1 pieces.

From Fabric XI, cut:
♦ Fifteen 3" x 42" strips for strip sets 5 and 6 (checkerboard borders).
♦ Four 1¾" x 42" strips for top and bottom inner borders.
♦ Six 2¾" x 42" strips.
  From these, cut:
  • Six 2¾" x 32" for side inner borders.
  • Two 2" x 10½" for top and bottom outer borders.
♦ Ten 2" x 42" strips for outer borders.

♦ Two 6½" x 42" strips.
  From these, cut:
  • Eight 6½" squares (20).
  • Eight 1¼" x 6½" (G-5).
  • Four 1¼" x 16".
    From these, cut:
    • Eight 1¼" x 8" (G-6).

Piecing the House Blocks

1. Using diagonal-corner technique, make one each of units 1 and 2 as shown in Block A Assembly diagram.

2. To make Unit 8, refer to diagram of Strip Set 1. Join ⅞" x 42" strips of Fabric V to sides of one 1" x 42" strip of Fabric VIII. Complete strip set with ⅞"-wide strips of Fabric VIII on outside edges. Make one strip set. From this, cut two 4½"-wide segments for Unit 8; set aside remainder of strip set for other fence units.

3. Join units 3, 4, and 5 in a row as shown. Join this combined unit to top of Unit 2.

4. Join Unit 1 to left side of 2-3-4-5 unit to complete roof section.

5. Join one of Unit 7 to both short sides of one Unit 8; then add Unit 6 to top of fence section.

6. Join a Unit 9 to both long sides of Unit 10. Add Unit 11 to top of 9-10 unit.

7. Join units 12, 13, and 14 in a row as shown in assembly diagram. Join a Unit 15 to top and bottom edges of combined unit; then add Unit 16 to right side.

8. Join three combined units in a row as shown to complete fence/house middle section.

9. Join roof to top of fence/house section. Join Unit 17 to right side of block; then add Unit 18 to bottom edge to complete block. Make two of Block A.

Strip Set 1—Make 9.

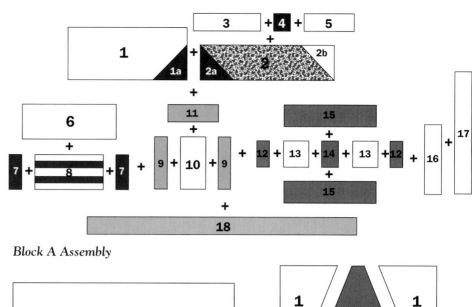

Block A Assembly

Strip Set 2—Make 2.

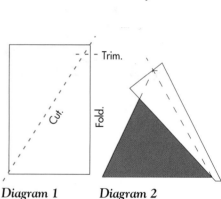

Block B/C/D Assembly

Strip Set 3—Make 1.

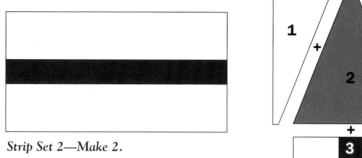

Diagram 1   *Diagram 2*

Piecing the Tree Blocks

1. Referring to diagrams of strip sets 2 and 3, join strips of Fabrics V and VIII as shown. Make two of Strip Set 2 and one of Strip Set 3. From Strip Set 2, cut eighty 1"-wide segments for B-3. From Strip Set 3, cut twelve 1¼"-wide segments for D-3. From remainder of Strip Set 3, trim ¾" from *each* long edge; then cut eight 1¾"-wide segments for Unit C-3.

2. With right sides facing, fold each 3¼" x 3⅞" piece of Fabric VII in half lengthwise as shown in Diagram 1. With fold at right, cut through both layers

from bottom left to top right as shown. Discard trimmed corners. Trim ⅜" from tops of remaining B-2/C-2 triangles.

3. For Block B, join Unit 1 triangles to both sides of each Unit 2, positioning righty and lefty triangles as shown. To sew each seam, align raw edges at top as shown in Diagram 2. Press seam allowances toward Unit 1. Add Unit 3 to bottom of Unit 2 to complete block. Make 80 of Block B.

4. For Block C, join units 1, 2, and 3 in the same manner as for Block B. Add Unit 4 to bottom to complete block. Make eight of Block C.

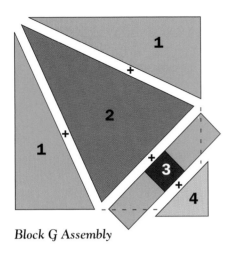

Block G Assembly

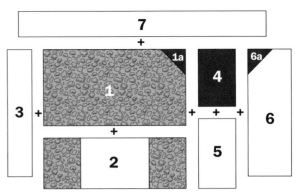

Block E Assembly

5. For Block D, fold and cut 4¾" x 6¼" pieces of Fabric VII in the same manner as for small trees. Trim ½" from tip of 12 D-2 triangles. Assemble Block D in the same manner as for Block B. Make 12 of Block D.

6. For Block G, use designated pieces of fabrics IV and V to make a miniature Strip Set 3 (3a). From this, cut four 1¾"-wide segments for Unit G-3.

7. Fold and cut 4⅞" x 7⅜" pieces of Fabric VII in the same manner as for other trees as shown in Diagram 1. Trim ¾" from tip of four G-2 triangles.

8. Referring to Block G Assembly diagram, join Unit 1 triangles to both sides of Unit 2, aligning points. Next, join Unit 3 to bottom of Unit 2, centering trunk. Press seam allowances toward Unit 3; then trim sides of Unit 3 even with Unit 1 triangles as shown in assembly diagram. Add Unit 4 as shown. Join Unit 5 to top and bottom edges; then add Unit 6 to sides to complete block. Make four of Block G.

Strip Set 4—Make 2.

Piecing the Cow Blocks

1. Referring to Block E Assembly diagram, use diagonal-corner technique to make one each of units 1 and 6. (If using scraps for faces, be sure to coordinate units 1a and 6a with Unit 4.)

2. To make Unit 2, refer to diagram of Strip Set 4. Join strips of fabrics VIII and X as shown. Make two strip sets. From these, cut thirty-six 2½"-wide segments for Unit 2. Join one Unit 2 to bottom of Unit 1.

3. Cut a 4" length of embroidery floss and tie a knot at each end. Pin one knot in side seam allowance at top left corner of Unit 1. Join Unit 3 to left side of 1-2 unit, catching tail in seam. Backstitch over tail to secure it.

4. Join units 4 and 5 as shown in assembly diagram; then add this to right side of 1-2 unit.

5. Join Unit 6 to right side of 4-5 unit. Add Unit 7 to top to complete block. Make 18 of Block E.

6. Block F is made in the same manner as Block E, but it is a mirror image. Units are made exactly the same as for Block E, but positions of units 1a and 6a are reversed. Follow Block F diagram on page 128 carefully to assemble blocks. Make 18 of Block F.

Piecing the Fence Sections

1. Referring to diagram of Strip Set 1, follow instructions given in Step 2 of Piecing the House Blocks to make eight more of Strip Set 1.

2. From these strip sets, cut the following segments:

♦ Eight 4⅞"-wide segments for First Round.
♦ Sixteen 5⅛"-wide segments for Third Round.
♦ Thirty-two 3¾"-wide segments for Fifth Round.
♦ Twenty-two 4½"-wide segments for Tree rows.

3. Referring to Quilt Assembly diagram and photograph, join posts (Unit 21) onto fence segments as shown for each round. All four sections of each round are assembled in the same manner.

Quilt Assembly

1. Referring to Quilt Assembly diagram and quilt photograph, join A blocks at top edges.

2. Join each First Round fence section to a Unit 22. Press seam allowances toward Unit 22; then join one B block to both ends of each fence.

3. Cut two 1" x 42" strips of Fabric VI in half. Aligning one end with side of Block B, join one half-strip to bottom of a First Round section. Trim strip even with patchwork. Repeat with remaining First Round sections.

4. Referring to Quilt Assembly diagram and quilt photograph, join a First Round section to top and bottom of combined house blocks. Note that tree tops always point into quilt center. Join Unit 19 squares to ends of remaining First Round sections; then add these to sides of center section.

5. Join an E block and an F block to sides of one Block D for each section of Second Round. Referring to Quilt Assembly diagram, join a Second Round section to top and bottom of First Round, again positioning tree tops toward quilt center. Join Unit 20 squares to ends of remaining Second Round sections and add these to First Round sides.

6. Join 1½"-wide sashing strips of Fabric VI to top and bottom of Second Round. Press seam allowances toward sashing; then trim sashing even with patchwork sides. Join sashing strips to sides in the same manner.

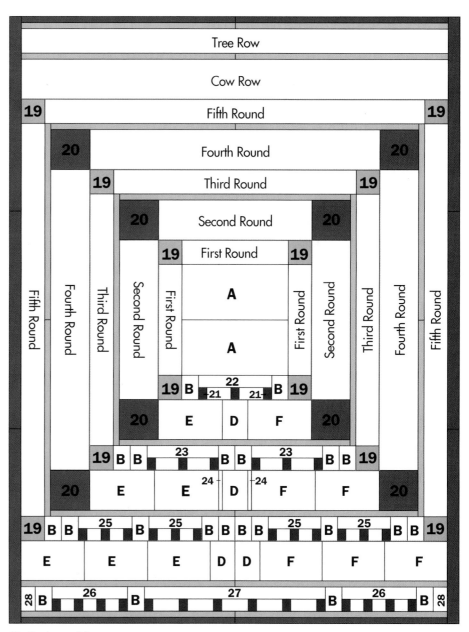

Quilt Assembly

7. Referring to Quilt Assembly diagram for number and placement of blocks, assemble Third Round sections in the same manner as for First Round, adding 1"-wide strips of Fabric VI to bottom of each section. Join Third Round sections to quilt.

8. Make Fourth Round sections in the same manner as for Second Round, adding Unit 24 strips to sides of D blocks as shown in Quilt Assembly Diagram. Join Fourth Round sections to quilt.

9. Join two 1½"-wide Fabric VI sashing strips end-to-end for each side of quilt. Matching centers of sashing strips and quilt, join sashing to Fourth Round in the same manner as Second Round sashing.

10. Referring to Quilt Assembly diagram, assemble Fifth Round sections. Join two 1"-wide Fabric VI strips end-to-end to make a sashing strip for bottom of each section. Join Fifth Round sections to quilt.

11. For each Cow Row, join three of Block E, two of Block D, and three of Block F as shown in Quilt Assembly diagram. Join Cow rows to top and bottom of quilt.

12. Join two 1½"-wide Fabric VI sashing strips end-to-end. Matching centers, join sashing to top edge of quilt. Press seam allowance toward sashing; then trim sashing ends even with quilt sides. Repeat to join sashing to bottom edge of quilt.

13. For each Tree Row, join fence sections with four B blocks as shown in Quilt Assembly diagram. Add a Unit 28 to both ends of each row. Join assembled rows to top and bottom of quilt.

14. Join two 1"-wide Fabric VI sashing strips end-to-end; then join two 1¾"-wide strips of Fabric XI in the same manner. Matching center seams, join strips. Matching centers, join combined strip to top edge of quilt. Press seam allowances toward sashing; then trim sashing ends even with quilt sides. Repeat to join sashing to bottom edge of quilt.

15. For each side inner border, join three 2¾" x 32" strips of Fabric XI end-to-end. Matching centers, join borders to quilt sides. Press and trim borders.

Piecing the Checkerboard Borders

1. Referring to diagrams of strip sets 5 and 6, join strips of fabrics IV and XI as shown. Make five of each strip set. From Strip Set 5, cut sixty-two 3"-wide segments. From Strip Set 6, cut sixty-five 3"-wide segments.

2. Select two Strip Set 5 segments and one Strip Set 6 segment. Use a seam ripper to remove stitching from these segments to get squares to add to tree blocks (Block C).

3. To make bottom border, begin with a Strip Set 6 segment. Add two more segments, alternating between strip sets 5 and 6 as shown in quilt photograph. For fourth segment, join a Fabric XI square to top of one C block and join this to border. Add 14 more segments to border, alternating fabrics as before. For next segment, join a Fabric IV square to bottom of a C block and join this to border. Add 10 more segments to complete border.

4. Make top border in the same manner, this time using 28 segments and one C block as shown in photograph.

5. Assemble right border in the same manner, using 35 segments and two C blocks. Assemble left border with 34 segments and three C blocks. Note that each border begins and ends with a Strip Set 6 segment.

6. Join a corner tree block (Block G) to both ends of each side border, positioning trees as shown.

7. Join top and bottom borders to quilt, easing as necessary. (See page 15 for tips on easing.) Join side borders in the same manner.

8. Join three 2" x 42" strips of Fabric XI end-to-end for each side border. Matching centers, join borders to quilt. Press seam allowances toward borders; then trim excess border fabric at ends.

9. Join a 2" x 42" border strip to both ends of each 10½"-long strip to make top and bottom borders. Join these to quilt in the same manner as for sides.

Quilting and Finishing

Mark desired quilting designs in Fabric XI borders and corner squares. The quilt shown has little houses quilted in corner squares and cross-hatching in borders and center section. Outline-quilt patchwork and add other quilting as desired.

Make 412" of binding. See page 23 for directions on making and applying straight-grain binding.

Strip Set 5—Make 5.

Strip Set 6—Make 5.

A **Moo**-vable Feast

Inspired by the motifs in Till the Cows Come Home, *this cheery tablecloth sets a happy tone for a party, picnic, or holiday meal. Select fabrics to represent your favorite breed—you can make a herd of Holsteins like ours, or use black fabric for Angus or tan and cream prints for Jerseys and Guernseys.*

Quick-Piecing Techniques:

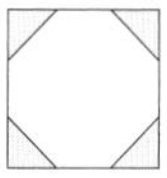

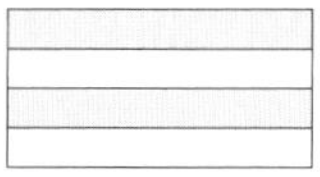

Finished Size
Blocks: 12 cow blocks, 6" x 10"
        14 tree blocks 4" x 6"
         4 fence blocks, 6" x 11"
         4 corner tree blocks, 7" square

Tablecloth: 60" x 90"

Materials

	Fabric I (black solid)	⅛ yard
	Fabric II (black-on-white spotted print)	⅜ yard
	Fabric III (light brown plaid)	⅛ yard
	Fabric IV (assorted green prints)	scraps
	Fabric V (black-on-green small check)	⅜ yard
	Fabric VI (brown solid)	⅛ yard
	Fabric VII (dark apple red)	5¾ yards
	Black embroidery floss	1 skein

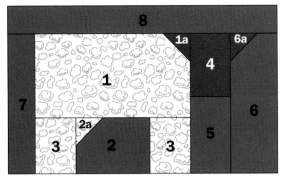

Block A—Make 6.

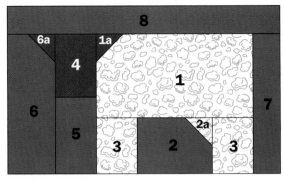

Block B—Make 6.

Cutting

From Fabric I, cut:

- One 2" x 42" strip.
  From this, cut:
  - Twelve 2" x 2¾" (A-4, B-4).
- One 1½" x 42" strip.
  From this, cut:
  - Twenty-four 1½" squares (A-1a, A-6a, B-1a, B-6a).

From Fabric II, cut:

- One 6¼" x 42" strip.
  From this, cut:
  - Twelve 3½" x 6¼" (A-1, B-1).
- Two 2" x 42" strips.
  From these, cut:
  - Twenty-four 2" x 2½" (A-3, B-3).
- One 1½" x 42" strip.
  From this, cut:
  - Twelve 1½" squares (A-2a, B-2a).

From Fabric III, cut:

- Two 1" x 42" strips for Strip Set 1 (C-2).
- Two 1¼" x 42" strips.
  From these, cut:
  - Twelve 1¼" x 4½" (C-1).

From Fabric IV scraps, cut:

- Fourteen 4¾" x 6¼" (D-2).
- Four 5¾" x 8⅝" (E-2).

From Fabric V, cut:

- Two 3¼" x 42" strips.
  From each of these, cut:
  - One 3¼" square. Cut both squares in half diagonally to get four E-4 triangles.
  - Two 1½" x 36½" strips for grass strips.
- Two 1½" x 42½" strips for grass strips.

From Fabric VI, cut:

- One 1" x 18" for Strip Set 2 (D-3).
- One 1¼" x 6" for Strip Set 3 (E-3).

From Fabric VII, cut:

- One 42½" x 72½" for center.
- One 42" x 72½" strip.
  From this, cut:
  - Two 9¾" x 72½" and two 9¾" x 60½" for facings.
  - One 2½" x 57½" for border.
  - One 8¼" x 16⅜" (E-1).
    Cut this as shown in Cutting diagram (page 127) to get eight triangles. Trim ¾" from narrow tip of each triangle. Each rectangle yields four triangles that point to the right and four that point left.
- Nine 2½" x 42" strips.
  From these, cut:
  - Six 2½" x 31" and two 2½" x 29" for borders.
  - Four 2½" x 12½" (C-3).
  - Twelve 2½" x 3¼" (A-2, B-2).
  - Twelve 2" x 3¼" (A-5, B-5).
- One 13¾" x 42" strip.
  From this, cut:
  - Four 5¼" x 13¾" (D-1).
    Cut these as shown in Cutting diagram (page 127) to get a total of 28 (and four extra). Trim 1⅛" from narrow tip of each triangle. Store righties and lefties separately.
  - Six 2¼" x 21" strips.
    From these, cut:
    - Two 2¼" x 18" for Strip Set 2 (D-3).
    - Twelve 2¼" x 5½" (A-6, B-6).
- Six 1½" x 42" strips.
  From these, cut:
  - Twelve 1½" x 10½" (A-8, B-8).
  - Twelve 1½" x 5½" (A-7, B-7).

- Three 1½" x 42" strips for Strip Set 1 (C-2).
- From scraps, cut:
  - Two 2¾" x 6" for Strip Set 3 (E-3).
  - Eight 1½" x 6½" (9).

Piecing the Cow Blocks

1. Referring to Block A diagram, use diagonal-corner technique to make one each of units 1, 2, and 6. *Note:* If desired, eliminate Unit 2a from some blocks to mix some bulls into the herd.

2. Join a Unit 3 to both sides of Unit 2. Join 2-3 unit to bottom of Unit 1.

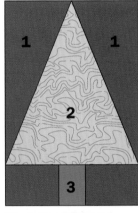

Block D—Make 14.

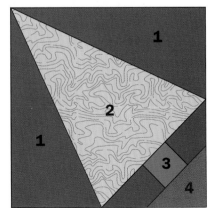

Block E—Make 4.

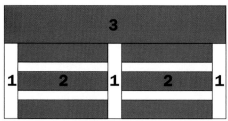

Block C—Make 4.

3. Join units 4 and 5. Add Unit 6 to right side of 4-5 unit. Join this to right side of cow body.

4. Cut a 4" length of embroidery floss and tie a small knot at each end. Pin one knot in side seam allowance at top left corner of Unit 1. Join Unit 7 to left side of cow body, catching tail in seam. Backstitch over tail to secure it.

5. Join Unit 8 to top edge to complete block. Make six of Block A.

6. Block B is made in the same manner as Block A, but it is a mirror image. Units are the same as for Block A, but positions of diagonal corners are reversed. Follow Block B diagram carefully to assemble six of Block B.

Piecing the Fence Blocks

1. Referring to diagram of Strip Set 1, join three 1½"-wide strips of Fabric VII to two 1"-wide strips of Fabric III. From this strip set, cut eight 4⅞"-wide segments for Unit C-2.

2. Join two segments with three of Unit 1 as shown in Block C diagram; then add Unit 3 to top of fence. Make four of Block C.

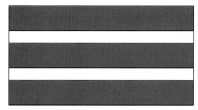

Strip Set 1—Make 1.

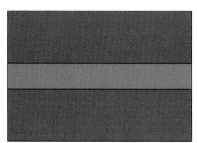

Strip Set 2—Make 1.

Piecing the Tree Blocks

1. Referring to diagram of Strip Set 2, join 2¼" x 18" strips of Fabric VII to both sides of 1" x 18" strip of Fabric VI. From this, cut fourteen 1¼"-wide segments for Unit D-3.

2. Fold and cut each 4¾" x 6¼" piece of Fabric IV as described in Step 2 of Piecing the Tree Blocks for *Till the Cows Come Home* (page 129). Trim ½" from tip of each triangle. Assemble block following instructions given in Step 3 of those instructions. Make 14 of Block D.

3. To make Strip Set 3, join 2¾" x 6" pieces of Fabric VII to sides of 1¼" x 6" piece of Fabric VI in the same manner as shown for Strip Set 2. From this, cut four 1¼"-wide segments for Unit E-3.

4. Fold and cut 5¾" x 8⅝" pieces of Fabric IV in the same manner as for other trees. Trim ⅝" from triangle tips. Assemble block following instructions given in Step 8 of Piecing the Tree Blocks for *Till the Cows Come Home* (page 130). Make four of Block E.

Tablecloth Assembly

1. Referring to Tablecloth Assembly diagram, join one A block, one B block, five D blocks, and two of Unit 9 to make a row for each end of tablecloth. Join a 42½" strip of Fabric V to bottom of each row.

2. Join remaining A, B, C, and D blocks to make side rows as shown.

3. Join two 36½"-long Fabric V strips end-to-end to make a grass strip for each side. Matching center seams, join grass strip to bottom of each long row.

4. Referring to Tablecloth Assembly diagram, join side rows to center section.

5. Add E blocks to ends of short rows as shown. Join rows to tablecloth ends.

6. Join 57½"-long border to one end of cloth. Press seam allowances toward border; then trim excess border fabric. Join two 29"-long strips to make another 57½" border and join this to opposite end in the same manner.

7. To make a border for each side, join three 31" strips end-to-end. Join these to sides of cloth.

8. On one long edge of each facing strip, press under a ¼" hem. On longer strips only, turn under another ¼" and press.

9. With right sides facing, join ends of long facings to hemmed edge of short facings as shown in Facing diagram. Press seam allowances toward short facings. Topstitch hemmed edges.

10. With right sides facing, pin facing to tablecloth and stitch around outer edge. Clip corners; then turn facing to back and press.

11. From right side, stitch in-the-ditch in patchwork seams through both layers to secure facing.

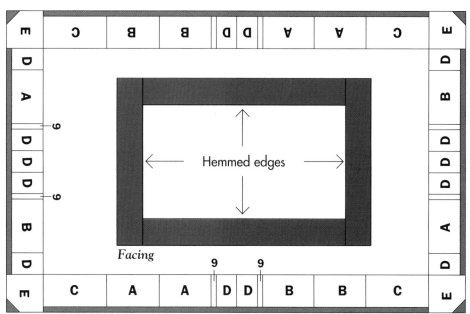

Tablecloth Assembly

Seminole Flower Bed

This quilt admirably demonstrates how Seminole Patchwork erases the difficulty of working with lots of little pieces. The clever combination of strip sets creates a design that looks intricate but is remarkably quick to sew. In this quilt, one floral print fabric has dramatic effect set amidst coordinating solids and subtle tone-on-tone prints.

Quick-Piecing Techniques:

Finished Size

Blocks: 20 blocks, 16" square   Quilt: 83" x 101"

Materials

	Fabric I (pink-and-green floral print)	2 yards
	Fabric II (dark mauve solid)	1½ yards
	Fabric III (pink-on-pink print)	4¼ yards
	Fabric IV (dark green-on-green print)	1⅝ yards
	Fabric V (white-on-ivory print)	5 yards
	Fabric VI (medium purple-on-purple print)	5 yards
	Backing fabric	7½ yards
	Square acrylic ruler, at least 12" square	
	Spray starch	

Cutting

From Fabric I, cut:

- Twenty 1⅛" x 42" strips for Strip Set A.
- Ten 1¼" x 42" strips for strip sets D and G.
- Eight 2" x 42" strips for Strip Set E.
- Six 1⅛" x 42" strips.
  From these, cut:
  - Eighty 1⅛" squares (2b).
  - Eighty 1⅛" x 1¾" (2c).
- Two 1¼" x 42" strips.
  From these, cut:
  - Forty 1¼" x 2" (G-1).

From Fabric II, cut:

- Ten 1⅝" x 42" strips for Strip Set A.
- Twenty 1¼" x 42" strips for strip sets B, D, F, and G.

From Fabric III, cut:

- Ten 1⅝" x 42" strips for Strip Set A.
- Twenty 4¼" x 42" strips for Strip Set A.
- Fifteen 1¼" x 42" strips for strip sets B, F, H, and L.
- Eight 2" x 42" strips for Strip Set C.
- Three 1⅛" x 42" strips.
  From these, cut:
  - Eighty 1⅛" squares (2a).
- Two 1¼" x 42" strips.
  From these, cut:
  - Forty 1¼" x 2" (F-1).

From Fabric IV, cut:

- Twenty-five 1¼" x 42" strips for strip sets B, D, H, J, and K.
- Eight 1⅛" x 42" strips.
  From these, cut:
  - Eighty 1⅛" x 1¾" (2d).
  - Eighty 1⅛" x 2⅜" (2e).
- Ten 1" x 42" strips for inner border.

From Fabric V, cut:

- Ten 3⅜" x 42" strips.
  From these, cut:
  - 120 3⅜" squares. Cut each square in quarters diagonally to get 480 triangles (7).
- Three 3" x 42" strips.
  From these, cut:
  - Forty 3" squares. Cut each square in half diagonally to get 80 triangles (8).

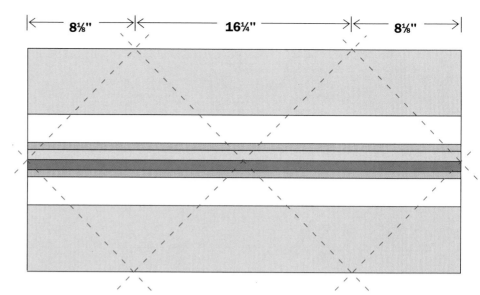

Strip Set A—Make 10.

- Twenty 2⅞" x 42" strips for Strip Set A.
- Thirty-seven 1¼" x 42" strips for strip sets B, C, D, E, H, and L.
- Five 2" x 42" strips for strip sets I and K.
- Ten 1½" x 42" strips for middle border.

From Fabric VI, cut:

- Nine 3" x 42" strips for binding.
- Eighteen 1¼" x 42" strips for strip sets H, I, J, K, and L.
- Five 2" x 42" strips for strip sets I and L.
- Four 2¾" x 42" strips for Strip Set J.
- Sixteen 2½" x 42" strips for sashing units.
  From 12 of these, cut:
  - Twenty-four 2½" x 14¼" for horizontal sashing.
- Twenty-seven 1" x 42" strips.
  From these, cut:
  - Forty 1" x 11½" (3).
  - Forty 1" x 12½" (4).
- Ten 3" x 42½" for outer border.

Piecing and Cutting the Strip Sets

Before beginning, review page 18 for general instructions on strip piecing and Seminole Patchwork.

1. Referring to diagram of Strip Set A, join strips of fabrics I, II, III, and V as shown. Make 10 of Strip Set A.

2. Starting at one corner of each strip set, measure and mark 8⅛" along one side as shown in diagram of Strip Set A. Measure and mark another 16¼" and then another 8⅛" as shown. Repeat on opposite side.

3. Align square ruler with center seam and marked points to cut Strip Set A as shown. Cut two 11½" squares from each strip set for block centers (Unit 1).

4. Referring to diagrams of strip sets B–L, join designated strips to make strip sets as shown.

5. From *each* of strip sets B, C, D, and E, cut 240 segments, each 1¼" wide. (To avoid confusion, store segments from each strip set in a zip-top plastic bag as described on page 13. Label each bag with strip set letter.)

6. From *each* of strip sets F and G, cut forty 1¼"-wide segments.

7. From *each* of strip sets H and I, cut twenty-four 1¼"-wide segments.

8. From Strip Set J, cut 129 segments, each 1¼" wide.

9. From *each* of strip sets K and L, cut 105 segments, each 1¼" wide.

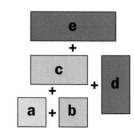

Unit 2 Assembly

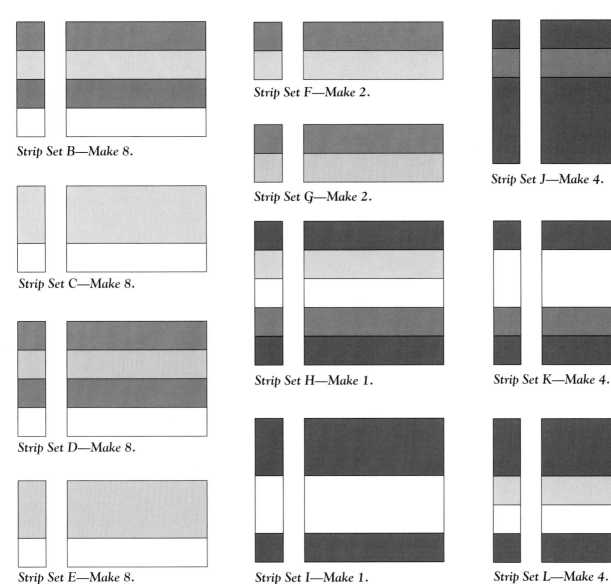

Strip Set B—Make 8.

Strip Set C—Make 8.

Strip Set D—Make 8.

Strip Set E—Make 8.

Strip Set F—Make 2.

Strip Set G—Make 2.

Strip Set H—Make 1.

Strip Set I—Make 1.

Strip Set J—Make 4.

Strip Set K—Make 4.

Strip Set L—Make 4.

Piecing the Blocks

The Seminole Flower block is made with pieces designated for units 2, 3, and 4, and segments from strip sets A–G.

To make the block center:

1. Referring to Unit 2 Assembly diagram, join 2a through 2e in alphabetical order as shown. Make 80 of Unit 2. Press under ¼" on Fabric IV edges only.

2. Aligning raw edges, position a Unit 2 at corners of Unit 1 squares. Topstitch or appliqué turned edges in place as shown in Block Assembly diagram.

3. Join a Unit 3 strip to top and bottom edges of each block. Press seam allowances toward Unit 3. Join Unit 4 strips to block sides in the same manner.

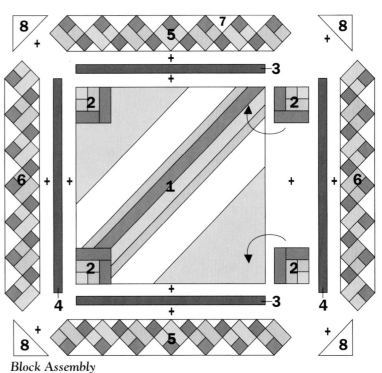

Block Assembly

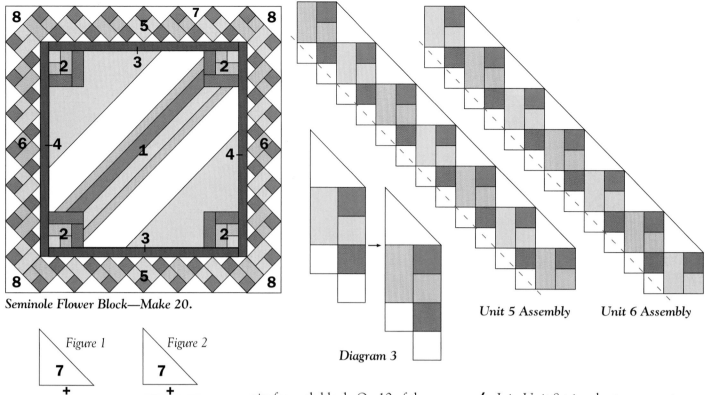

Seminole Flower Block—Make 20.

Diagram 1

Figure 1
7
+
Strip Set C
+
Strip Set B

Figure 2
7
+
Strip Set E
+
Strip Set D

Diagram 2

Figure 1
7
+
Strip F-1
+
Strip Set F

Figure 2
7
+
Strip G-1
+
Strip Set G

Unit 5 Assembly   Unit 6 Assembly

Diagram 3

To make the Seminole-pieced block borders:

1. Referring to Diagram 1, Figure 1, join one segment of Strip Set B to one from Strip Set C, aligning top edges and seam lines. Make 12 B-C flower units for each block. On 10 of these, add a Unit 7 triangle to top as shown. Referring to Diagram 1, Figure 2, make D-E flower units in the same manner.
2. Referring to Diagram 2, Figure 1, join Strip Set F segments with F-1 pieces. Add a Unit 7 triangle to top as shown to complete flower unit. Make two F units for each block. Referring to Diagram 2, Figure 2, make G flower units in the same manner.
3. Referring to Unit 5 Assembly diagram, join flower units in a row, aligning edges and seams as shown in Diagram 3. Make two of Unit 5 for each block. Referring to Unit 6 Assembly diagram, join flower units to make two of Unit 6 for each block. Press units 5 and 6, using a light spray of starch to prevent stretching bias edges when cutting.
4. Referring to assembly diagrams, trim bottom edges of each unit 5 and unit 6 strip, being careful to leave ¼" seam allowance below each seam.
5. Join a Unit 5 to top and bottom edges of each block, beginning and ending seams ¼" from each corner. Backstitch to secure. Join Unit 6 to block sides in the same manner. Join units 5 and 6 at each corner, stitching from outer edges to inside corners. Press mitered seams open.

6. Join Unit 8 triangles to corners to complete blocks. Completed blocks should measure 16½" square.

Piecing the Sashing

Separate units are assembled for horizontal and vertical sashing. Horizontal sashing is made with segments from strip sets H, I, J, and 2½" x 14¼" pieces of Fabric VI. Vertical sashing is made with segments from strip sets J, K, L, and remaining 2½"-wide strips of Fabric VI.

To make horizontal sashing:

1. Referring to Diagram 4, Figure 1, join segments of strip sets H, I, and J to make one flower unit, aligning seams as shown. Make 24 flower units. Press units with spray starch as before.
2. Align ruler with edges and trim flower units as shown in Diagram 4, Figure 2. Be careful to leave seam allowance below each seam.
3. Referring to Diagram 5, measure and mark 6⅜" from bottom left corner of each 2½" x 14¼" piece of Fabric VI. Next, measure and mark 5⅜" from top right corner as shown. Align ruler on diagonal line between marks and cut as shown to get two sashing units from each piece.

140

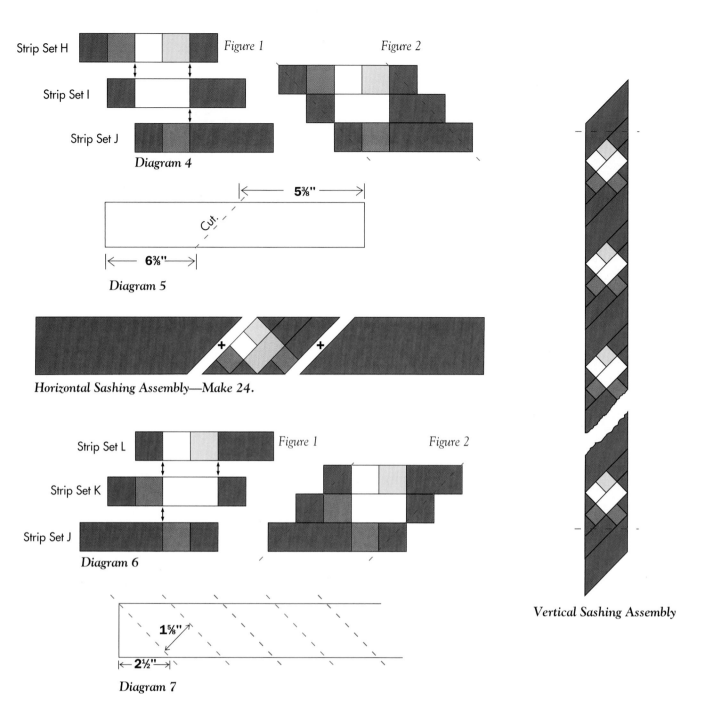

Strip Set H

Figure 1

Figure 2

Strip Set I

Strip Set J

Diagram 4

5⅜"

Cut

6⅜"

Diagram 5

Horizontal Sashing Assembly—Make 24.

Strip Set L

Figure 1

Figure 2

Strip Set K

Strip Set J

Diagram 6

1⅝"

2½"

Diagram 7

Vertical Sashing Assembly

4. Referring to Horizontal Sashing Assembly diagram, join sashing units to flower unit sides. Make 24 horizontal sashing strips. Each strip should measure 16½" long.

To make vertical sashing:
1. Referring to Diagram 6, Figure 1, join segments of strip sets J, K, and L to make one flower unit, aligning seams as shown. Make 105 flower units. Press units with spray starch as before.

2. Align ruler with edges and trim flower units as shown in Diagram 6, Figure 2. Be careful to leave seam allowance below each seam.
3. Referring to Diagram 7, measure and mark 2½" from bottom left corner of each remaining 2½"-wide strip of Fabric VI. Align ruler on diagonal line between mark and top left corner as shown and cut. Discard trimmed triangle. Align ruler with cut edge and cut 1⅝"-wide segments from remainder of strip. In this manner, cut a total of 110 sashing units.

4. Referring to Vertical Sashing Assembly diagram, join 21 flower units in a vertical row with sashing units between them. Add sashing units to top and bottom of row. Make five vertical sashing rows.
5. Trim bottom and top of each sashing row as shown, leaving seam allowances beyond flower seams. Each trimmed sashing row should measure 92½" long.

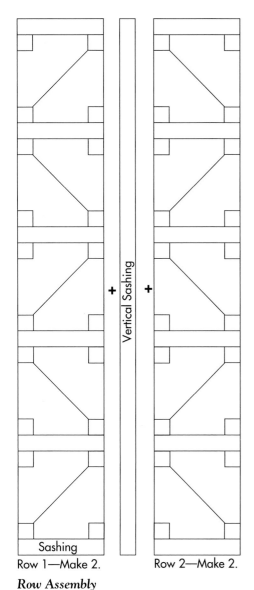

Vertical Sashing

Sashing

Row 1—Make 2.   Row 2—Make 2.

Row Assembly

Quilt Assembly

1. Referring to Row Assembly diagram, join five blocks and six horizontal sashing units as shown to make one of Row 1. Pay careful attention to diagram for correct positioning of diagonal center of each block. Ease blocks to fit sashing units as necessary. (See page 15 for tips on easing.) Make two of Row 1. Repeat to make two of Row 2.

2. Join rows in 1-2-1-2 order as shown in Row Assembly diagram, with a vertical sashing row between block rows. Ease block rows to fit vertical sashing rows as necessary. Add remaining vertical sashing rows to quilt sides.

3. Join two 1" x 42" strips of Fabric IV end-to-end for top inner border. Repeat for bottom border. Join two 1½" x 42" strips of Fabric V in the same manner for top and bottom middle borders. Join two 3" x 42½" strips of Fabric VI in the same manner for top and bottom outer borders.

4. Matching center seams, join three strips for top border. Aligning centers of border and quilt, join border to top edge, starting and stopping seam ¼" from each corner. Repeat for bottom border.

5. Join three 1" x 42" strips of Fabric IV end-to-end for each side inner border. Join strips of fabrics V and VI in the same manner for middle and outer borders. Matching seams, join three strips to make one border for each side. Trim 8" or 9" from both ends of each strip.

6. Aligning centers of border and quilt, join border to one side edge, starting and stopping seam ¼" from each corner. Repeat for opposite side.

7. Miter border corners.

Quilting and Finishing

Hand quilting is recommended for this quilt to minimize stretching all the bias edges. Quilt in-the-ditch in diagonal seam lines of all Seminole Patchwork. Continue the diagonal lines of the patchwork by quilting into solid areas of sashing units and triangle units 7 and 8.

Make 378" of binding. See page 23 for directions on making and applying straight-grain binding.

143

Blue Stars

Three simple blocks combine to make a galaxy of stars framed with a two-strip border. The monochromatic color scheme makes this quilt an ideal project in the color of your choice.

Quick-Piecing Techniques:

Finished Size

Blocks: 165 blocks, 6" square
        52 half blocks, 3" x 6"

Quilt: 78" x 102"

Materials

	Fabric I (medium blue solid)	3½ yards
	Fabric II (dark blue mini-print)	3¼ yards
	Fabric III (dark blue check or mini-print)	1¾ yards
	Fabric IV (light blue print)	2 yards
	Fabric V (medium blue print)	1¾ yards
	Fabric VI (light blue check or print)	2 yards
	Backing fabric	6 yards

Cutting

Refer to diagrams on page 146 to identify blocks and units designated in cutting list.

From Fabric I, cut:

♦ Eighteen 6½" x 42" strips.
  From these, cut:
  • Eighty-two 6½" squares (C-1).
  • Twenty-eight 3½" x 6½" (D-1).

From Fabric II, cut:

♦ Nine 2½" x 42" strips for outer border.
♦ Nine 2½" x 42" strips for binding.
♦ Nine 6½" x 42" strips.
  From these, cut:
  • Thirty-five 6½" squares (B-1).
  • Twenty-four 3½" x 6½" (E-1).
♦ One 6" x 10" for half-square triangles (F).

From Fabric III, cut:

♦ Twenty-eight 2" x 42" strips.
  From these, cut:
  • 576 2" squares (A-1a, C-1a, D-1a).

From Fabric IV, cut:

♦ Nine 1½" x 42" strips for inner border.
♦ Four 3½" x 42" strips.
  From these, cut:
  • Forty-eight 3½" squares (A-1).
♦ Eighteen 2" x 42" strips.
  From these, cut:
  • 192 2" squares (A-3a).
  • Ninety-six 2" x 3½" (A-2).

From Fabric V, cut:

♦ Twenty-six 2" x 42" strips.
  From these, cut:
  • 192 2" squares (A-2a).
  • 192 2" x 3½" (A-3).

From Fabric VI, cut:

♦ Sixteen 3½" x 42" strips.
  From these, cut:
  • 188 3½" squares (B-1a, E-1a).
♦ One 6" x 10" for half-square triangles (F).

Piecing the Blocks

1. Referring to Block A Assembly diagram, use diagonal-corner technique to make one of Unit 1, two of Unit 2, and four of Unit 3 for each Block A. Join units in horizontal rows as shown; then join rows. Make 48 of Block A.

2. Using diagonal-corner technique, make blocks B, C, D, and E as shown.

3. To make Block F, see page 17 for instructions on half-square triangles. On wrong side of the 6" x 10" piece of Fabric VI, draw a 1 x 2-square grid of 3⅞" squares. With right sides facing, match marked fabric with the 6" x 10" piece of Fabric II. Stitch grid as directed on page 17. Cut 4 triangle-squares from this grid.

Quilt Assembly

1. Referring to Row Assembly diagram, join blocks in rows as shown. Make two edge rows, eight of Row 1, and seven of Row 2.

2. Starting with a Row 1, join all rows 1 and 2, alternating row types.

3. Referring to photograph, add an edge row to top. Turn remaining edge row upside down and join it to bottom.

4. For side inner borders, cut in half one 1½"-wide strip of Fabric IV. Stitch one of these short strips between two full-length strips to make a 104"-long border strip for each side. For top and bottom borders, join two full-length strips end-to-end for each border.

5. Join long borders to sides of quilt. Press seam allowances toward border and trim excess border length. Add top and bottom borders in same manner.

6. Assemble 2½"-wide strips of Fabric II in same manner to make outer borders. Join outer borders to quilt in same manner as inner border.

Quilting and Finishing

Outline-quilt patchwork and borders or quilt as desired.

Make 370" of binding. See page 23 for directions on making and applying straight-grain binding.

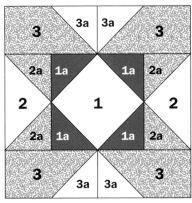

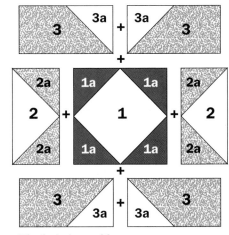

Block A—Make 48.

Block A Assembly

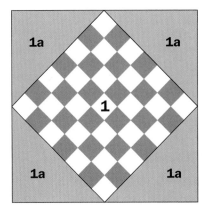

Block B—Make 35.

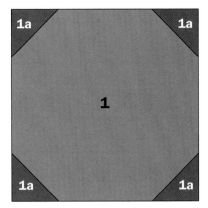

Block C—Make 82.

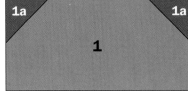

Block D—Make 28.

Block F—Make 4.

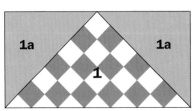

Block E—Make 24.

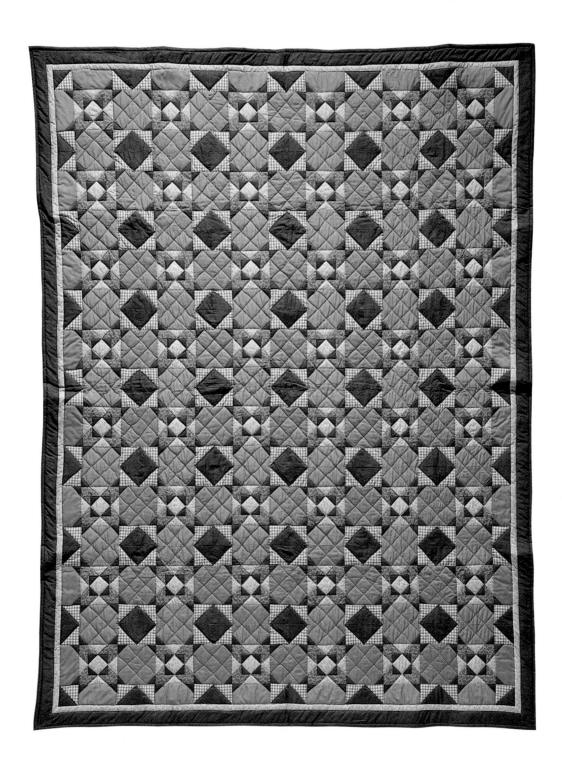

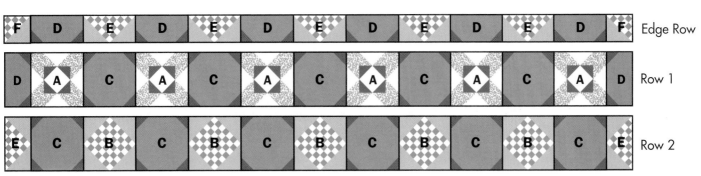

Edge Row

Row 1

Row 2

Row Assembly

Formal Garden

A medley of four colors harmonizes in this patchwork interpretation of the elaborate landscapes of stately homes. The fabrics—in pastels or another theme of your choice—create a lovely diversity that disguises how easy this quilt is to make. Because this quilt uses just two basic quick-piecing techniques, we recommend it for beginners.

Quick-Piecing Techniques:

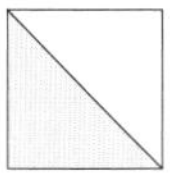

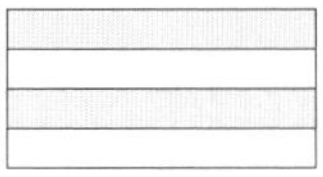

Finished Size

Blocks: 90 flower blocks, 6" x 10"
      20 half blocks, 6" square
       8 corner leaf blocks, 6" square
       8 nine-patch blocks, 6" square
       4 checkerboard blocks, 10" square

Quilt: 92" x 116"

Materials

	Fabric I (blue print)	¾ yard
	Fabric II (light blue solid)	¾ yard
	Fabric III (yellow print)	¾ yard
	Fabric IV (light yellow solid)	¾ yard
	Fabric V (lavender print)	¾ yard
	Fabric VI (light lavender solid)	¾ yard
	Fabric VII (pink-on-pink print)	¾ yard
	Fabric VIII (light pink print)	¾ yard
	Fabric IX (light green texture-look print)	2⅝ yards
	Fabric X (dark green solid)	3⅞ yards
	Fabric XI (white solid)	6⅝ yards
	Backing fabric	8½ yards
	⅛"-wide dark green double-faced satin ribbon	12 yards

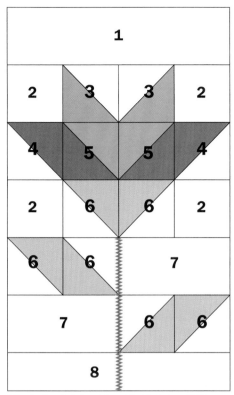

Block A—Make 19 with Fabrics I/II.
Make 26 with Fabrics V/VI.

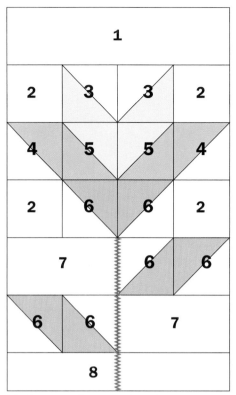

Block B—Make 27 with Fabrics III/IV.
Make 18 with Fabrics VII/VIII.

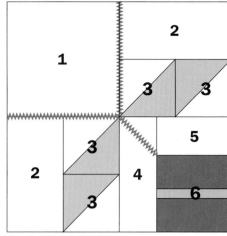

Block C—Make 8.

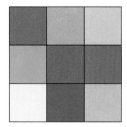

Block D—Make 8.

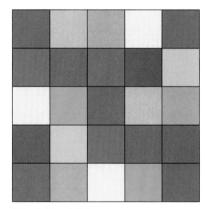

Block E—Make 4.

Cutting

From *each* of Fabrics I through VIII, cut:

- One 11" x 42" strip.
  From this, cut:
  - Two 11" x 18¼" for triangle-squares (A-3, A-4, A-5, B-3, B-4, B-5).
- Two 2½" x 42" strips.
  From these, cut:
  - Eighteen 2½" squares (Blocks D and E).
- Three 1½" x 42" strips.
  From these, cut:
  - Ten 1½" x 10½" (outer border sashing).

From Fabric IX, cut:

- Six 11" x 42" strips.
  From these, cut:
  - Twelve 11" x 16" for triangle-squares (A-6, B-6, C-3).
- Nine ¾" x 43" strips for Strip Set X.
- Eighteen 1" x 42" strips for Strip Set Y.

From Fabric X, cut:

- Eighteen 1⅜" x 42" strips for Strip Set X.
- Thirty-six 1¾" x 42" strips for Strip Set Y.
- Eleven 3" x 42" strips for binding.

- Two 2½" x 42" strips.
  From these, cut:
  - Twenty-eight 2½" squares (Blocks D and E).
- Two 1½" x 42" strips.
  From these, cut:
  - Eight 1½" x 10½" (outer border sashing).

From Fabric XI, cut:

- Ten 11" x 42" strips.
  From these, cut:
  - Eight 11" x 18¼" for triangle-squares (A-3, A-4, B-3, B-4).
  - Twelve 11" x 16" for triangle-squares (A-6, B-6, C-3).
- Ten 3½" x 42" strips.
  From these, cut:
  - 196 2" x 3½" (A-7, B-7, C-2).
  - Eight 3½" squares (C-1).
- Fifteen 1½" x 42½" strips.
  From these, cut:
  - Ninety 1½" x 6½" (A-8, B-8).
  - Eight 1½" x 2½" (C-5).
  - Eight 1½" x 3½" (C-4).
- Thirty 2" x 42" strips.
  From these and scraps, cut:
  - 110 2" x 6½" (A-1, B-1).
  - 440 2" squares (A-2, B-2).

Piecing the Flower Blocks

1. See page 17 for complete instructions on half-square triangles. On wrong side of one 11" x 18¼" piece of Fabric II, draw a 4 x 7-square grid of 2⅜" squares. Repeat with 11" x 18¼" pieces of fabrics IV, VI, and VIII.
2. With right sides facing, match each marked fabric with an 11" x 18¼" piece of second fabric in the same color family (fabrics I, III, V, and VII). Stitch each grid as directed on page 17. Cut 56 triangle-squares from each grid for units A-5 and B-5.

3. On wrong side of each 11" x 18¼" piece of Fabric XI, draw a 4 x 7-square grid of 2⅜" squares. With right sides facing, match one marked piece with each remaining 11" x 18¼" piece of colored fabric (fabrics I–VIII). Stitch grids as before and cut 56 triangle-squares from each grid for units A-3, A-4, B-3, and B-4.

4. On wrong side of each 11" x 16" piece of Fabric XI, draw a 4 x 6-square grid of 2⅜" squares. With right sides facing, match marked pieces with corresponding pieces of Fabric IX. Stitch grids as directed on page 17. Cut 48 triangle-squares from each grid to get 572 triangle-squares (and four extra) for units A-6, B-6, and C-3.

5. Referring to Block A Assembly diagram, join blue triangle-squares and white units in horizontal rows, turning triangle-squares as shown. Join rows to complete one each of sections A and B.

6. Add ribbon stem to Section B before joining sections. (A walking foot or even-feed foot is helpful for applying ribbon.) Center ribbon over Section B center seam (between units 6 and 7), extending ribbon to bottom of Unit 8. Topstitch down one side of ribbon; then lift presser foot, pivot block, and stitch opposite side.

7. Join sections A and B to complete one block. Make 19 of Block A with blue triangle-squares and 26 blocks with lavender triangle-squares.

8. The flower part (Section A) of each Block B is exactly the same as for Block A. Section B is made with the same units, but Unit 6 (leaves) positions are reversed. Following block diagram carefully, make 27 of Block B with yellow triangle-squares and 18 blocks with pink triangle-squares.

9. Use remaining units to make half blocks. Referring to Block A Assembly diagram, make Section A only. Make nine blue half blocks, one yellow half block, one lavender half block, and nine pink half blocks. Before beginning quilt assembly, you should have 90 blocks and 20 half blocks.

Piecing the Corner Blocks

1. Referring to Strip Set X diagram, join two 1⅜" strips of Fabric X to both sides of each ¾" strip of Fabric IX. Make nine strip sets. From these, cut four 36½" lengths, four 30½" lengths, and four 12½" lengths. Set these aside for inside borders. From remainder, cut eight 2½" lengths for Unit C-6.

2. To assemble top half of corner leaf block, begin by joining two of Unit 3 as shown at top right of Block C Assembly diagram. Join Unit 2 to top of Unit 3 pair. Add Unit 1 to left side of combined unit.

3. Before joining bottom half of Block C, add ribbon to Unit 4 as follows. Cut 2½" of ribbon. Starting at top left corner of Unit 4 piece, center ribbon at a 45° angle across width of unit. Topstitch both sides of ribbon.

4. To assemble bottom half of corner leaf block, begin by joining two of Unit 3 as shown at bottom left of Block C Assembly diagram. Join Unit 2 to left side of Unit 3 pair; then join Unit 4 to right side. Join units 5 and 6; then join this to right side of combined unit.

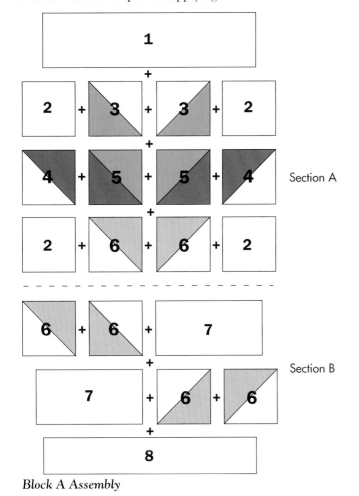

Section A

Section B

Block A Assembly

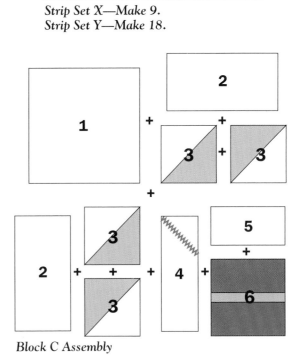

Strip Set X—Make 9.
Strip Set Y—Make 18.

Block C Assembly

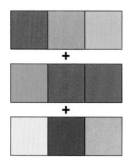

Block D Assembly

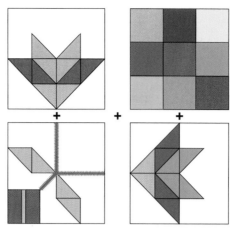

Corner Assembly

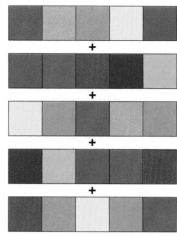

Block E Assembly

5. Join top and bottom sections to complete block. Make eight of Block C.
6. Cut 6¾" of ribbon for each C block. Topstitch ribbon in place atop Unit 1 seam, mitering ribbon at corner.
7. Referring to Block D Assembly diagram, join 2½" squares of fabrics I–VIII in three horizontal rows of three squares each, placing a Fabric X square in middle of center row as shown. Join rows to complete Block D. Make eight of Block D.
8. Referring to Corner Assembly diagram, join pink and blue half blocks with C and D blocks. Make eight corner blocks.
9. Referring to Block E Assembly diagram, join twenty-five 2½" squares of colored fabrics in five horizontal rows of five squares each, placing Fabric X squares in rows as shown. Make two of Block E as shown. Make two more blocks in the same manner, reversing placement of light and dark values of each color family.

Quilt Assembly

1. Referring to Quilt Assembly diagram, join four remaining half blocks as shown to make center square. (Arrows on diagram indicate color and direction of each flower.)
2. Join a lavender block to right sides of four yellow blocks. Add 12½" lengths of Strip Set X to bottoms of all four pairs. Matching strip-set edge to center square, join two pairs to sides of center square. Join assembled corner blocks to sides of both remaining pairs, aligning seams of strip-set units. Referring to Quilt Assembly diagram, join these to top and bottom of center square.

3. Starting with a yellow block, join six blocks in a horizontal row as shown in Quilt Assembly diagram, ending with a lavender block. Make four rows. Join a 36½" length of Strip Set X to bottom of each row, easing blocks to fit as necessary. (See page 15 for tips on easing.)
4. Matching strip-set edge to center section, join two rows to sides of center square as shown in Quilt Assembly diagram. Join corner blocks to ends of both remaining rows. Referring to Quilt Assembly diagram, join these rows to top and bottom of center section.
5. Join two 30½" lengths of Strip Set X end-to-end to make 60½"-long top and bottom borders. Matching center seams, join borders to top and bottom of center section.
6. Referring to top of Quilt Assembly diagram, join 10 blocks in a horizontal row, starting with a pink block and ending with a lavender block. Matching top of block row with top border, join row to top of quilt.
7. Referring to bottom of assembly diagram, join 10 more blocks in a row, starting with a blue block and ending with a yellow block. Join this row to quilt bottom, again matching top of block row to border.
8. For Strip Set Y, join two 1¾" strips of Fabric X to sides of 1" strip of Fabric IX. Make 18 strip sets.
9. Join two of Strip Set Y end-to-end to make an 84½"-long border. Join these to quilt sides, easing quilt to fit border as necessary. From four of Strip Set Y, cut four 33½"-long strips. Join

two of these end-to-end to make a 66½" border for top and bottom edges. Matching center seams, join borders to top and bottom of center section.
10. Join yellow 1½" x 10½" sashing strips in pairs. Join one pair to each remaining yellow block, matching lighter sashing strip to *right side* of block. Using pink sashing strips, repeat with all but two pink blocks. Join each of the four remaining pink sashing strips to Fabric X strips.
11. Join lavender sashing strips in pairs. Join one pair to each remaining lavender block, matching lighter sashing strip to *left side* of block. Using blue sashing strips, repeat with all but two blue blocks. Join each of the four remaining blue sashing strips to Fabric X strips.
12. Referring to right side of Quilt Assembly diagram, join 11 blocks in a vertical row, starting with a yellow block and ending with a pink block. Note arrow directions for positioning of blocks. Add blue/green and pink/green sashing strips to row ends as shown. Join this row to right side of quilt. Referring to left side of assembly diagram, join blocks for left side of quilt as shown.
13. Use remaining blocks to assemble horizontal rows for top and bottom of quilt as shown in Quilt Assembly diagram. Add blue/green and pink/green sashing strips to row ends as shown; then join E blocks to row ends, positioning diagonal rows of Fabric X squares as shown. Join these rows to top and bottom of quilt.

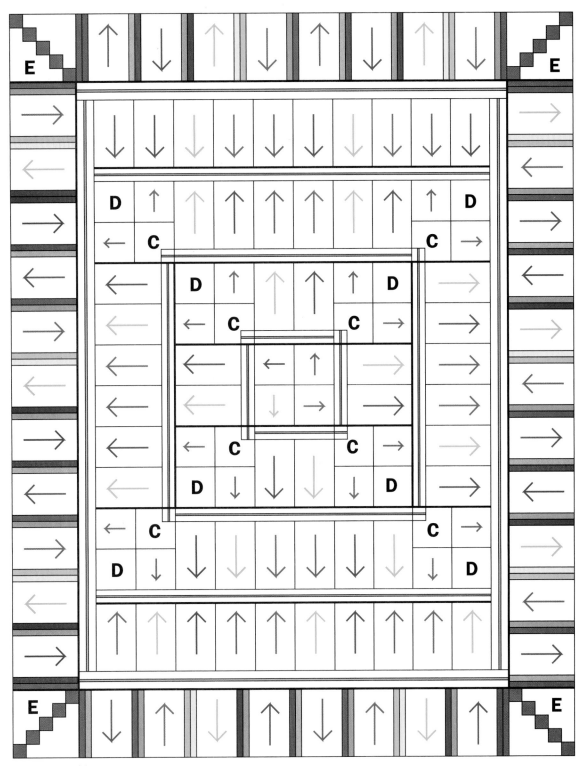

Quilt Assembly

14. From remaining Y strip sets, cut six 37½" lengths, four 38½" lengths, and four 9" lengths. Join three 37½" lengths end-to-end to make 111½"-long borders for each side. Matching centers of border and quilt side, join one of these to each side of quilt. For each of the top and bottom borders, join two 38½" lengths end-to-end and then add a 9" length to each end. Join these to top and bottom of quilt in the same manner as for side borders.

Quilting and Finishing

Outline-quilt patchwork or quilt as desired.

Make 430" of binding. See page 23 for directions on making and applying straight-grain binding.

South of the Border

Add a little salsa to your home decor with a quilt that says, "Olé, amigos!" A palette of colors from the American desert enhances four classic southwestern motifs that you can assemble with just two quick-piecing techniques. See page 161 for a spicy tablecloth made with the same chili blocks.

Quick-Piecing Techniques:

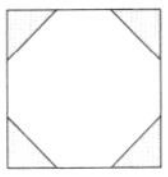

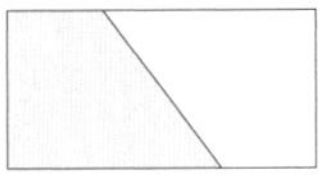

Finished Size

Blocks: 24 chili blocks, 7" x 9"
       12 cactus blocks, 7½" x 13"
        4 coyote blocks, 10" x 11¾"
  102 border blocks, 4" x 6"

Quilt: 87" x 105"

Materials

	Fabric I (orange-and-brown sunset-look print)	¼ yard
	Fabric II (dark brown print)	¼ yard
	Fabric III (light rust solid)	2¾ yards
	Fabric IV (light peach solid)	1¾ yards
	Fabric V (dusty green solid)	¼ yard
	Fabric VI (light dusty green solid)	⅜ yard
	Fabric VII (pink print)	2¾ yards
	Fabric VIII (burgundy print)	1⅛ yards
	Fabric IX (green texture-look print)	½ yard
	Fabric X (mauve solid)	2½ yards
	Fabric XI (dark turquoise solid)	2¾ yards
	Backing fabric	8 yards

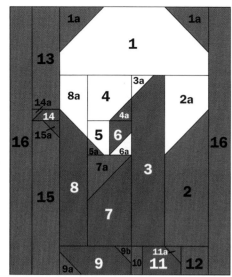

Block A—Make 2.

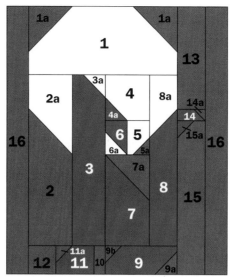

Block B—Make 2.

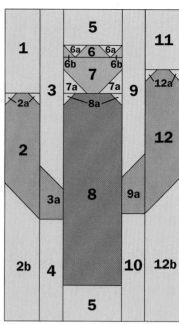

Block C—Make 12.

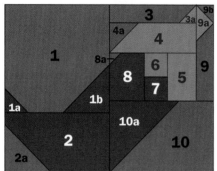

Block D—Make 12.

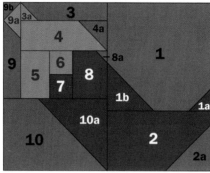

Block E—Make 12.

Block F—Make 102.

Cutting

From Fabric I, cut:

♦ One 3½" x 42" strip.
  From this, cut:
  • Four 3½" x 7¼" (A-1, B-1).
  • Four 1¾" x 3¼" (A-8a, B-8a).
  • Eight 1½" squares (A-3a, A-6a, B-3a, B-6a).

♦ One 2½" x 42" strip.
  From this, cut:
  • Four 2½" x 4" (A-2a, B-2a).
  • Four 2½" squares (A-4, B-4).
  • Four 1½" x 2" (A-5, B-5).

From Fabric II, cut:

♦ One 2" x 42" strip.
  From this, cut:
  • Four 2" x 8" (A-3, B-3).
  • Four 1½" x 2" (A-6, B-6).

♦ One 2½" x 42" strip.
  From this, cut:
  • Four 2½" x 4½" (A-7, B-7).
  • Four 1¾" x 2¼" (A-11, B-11).

♦ One 1¾" x 42" strip.
  From this, cut:
  • Four 1¾" x 6½" (A-8, B-8).
  • Four 1¾" x 3¾" (A-9, B-9).

♦ From scraps, cut:
  • Four 1" x 1¾" (A-14, B-14).
  • Four 1½" squares (A-4a, B-4a).
  • Four 1¼" squares (A-15a, B-15a).

From Fabric III, cut:

♦ Four 2½" x 42" strips.
  From these, cut:
  • Eight 2½" x 7½" (25).
  • Four 2½" x 6½" (A-2, B-2).
  • Thirty-six 2½" squares (A-1a, A-7a, B-1a, B-7a, D-2a, E-2a).

♦ Six 1¼" x 42" strips.
  From these, cut:
  • Thirty-six 1¼" squares (A-5a, A-9b, A-11a, B-5a, B-9b, B-11a, D-9b, E-9b).
  • Twenty-four 1¼" x 4¼" (D-3, E-3).
  • Twenty-four 1¼" x 3¾" (D-9, E-9).

♦ One 1⅝" x 42" strip.
  From this, cut:
  • Four 1⅝" x 10½" (17).

♦ Sixteen 1¾" x 42" strips.
  From these, cut:
  • Sixteen 1¾" x 21½" (26).
  • Eight 1¾" x 13½" (27).
  • Eight 1¾" x 11½" (29).
  • Four 1¾" x 7¼" (A-15, B-15).
  • Four 1¾" x 5" (A-13, B-13).
  • Twenty-eight 1¾" squares (A-12, B-12, D-4a, E-4a).
  • Four 1" x 1¾" (A-10, B-10).

♦ Nine 1½" x 42" strips.
  From these, cut:
  • Eight 1½" x 12¼" (A-16, B-16).
  • Thirty-two 1½" x 7½" (24).
  • Four 1½" squares (A-9a, B-9a).
  • Twenty-eight 1" squares (A-14a, B-14a, D-8a, E-8a).

♦ Five 5" x 42" strips.
  From these, cut:
  • Twenty-four 5" squares (D-1, E-1).
  • Twenty-four 3½" x 5" (D-10, E-10).

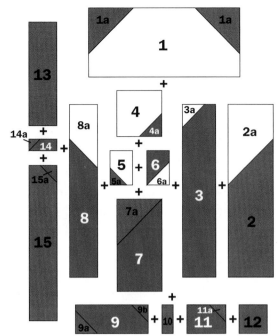

Block A Assembly

♦ One 2⅛" x 42" strip.
   From this, cut:
   • Four 2⅛" x 10½" (21).

From Fabric IV, cut:
♦ Eight 2" x 42" strips.
   From these, cut:
   • Twelve 2" x 4" (C-1).
   • Twelve 2" x 6" (C-2b).
   • Thirty-six 2" x 3" (C-5, C-11).
   • Twelve 2" x 6½" (C-12b).
♦ Nine 1½" x 42" strips.
   From these, cut:
   • Twelve 1½" x 8" (C-3).
   • Twelve 1½" x 4½" (C-4).
   • Twelve 1½" x 7½" (C-9).
   • Twelve 1½" x 5" (C-10).
   • Twenty-four 1½" squares (C-7a).
   • Twenty-four 1" x 1½" (C-6a).
♦ Twelve 1" x 42" strips.
   From these, cut:
   • Six 1" x 35" and six 1" x 29" for middle borders.
♦ Seventy-two 1" squares (C-2a, C-8a, C-12a).
♦ One 12½" x 42" strip.
   From this, cut:
   • Ten 2½" x 12½" (22).
   • Four 3" x 12½" (23).

From Fabric V, cut:
♦ One 8½" x 42" strip.
   From this, cut:
   • Twelve 3" x 8½" (C-8).

From Fabric VI, cut:
♦ Four 2" x 42" strips.
   From these, cut:
   • Twelve 2" x 6½" (C-12).
   • Twelve 2" x 6" (C-2).
♦ One 3" x 42" strip.
   From this, cut:
   • Twenty-four 1½" x 3" (C-3a, C-9a).

From Fabric VII, cut:
♦ One 3" x 42" strip.
   From this, cut:
   • Twelve 2" x 3" (C-7).
♦ Fifty-seven 1½" x 42" strips.
   From these, cut:
   • 204 1½" x 4½" (F-1).
   • 408 1½" x 3½" (F-2).
♦ From scraps, cut:
   • Twelve 1" x 2" (C-6).
   • Twenty-four 1" squares (C-6b).

From Fabric VIII, cut:
♦ Three 3" x 42" strips.
   From these, cut:
   • Twenty-four 3" x 5" (D-2, E-2).
♦ Two 3½" x 42" strips.
   From these, cut:
   • Twenty-four 3½" squares (D-10a, E-10a).
♦ Three 2½" x 42" strips.
   From these, cut:
   • Twenty-four 2½" squares (D-1b, E-1b).
   • Twenty-four 2" x 2½" (D-8, E-8).

♦ Two 4½" x 42" strips.
   From these, cut:
   • Twelve 4½" squares (19).
♦ From scraps, cut:
   • Forty-eight 1½" squares (D-1a, D-7, E-1a, E-7).

From Fabric IX, cut:
♦ Four 1¾" x 42½" strips.
   From these, cut:
   • Twenty-four 1¾" x 4¼" (D-4, E-4).
   • Twenty-four 1¾" x 2½" (D-5, E-5).
♦ One 1½" x 42" strip.
   From this, cut:
   • Twenty-four 1½" squares (D-6, E-6).
♦ Two 1¼" x 42" strips.
   From these, cut:
   • Twenty-four 1¼" squares (D-3a, E-3a).
   • Twenty-four 1¼" x 2" (D-9a, E-9a).

From Fabric X, cut:
♦ Fifty-four 1½" x 42½" strips.
   From these, cut:
   • 408 1½" x 2½" (F-1a).
   • 816 1½" squares (F-2a).

From Fabric XI, cut:
♦ Ten 3" x 42" strips for binding.
♦ Thirty-two 2" x 42½" strips.
   From 20 of these, cut:
   • Six 2" x 31" for center quilt sashing.
   • Four 2" x 26" for center quilt sashing.
   • Six 2" x 30" for outer border.
   • Two 2" x 20" for outer border.
   • Two 2" x 16" for inner border.
   • Twelve 2" x 10" (28).
   • Five 2" x 10½" (18).
   • Two 2" x 18½" (20).

Piecing the Coyote Blocks

1. Referring to Block A Assembly diagram, use diagonal-corner technique to make one each of units 1, 3, 4, 5, 6, 7, 9, 11, 14, and 15 as shown.

2. Using diagonal-end technique, make one each of units 2 and 8.

3. To begin block assembly, join units 5 and 6 as shown. Then join Unit 4 to top of 5-6 unit and Unit 7 to bottom.

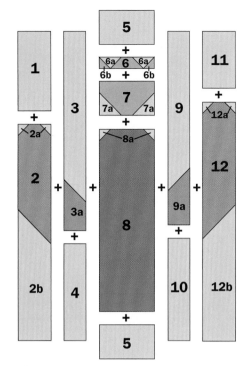

Block C Assembly

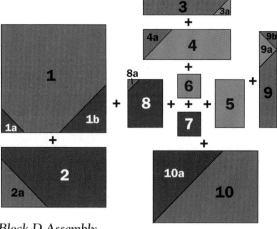

Block D Assembly

4. Join units 2 and 3 as shown; then join 2-3 unit to side of 4-5-6-7 unit. Join Unit 8 to opposite side.

5. Join units 9, 10, 11, and 12 in a horizontal row as shown; then join this to bottom of combined units. Join Unit 1 to top of combined units.

6. Join units 13, 14, and 15 in a vertical row as shown. Add 13-14-15 unit to side of combined units to complete block. Make two of Block A.

7. Block B is made in the same manner as Block A, but it is a mirror image. Units are made exactly the same as for Block A, but positions of diagonal corners and angles of diagonal ends are reversed. Make two of Block B, referring to block diagram carefully.

Piecing the Cactus Blocks

1. Referring to Block C Assembly diagram, use diagonal-corner technique to make one each of units 7 and 8.

2. Using diagonal-end technique, make one each of units 3 and 9.

3. For Unit 2, use diagonal-corner technique to add 2a to piece 2. Use diagonal-end technique to join 2b to opposite end of piece 2. Make one of Unit 12 in the same manner.

4. To make Unit 6, add diagonal ends 6a to piece 6. Then add diagonal corners 6b to both ends of unit.

5. Referring to Block C Assembly diagram, join units in vertical rows as shown; then join rows to complete block. Make 12 of Block C.

Piecing the Chili Blocks

1. Referring to Block D Assembly diagram, use diagonal-corner technique to make one each of units 1, 2, 3, 4, 8, and 10.

2. To make Unit 9, first join diagonal end 9a to piece 9; then add diagonal corner 9b to end of unit as shown.

3. Join units 6 and 7; then add units 5 and 8 to sides of 6-7 unit as shown.

4. Join units 3 and 4; then join 3-4 unit to top of 5-6-7-8 unit. Add Unit 9 to side of combined unit as shown. Join Unit 10 to bottom to complete half of block.

5. Join units 1 and 2 to make other block half. Join halves to complete block. Make 12 of Block D.

6. Block E is made in the same manner as Block D, but it is a mirror image. Units are made the same as for Block D, but diagonal corners and ends are reversed. Make 12 of Block E, referring to block diagram carefully.

Piecing the Southwest Borders

1. Referring to Block F Assembly diagram, use diagonal-end technique to make two of Unit 1. Use diagonal-corner technique to make four of Unit 2.

2. Join two of Unit 2 to make two horizontal rows as shown. Join rows to complete block. Make 102 of Block F for Southwest borders 1–6.

3. Join F blocks end-to-end to assemble two of each border as follows. For each Border 1, join two blocks. Join five blocks for each Border 2, seven blocks for each Border 3, 10 blocks for each Border 4, 12 blocks for each Border 5, and 15 blocks for each Border 6.

4. Join Unit 19 squares to both ends of each of Border 2, Border 4, and Border 6.

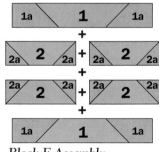

Block F Assembly

Center Quilt Assembly

1. Join Unit 17 strips to top and bottom of one Block A and one Block B. Join these blocks head-to-head, sewing one Unit 18 between them as shown in Quilt Assembly diagram.

2. Matching centers, join Border 1 to opposite ends of center coyote blocks as shown. Then join a Border 2 to each side of center unit as shown.

3. Join Unit 20 strips to both short ends of center unit as shown in assembly diagram.

4. Join Unit 21 to top and bottom edges of both remaining coyote blocks; then add Unit 18 to each Unit 21 as shown. Join these blocks to ends of center unit, referring to diagram and quilt photograph for correct positioning.

5. Join four of Block C in a row, sewing Unit 22 strips between them as shown in Quilt Assembly diagram. Join Unit 23 strips to ends of row; then add another of Block C to each end. Complete row by adding a Unit 22 strip to both ends. Make another row of cactus blocks in the same manner. Referring to assembly diagram and photograph for positioning, join cactus rows to center section.

6. Join Border 3 to each short end of center section; then join Border 4 to sides, easing quilt to fit borders. (See page 15 for tips on easing.)

7. Join two 2" x 26" strips of Fabric XI end-to-end to make a border strip. Repeat to make second strip. Matching center seam to center of Border 3, join each border strip to center section as shown in assembly diagram.

Outer Quilt Assembly

1. Referring to center bottom of Quilt Assembly diagram, join one D block and one E block, sewing a Unit 24 strip between them. Add Unit 24 strips to sides of joined blocks; then add Unit 26 strips to top and bottom edges. Make eight of these units in this manner.

2. On each of two D blocks and two E blocks, join Unit 25 strips to block sides; then add Unit 27 strips to top and bottom edges.

3. Referring to right side of Quilt Assembly diagram, join Unit 28 strips to sides of one double-chili unit. Add Block D unit to right end of row and Block E unit to left end of row. Repeat to make a second row. Join rows to ends of center quilt section as shown.

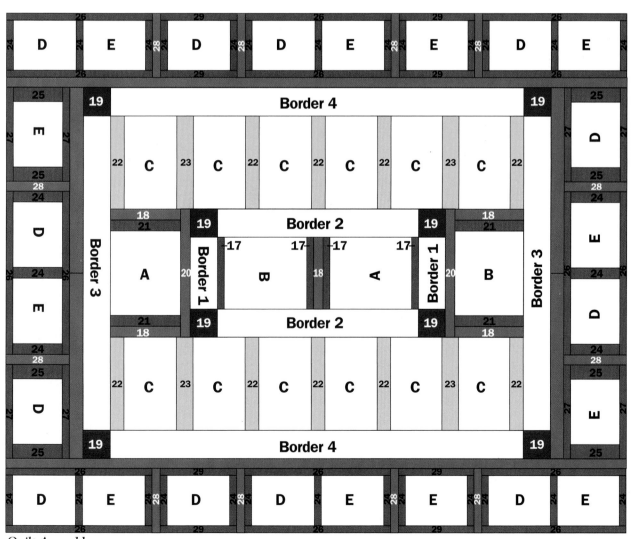

Quilt Assembly

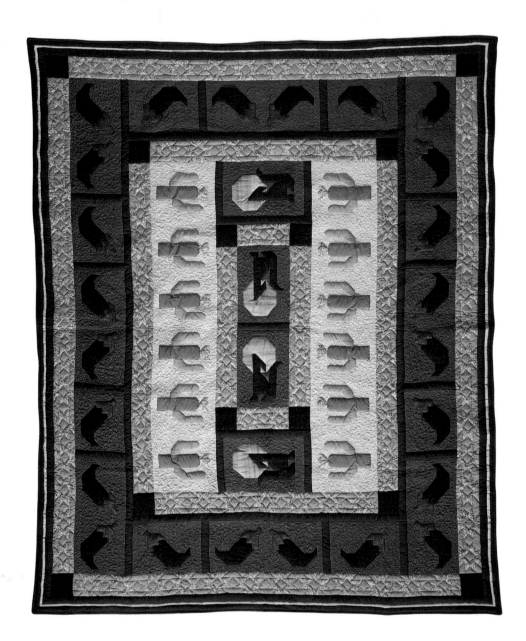

4. Join three 2" x 31" strips of Fabric XI end-to-end to make a 92"-long border for each quilt side. Matching centers, join borders to quilt. Press seam allowances toward borders; then trim excess border fabric at ends of strip.

5. On each remaining chili block, join a Unit 24 strip to both sides; then join Unit 29 strips to top and bottom.

6. Referring to bottom of Quilt Assembly diagram, join double-chili units and single chili units in a row, sewing Unit 28 strips between units as shown. Repeat to make a second row. Join rows to quilt sides as shown.

7. Referring to photograph, join Border 5 to ends of quilt, easing quilt to fit as necessary. Join Border 6 to quilt sides.

8. For each inner side border, join two 42½" strips and one 16" strip of Fabric XI. Matching centers of borders and quilt, join borders to quilt sides.

9. For each inner end border, join two 42½" strips end-to-end. Matching center seam with center of quilt, join borders to top and bottom edges.

10. For each middle side border, join three 1" x 35" strips of Fabric IV end-to-end. Join borders to quilt sides. For each middle end border, join three 1" x 29" strips and join borders to top and bottom edges in the same manner.

11. For each outer side border, join three 2" x 30" strips of Fabric XI. Join borders to quilt sides. For each outer end border, join two 42½" strips and one 20" strip of Fabric XI. Join borders to top and bottom edges.

Quilting and Finishing

The quilt shown was machine quilted with outline quilting around patchwork and stippling around chilies, coyotes, and cacti. Quilt as desired.

Make 400" of binding. See page 23 for directions on making and applying straight-grain binding.

Chili Pepper Tablecloth

Use a southwestern theme to decorate for Christmas with this merry tribute to the great American chili pepper. A red-hot accent for any occasion, this easy-to-make tablecloth will make you the hostess with the spiciest parties in town!

Quick-Piecing Techniques:

Finished Size
Blocks: 28 blocks, 7" x 9"   Tablecloth: 66" x 84"

Materials

	Fabric I (white-on-white print)	4 yards
	Fabric II (bright red print)	1¼ yards
	Fabric III (black-on-green print)	1⅜ yards
	Fabric IV (dark green solid)	¼ yard
	Backing fabric	4 yards

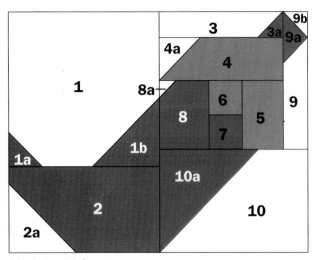

Block A—Make 12.

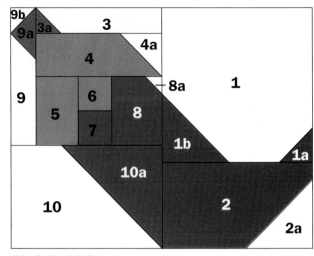

Block B—Make 16.

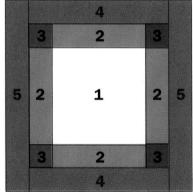

Block C—Make 1.

Cutting

From Fabric I, cut:

- One 23½" x 42" strip.
  From this, cut:
  - Two 20" x 23½" (12).
  - 28 1" squares (A-8a, B-8a).
- Four 11" x 42" strips.
  From these, cut:
  - Four 11" x 31½" (13).
  - Four 7½" squares (11).
- Six 5" x 42" strips.
  From these, cut:
  - 29 5" squares (A-1, B-1, C-1).
  - 28 3½" x 5" (A-10, B-10).
- Five 2½" x 42" strips.
  From these, cut:
  - 16 2½" x 7½" (15).
  - 28 2½" squares (A-2a, B-2a).
- Three 1¼" x 42½" strips.
  From these, cut:
  - 28 1¼" x 4¼" (A-3, B-3).
- 16 1½" x 42" strips.
  From these, cut:
  - 16 1½" x 31½" (inner borders).
  - Eight 1½" x 9½" (16).
  - 28 1¼" squares (A-9b, B-9b).
- From scraps, cut:
  - 28 1¾" squares (A-4a, B-4a).
  - 28 1¼" x 3¾" (A-9, B-9).

From Fabric II, cut:

- Two 5" x 42" strips.
  From these, cut:
  - 28 3" x 5" (A-2, B-2).
- Three 2½" x 42" strips.
  From these, cut:
  - 28 2½" squares (A-1b, B-1b).
  - 28 2" x 2½" (A-8, B-8).

- Four 1½" x 42" strips for Strip Set 1.
- Three 3½" x 42" strips.
  From these, cut:
  - 28 3½" squares (A-10a, B-10a).
  - Four 1⅝" squares (C-3).
  - Eight 1½" squares for outer border.
- Two 1½" x 42" strips.
  From these, cut:
  - 56 1½" squares (A-1a, A-7, B-1a, B-7).

From Fabric III, cut:

- Eight 2" x 42" for binding.
- Four 4½" x 42" strips for Strip Set 1.
- Two 1½" x 42" strips.
  From these, cut:
  - Four 1½" x 5½" (C-2).
  - Six 1½" x 2½" (14).
  - 28 1½" squares (A-6, B-6).
- Five 1⅞" x 42" strips.
  From these, cut:
  - 28 1⅞" x 4¼" (A-4, B-4).
  - 28 1⅞" x 2½" (A-5, B-5).

From Fabric IV, cut:

- One 1⅝" x 42" strip.
  From this, cut:
  - Two 1⅝" x 7¼" (C-4).
  - Two 1⅝" x 9½" (C-5).
- Three 1¼" x 42" strips.
  From these, cut:
  - 28 1¼" squares (A-3a, B-3a).
  - 28 1¼" x 2" (A-9a, B-9a).

Piecing the Blocks

1. Refer to Piecing the Chili Blocks instructions for *South of the Border* quilt

on page 158. Following those instructions and referring to diagrams above, make 12 of Block A and 16 of Block B.

2. Referring to Block C diagram, join two C-2 strips to opposite sides of C-1. Join C-3 squares to ends of remaining C-2 strips; then add these to top and bottom of C-1. Join C-4 strips to top and bottom of block. Join C-5 strips to sides to complete block.

Tablecloth Assembly

1. Join a B block to top and bottom of Block C, turning each chili so its stem is adjacent to Block C.

2. Join a Unit 11 square to both sides of two B blocks. Referring to Tablecloth Assembly diagram, join these rows to sides of center unit, positioning chilies with stems pointing toward Block C.

3. Join Unit 12 to sides of center unit.

4. Join two of Unit 13 end-to-end; then add this strip to top of center unit. Repeat at bottom.

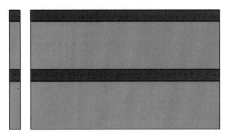

Strip Set 1—Make 2.

5. To make Strip Set 1, join two 4½" x 42" strips of Fabric III and two 1½" x 42" strips of Fabric II as shown. Make two strip sets. From these, cut fifty 1½"-wide segments.

6. Join three segments end-to-end. Make three more three-segment strips in the same manner. Join two of these strips with one Unit 14 between them, *always sewing red fabric to green fabric*. Repeat to make a second strip. Join assembled borders to Unit 13s at top and bottom of center section as shown

in assembly diagram. (*Note:* Shaded areas of Tablecloth Assembly diagram indicate strip-pieced borders. Seams shown indicate strip-set segments.)

7. For each side border, join five segments end-to-end. Remove green fabric from bottom of last segment so border has a red square at both ends. Join borders to sides of cloth, easing cloth to fit. (See page 15 for tips on easing.)

8. Referring to bottom of Tablecloth Assembly diagram, join three A blocks and three B blocks as shown, sewing Unit 15 strips between them (except for center seam).

9. Join 1½" x 31½" strips of Fabric I in pairs to make eight 1½" x 62½" strips. Join one of these to top and bottom of chili pepper row. Complete row by joining Unit 16 strips to both ends.

10. Join two sets of three strip-set segments. Add a 1½" square of Fabric II to

green end of last segment so there is a red square at both ends of each strip. Join these strips end-to-end, sewing one Unit 14 between them. Join border to bottom of chili pepper row.

11. Repeat steps 8, 9, and 10 to make three more rows in the same manner.

12. Join one completed row to bottom of tablecloth. Repeat at top of cloth.

13. Join one strip-set segment to ends of both remaining chili pepper rows. Join these rows to tablecloth sides.

Quilting and Finishing

Outline-quilt chili peppers and quilt in-the-ditch in Block C to secure backing. Add additional quilting as desired.

Make 310" of binding. See page 23 for directions on making and applying straight-grain binding.

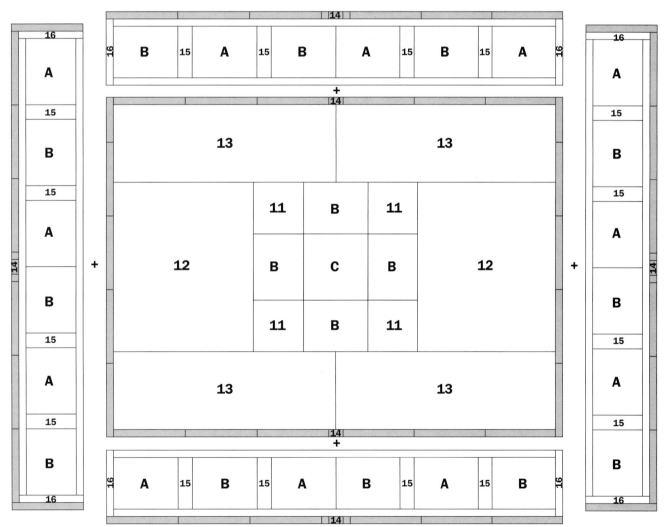

Tablecloth Assembly

Amish Triangles

Looking for a small, easy project? Here it is—a strip-pieced wall hanging that blends tradition with today's quick techniques. The design and fabrics, adapted from classic antique Amish quilts, have a strikingly contemporary appeal. For a different look, try nontraditional fabrics such as pastel prints on an ivory background.

Quick-Piecing Techniques:

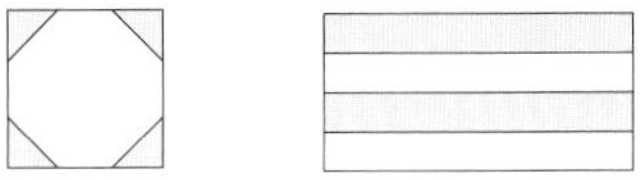

Finished Size
Blocks: 44 Triangle blocks, 6" square
      4 Arrow blocks, 6" x 8"

Quilt: 60" x 60"

Materials

	Fabric I (black solid)	2 yards
	Fabric II (purple solid)	1⅝ yards
	Fabric III (yellow solid)	¼ yard
	Fabric IV (teal solid)	¼ yard
	Fabric V (red solid)	¼ yard
	Fabric VI (gray solid)	1 yard
	Fabric VII (aqua solid)	¾ yard
	Backing fabric	3¾ yards

Cutting
Refer to diagrams on page 166 to identify blocks and units designated in cutting list.

From Fabric I, cut:
◆ Six 3" x 42" strips for binding.
◆ Two 3½" x 42" strips.
  From these, cut:
    • Sixteen 3½" squares (2a).
    • Four 3½" x 4½" (6).

◆ Four 6⅞" x 42" strips.
  From these, cut:
    • Twenty-two 6⅞" squares. Cut squares in half diagonally to get 44 triangles (1).
◆ One 2½" x 42" strip.
  From this, cut:
    • Eight 2½" squares (4).
◆ Six 1¼" x 42" strips for Strip Set Y.

From Fabric II, cut:
◆ Six 2½" x 42" strips for borders.
  From four of these strips, cut:
    • Four 2½" x 29".
    • Four 2½" x 11".
◆ Two 6½" x 42" strips.
  From these, cut:
    • Eight 3½" x 6½" (2).
    • Eight 6½" squares (9).
◆ One 4½" x 42" strip.
  From this, cut:
    • Eight 4½" squares (8).
◆ One 3½" x 42" strip.
  From this, cut:
    • Four 3½" x 4½" (7).
◆ Fourteen 1⅛" x 42" strips for Strip Set X.

From each of fabrics III, IV, and V, cut:
◆ Seven 1⅛" x 42" strips for Strip Set X.

From Fabric VI, cut:
◆ Seven 1⅛" x 42" strips for Strip Set X.
◆ Six 2⅛" x 42" strips for Strip Set Y.
◆ One 4½" square (5).
◆ Four 2½" squares (3).

From Fabric VII, cut:
◆ Seven 1⅛" x 42" strips for Strip Set X.
◆ Six 2⅛" x 42" strips for Strip Set Y.

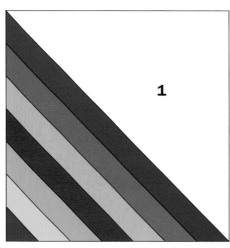

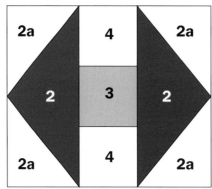

Block A—Make 24.

Block B—Make 20.

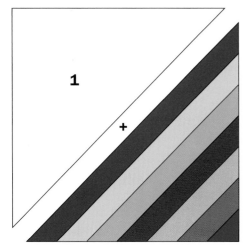

Block A Assembly

2a | **4** | **2a**
2 | **3** | **2**
2a | **4** | **2a**

Block C—Make 4.

Strip Set X—Make 7.

Strip Set Y—Make 6.

Block C Assembly

Piecing the Blocks

1. Referring to diagram of Strip Set X, join all 1⅛" strips as shown. Make seven of Strip Set X. Square off left edge of each strip set.

2. Measuring from bottom left corner of strip set, cut a 45° angle as shown in Strip Set X Cutting diagram. If your acrylic ruler does not have a marked 45° angle, find the angle by measuring the strip set width (which, ideally, is 4⅞"); then measure the same distance along top edge. Cut from bottom left corner to marked point on top edge. Discard cut portion.

3. Make next cut perpendicular to diagonal edge. Cut triangles from each strip set as shown, cutting four triangles for A blocks and three for B blocks. See page 13 for tips on stabilizing bias edge of triangles.

4. Referring to Block A Assembly diagram, join Unit 1 to striped triangles. Make 24 of Block A and 20 of Block B. Press seam allowances toward Unit 1.

5. Using diagonal-corner technique, make two of Unit 2 for each Arrow block. Referring to Block C Assembly diagram, join units 3 and 4 in a vertical row as shown. Join rows to complete each block. Make four of Block C.

Center Section Assembly

1. Referring to Center Section Assembly diagram, join two pair of units 6 and 7. Positioning blocks as shown, join A blocks to top and bottom edges of combined 6-7 units. Join remaining units 5, 6, and 7 in a vertical row as shown. Join rows to complete center section.

2. Referring to diagram of Strip Set Y, join 2⅛" strips of fabrics VI and VII to sides of 1¼" strip of Fabric I. Make six strip sets. Cut two of Strip Set Y in half.

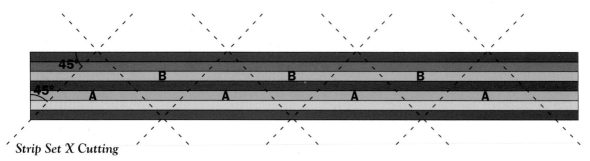

Strip Set X Cutting

3. Measure all sides of center section. Trim four Y half-strip sets to match *shortest* measurement. Join trimmed strips to top and bottom edges of center section, easing as necessary (see page 15 for tips on easing).

4. Join a Unit 8 to ends of two remaining half-strip sets. Join these to sides of center section.

Middle Section Assembly

1. Referring to Quilt Assembly diagram, join four of Block A in a row as shown for each side section. Join rows to sides of center section.

2. For top and bottom edges, join two rows of four B blocks as shown. Add one of Unit 9 to each end of these rows; then join rows to quilt.

3. Measure all sides of assembled quilt. Trim remaining Y strip sets to match shortest measurement. Join trimmed strips to top and bottom edges of quilt, easing as necessary.

4. Join a Unit 8 to ends of two remaining strips. Join these to quilt sides.

Outer Section Assembly

1. Referring to Quilt Assembly diagram, join six of Block A and one of Block C in a row as shown for each side section. Join rows to quilt sides.

2. For top and bottom rows, join six of Block B and one of Block C as shown; then join one Unit 9 to each end. Join rows to top and bottom edges of quilt.

3. Join two 29"-long border strips end-to-end. Matching centers of border and quilt, join border to top edge. Repeat for bottom edge.

4. Join an 11" border strip to ends of each 42" strip. Join borders to quilt sides.

Quilting and Finishing

Outline-quilt patchwork or quilt as desired.

Make 250" of binding. See page 23 for directions on making and applying straight-grain binding. To make a hanging sleeve, see directions on page 23.

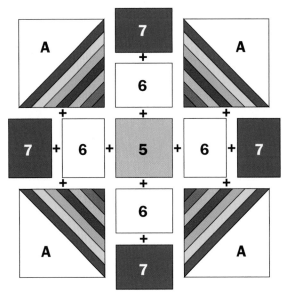

Center Section Assembly

Quilt Assembly

Safari Path

Elephants parade around a trio of exotic animals in this delightful tribute to our favorite beasts of the African plains. Each animal is made with a combination of three quick-piecing techniques, and strip piecing creates paths that connect one critter to another. The fabrics are solids and subtle prints that allow one bold print to stand out. Because there is so much piecing in this quilt, we recommend it for experienced quiltmakers.

Quick-Piecing Techniques:

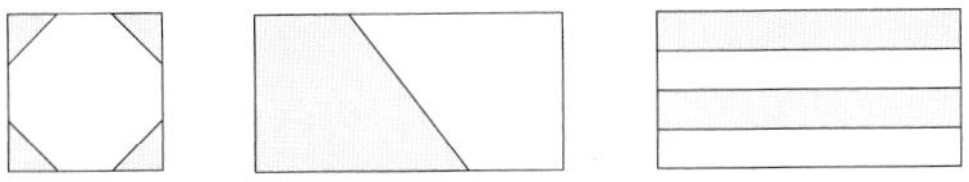

Finished Size

Blocks: 14 elephant blocks, 12⅜" x 18¾"
      2 turtle blocks, 6¾" x 12"
      4 lion blocks, 11⅝" x 17⅝"
      4 giraffe blocks, 8⅝" x 23¼"

Quilt: 101½" x 109"

Materials

	Fabric I (pale yellow print)	2⅜ yards
	Fabric II (gold mini-stripe)	2¾ yards
	Fabric III (rust solid)	1 yard
	Fabric IV (dark brown solid)	2⅝ yards
	Fabric V (brown-on-cream print)	1¼ yards
	Fabric VI (rust-on-dark brown print)	1¾ yards
	Fabric VII (dark brown check)	2 yards
	Fabric VIII (medium brown print)	1⅛ yards
	Fabric IX (tan solid)	1⅛ yards
	Backing fabric	9 yards

Cutting

From Fabric I, cut:

♦ Eighteen 2" x 42" strips.
  From these, cut:
  • Twelve 2" x 35" for middle border.
  • Four 2" x 25" (30).
  • Four 2" x 12⅛" (27).
  • Four 2" x 9½" (H-1).
  • Four 2" x 8⅜" (E-13, F-13).
  • Four 2" x 4¼" (C-21, D-21).
  • Thirty 1¼" x 2" (A-3a, A-6a, A-8, B-3a, B-6a, B-8, C-16, C-18a, D-16, D-18a, E-2a, E-9a, F-2a, F-9a).
  • Two 1⅝" x 2" (A-10, B-10).
  • Six 2" squares (A-11, B-11, C-8b, D-8b).
  • Four 2" x 2¾" (E-10, F-10).

♦ Two 1¼" x 42" strips.
  From these, cut:
  • Fifty-eight 1¼" squares (A-2b, A-9a, B-2b, B-9a, C-11a, C-13a, C-19a, D-11a, D-13a, D-19a, E-12a, E-15b, F-12a, F-15b).
  • Four 1¼" x 2⅜" (C-10, D-10).

♦ Two 3⅛" x 42" strips.
  From these, cut:
  • Four 3⅛" x 11" (C-4, D-4).
  • Four 3⅛" x 4¼" (C-20, D-20).
  • Four 3⅛" squares (C-1a, D-1a).
  • Two 2⅜" squares (A-5a, B-5a).

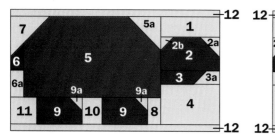

Block A—Make 1.

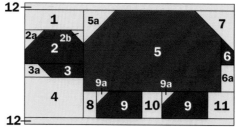

Block B—Make 1.

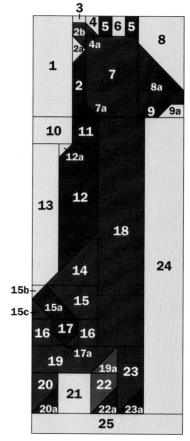

Block E—Make 2.

♦ Seven 1⅝" x 42" strips.
  From these, cut:
  • Four 1⅝" x 25" (31).
  • Four 1⅝" x 18⅛" (C-22, D-22).
  • Four 1⅝" x 9⅛" (E-25, F-25).
  • Four 1⅝" x 7¼" (26).
  • Two 1⅝" x 3⅞" (A-1, B-1).
  • Two 1⅝" squares (A-2a, B-2a).
  • Eight 1¼" x 1⅝" (E-4, E-6, F-4, F-6).

♦ Two 4⅝" x 42" strips.
  From these, cut:
  • Four 4⅝" x 12⅛" (28).
  • Four 3⅛" x 4⅝" (E-8, F-8).
  • Four ⅞" x 20".
    From these, cut:
    • Four ⅞" x 12½" (A-12, B-12).
    • Four ⅞" x 1¼" (E-3, F-3).

♦ Four 2¾" x 42" strips.
  From these, cut:
  • Four 2¾" x 17" (E-24, F-24).
  • Two 2¾" x 9⅛" (29).
  • Four 2¾" x 6⅛" (E-1, F-1).
  • Two 2¾" x 3⅞" (A-4, B-4).
  • Two 2¾" squares (A-7, B-7).
  • Four 2⅜" x 2¾" (E-21, F-21).
  • Twelve 1¼" x 2¾" (C-14, D-14).

From Fabric II, cut:

♦ Nine 1¼" x 42" strips.
  From these, cut:
  • Fourteen 1¼" x 11¾" (G-15).
  • Fourteen ¼" x 5" (G-13a).
  • Thirty-four 1¼" x 2" (C-15, C-18, D-15, D-18, G-9a).
  • Eighteen 1¼" x 2⅜" (C-12, D-12, G-5).
  • Twenty-two 1¼" squares (C-13b, D-13b, G-12).

♦ Twenty-two 2" x 42" strips.
  From these, cut:
  • Eight 2" x 32" and twelve 2" x 29" for elephant section borders.
  • Four 2" x 12⅞" (33).
  • Four 2" x 12½" (C-17, D-17).
  • Sixteen 2" x 3½" (C-19, D-19).
  • Twenty-eight 2" x 3⅛" (G-6, G-10).
  • Eighteen 2" squares (C-8a, D-8a, G-2c).

♦ Six 3⅛" x 42" strips.
  From these, cut:
  • Fourteen 3⅛" x 5⅜" (G-16b).
  • Fourteen 3⅛" x 9⅛" (G-17).
  • Fourteen 2¾" x 3⅛" (G-19).

♦ Two 2⅜" x 42" strips.
  From these, cut:
  • Twenty-eight 2⅜" squares (G-14, G-16a).

♦ One 12⅞" x 42" strip.
  From this, cut:
  • Four 3½" x 12⅞" (35).
  • Six 3" x 12⅞" (34).
  • Four 4⅝" x 6⅛" (C-9, D-9).

From Fabric III, cut:

♦ Four 2" x 42" strips.
  From these, cut:
  • Fifty-six 2" squares (G-3a, G-4b, G-7a, G-8a).
  • Fourteen 1¼" x 2" (G-5a).
  • Eight 2" x 3⅛" (C-6, D-6).

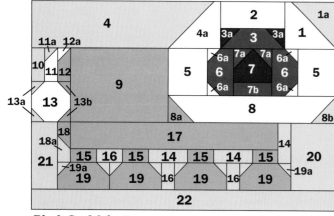

Block C—Make 2.

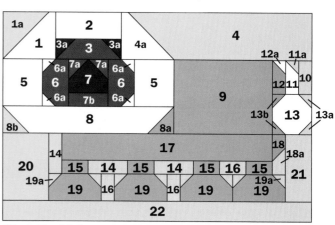

Block D—Make 2.

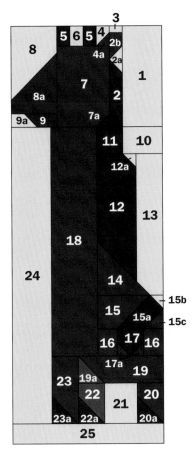

Block F—Make 2.

♦ Two 8¾" x 42" strips.
  From these, cut:
  • Fourteen 5" x 8¾" (G-2).
  • One 7" square.
    From this, cut:
    • Four 3½" squares (32).
    • Four 1⅝" x 8¾".
      From these, cut:
      • Four 1⅝" x 4¼" (C-3, D-3).
      • Eight 1⅝" squares (C-7a, D-7a).
♦ Five 1¼" x 42" strips.
  From these, cut:
  • Fourteen 1¼" x 8⅜" (G-13).
  • Four 1¼" x 2¾" (C-7b, D-7b).
  • Twenty-eight 1¼" squares (G-10a, G-11).
  • Fourteen 1¼" x 3½" (G-15a).

From Fabric IV, cut:
♦ Four 2¾" x 42" strips.
  From these, cut:
  • Four 2¾" x 8⅜" (E-12, F-12).
  • Fourteen 2¾" x 3⅞" (G-4).
  • Fourteen 2¾" x 3⅛" (G-7).
  • Four 2⅜" x 2¾" (C-7, D-7).
  • Four 2⅜" x 3⅛" (E-15a, F-15a).
  • Four 2" x 3⅛" (A-9, B-9).

♦ Eleven 3" x 42" strips for binding.
♦ One 1¼" x 42" strip.
  From this, cut:
  • Two 1¼" x 3⅞" (A-3, B-3).
  • Two 1¼" x 3½" (A-6, B-6).
  • Four 1¼" x 4¼" (E-2, F-2).
  • Four 1¼" squares (E-7a, F-7a).
♦ One 1⅝" x 42" strip.
  From this, cut:
  • Eight 1¼" x 1⅝" (E-5, F-5).
  • Eight 1⅝" squares (C-3a, D-3a).
♦ One 2" x 42" strip.
  From this, cut:
  • Twenty 2" squares (E-11, E-17,
    E-20a, E-22a, E-23a, F-11, F-17,
    F-20a, F-22a, F-23a).
♦ One 2⅜" x 42" strip.
  From this, cut:
  • One 2⅜" x 20" for Strip Set 1.
  • One 2⅜" x 12" for Strip Set 3.
  • Two 2⅜" x 3⅞" (A-2, B-2).
♦ One 4¼" x 42" strip for Strip Set 4.
♦ Four 2⅜" x 42" strips for Strip Set 5.
♦ Ten 2" x 42" strips for Strip Set 6.

From Fabric V, cut:
♦ Twelve 2½" x 42" strips.
  From these, cut:
  • Twelve 2½" x 36" for outer border.
  • Four 2" x 4¼" (C-2, D-2).
  • Four 1¼" x 2⅜" (C-11, D-11).
  • Twenty 1¼" squares (C-6a, C-12a,
    D-6a, D-12a).
♦ One 3⅛" x 42" strip.
  From this, cut:
  • Eight 3⅛" x 3½" (C-1, C-4a, D-1,
    D-4a).
♦ One 2" x 42" strip.
  From this, cut:
  • Four 2" x 10¼" (C-8, D-8).

♦ One 2¾" x 42" strip.
  From this, cut:
  • Eight 2¾" x 3⅛" (C-5, D-5).
  • Four 2¾" squares (C-13, D-13).

From Fabric VI, cut:
♦ One 5" x 42" strip.
  From this, cut:
  • Two 5" x 8⅜" (A-5, B-5).
  • Four 5" squares (36).
♦ One 3½" x 42" strip.
  From this, cut:
  • Four 3½" x 5" (E-7, F-7).
  • Four 3½" squares (E-14, F-14).
♦ Two 3⅛" x 42" strips.
  From these, cut:
  • Four 3⅛" x 13¼" (E-18, F-18).
  • Four 3⅛" x 3⅞" (E-8a, F-8a).
♦ Two 2" x 42" strips.
  From these, cut:
  • Four 2" x 2¾" (E-20, F-20).
  • Four 2" x 4¼" (E-23, F-23).
  • Eight 1⅝" x 2" (E-16, F-16).
  • Four 2" x 5⅜" (E-19, F-19).
  • Four 1¼" x 2" (E-2b, F-2b).
  • Four 1⅝" squares (E-15c, F-15c).
♦ From scraps, cut:
  • Four 2⅜" x 3½" (E-15, F-15).
  • Four 1¼" x 2⅜" (E-9, F-9).
  • Twelve 1¼" squares (E-4a, E-17a,
    F-4a, F-17a).

From Fabric VII, cut:
♦ Five 3⅛" x 42" strips.
  From these, cut:
  • Fourteen 3⅛" x 10⅝" (G-16).
  • Fourteen 2" x 3⅛" (G-18).
♦ One 2⅜" x 42" strip.
  From this, cut:
  • Fourteen 2⅜" squares (G-2b).

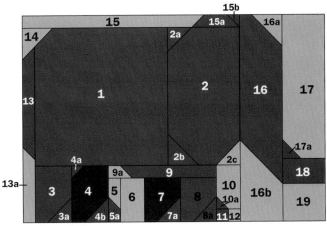

Block G—Make 14.

- ◆ Four 8¾" x 42" strips.
  From these, cut:
  - • Fourteen 8¾" squares (G-1).
  - • Three 2¾" x 24".
    From these, cut:
    - • Fourteen 2¾" x 3⅞" (G-3).
    - • Four 2" x 2¾" (E-22, F-22).
    - • Seven 2¾" x 7".
      From these, cut:
      - • Fourteen 2¾" x 3⅛" (G-8).
- ◆ Three 1¼" x 42" strips.
  From these, cut:
  - • Fourteen 1¼" x 6½" (G-9).
  - • Fourteen 1¼" squares (G-15b).
- ◆ One 2" x 42" strip.
  From this, cut:
  - • Eighteen 2" squares (E-19a, F-19a, G-2a).
- ◆ From scraps, cut:
  - • Fourteen 1⅝" squares (G-17a).
  - • Fourteen 1¼" squares (G-4a).

From Fabric VIII, cut:

- ◆ One 2⅜" x 42" strip.
  From this, cut:
  - • One 2⅜" x 20" for Strip Set 1.
  - • One 2⅜" x 15" for Strip Set 2.
- ◆ One 4¼" x 42" for Strip Set 4.
- ◆ Four 2⅜" x 42" for Strip Set 5.
- ◆ Ten 2" x 42" strips for Strip Set 6.

From Fabric IX, cut:

- ◆ One 2⅜" x 42" strip.
  From this, cut:
  - • One 2⅜" x 15" for Strip Set 2.
  - • One 2⅜" x 12" for Strip Set 3.
- ◆ One 4¼" x 42" for Strip Set 4.
- ◆ Four 2⅜" x 42" for Strip Set 5.
- ◆ Ten 2" x 42" strips for Strip Set 6.

Piecing the Turtle Blocks

1. Referring to Block A Assembly diagram, use diagonal-corner technique to make one each of units 2 and 5 and two of Unit 9.

2. Using diagonal-end technique, make one of Unit 3.

3. Join units 6 and 6a as shown.

4. Join units 1, 2, 3, and 4 in a vertical row as shown in assembly diagram to complete head section.

5. Join Unit 6 to Unit 5 as shown. Use

diagonal-corner technique to add Unit 7 to 5-6 unit.

6. Join units 8, 9, 10, and 11 in a horizontal row. Join this row to bottom of 5-6 unit to complete body section.

7. Join head and body sections as shown. Add Unit 12 to top and bottom edges to complete one of Block A.

8. Block B is made in the same manner as Block A, but it is a mirror image. Units are made exactly the same as for Block A, but positions and angles of diagonal corners and ends are reversed. Make one of Block B, referring to block diagram carefully.

Piecing the Lion Blocks

1. Referring to Block C Assembly diagram, use diagonal-corner technique to make two of Unit 6, four of Unit 19, and one each of units 1, 3, 8, 11, 12, and 13. To make Unit 7, add diagonal corners as shown; then add piece 7b to bottom of unit.

2. Using diagonal-end technique, make one each of units 4 and 18.

3. To assemble Section A, begin by joining units 2 and 3. Add units 1 and 4 to sides of 2-3 unit as shown in assembly diagram to complete Section A.

4. To assemble Section B, begin by joining two of units 5 and 6 and one Unit 7 in a horizontal row as shown. Add Unit 8 to bottom of 5-6-7 unit. Join Unit 9 to left side of combined unit. Next, join units 10, 11, and 12 in a row as shown; then join 10-11-12 unit to top of Unit 13. Join combined unit to side of Unit 9 to complete Section B.

5. To assemble Section C, begin by joining two of Unit 14, four of Unit 15, and one Unit 16 in a horizontal row as shown. Join this row to bottom of Unit 17. Add a Unit 14 to right side of combined row and Unit 18 to left side. Next, join two of Unit 16 and four of Unit 19 in a row as shown. Join this row to bottom of combined unit. Add

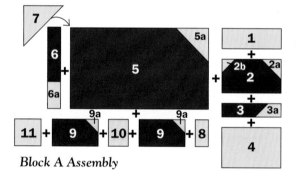

Block A Assembly

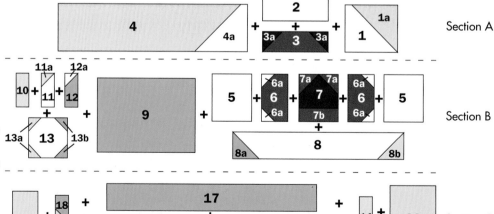

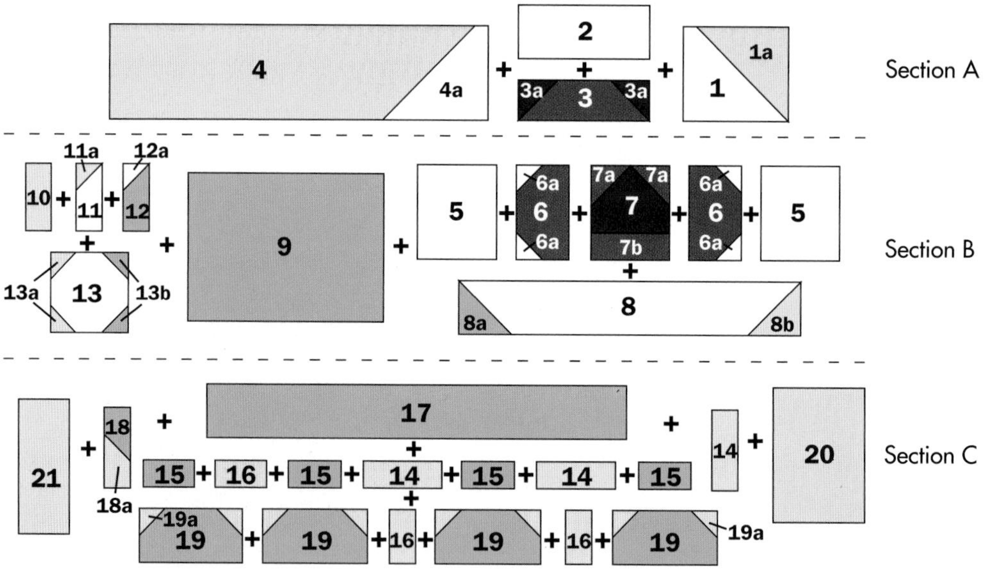

Block C Assembly

units 20 and 21 to sides of unit as shown to complete Section C.

6. Join sections A, B, and C. Add Unit 22 to bottom to complete Block C. Make two of Block C.

7. Block D is made in the same manner as Block C, but it is a mirror image. Units are made exactly the same, but diagonal corners and diagonal ends are reversed. Make two of Block D, referring to block diagram carefully.

Piecing the Giraffe Blocks

1. Referring to Block E Assembly diagram, use diagonal-corner technique to make one each of units 4, 7, 12, 17, 19, 20, 22, and 23.

2. Using diagonal-end technique, make one each of units 8 and 9.

3. To make Unit 2, add diagonal end 2a to piece 2; then add 2b to combined unit as a second diagonal end.

4. To make Unit 15, add diagonal end 15a to piece 15; then add diagonal corners 15b and 15c.

5. To assemble Section A, begin by joining units 2 and 3. Add this to side of Unit 1. Next, join units 4 and 6 and two of Unit 5 in a horizontal row as shown. Join this row to top of Unit 7; then join combined unit to side of 2-3 unit. Join Unit 9 to bottom of Unit 8; then join this to side of combined unit to complete Section A.

6. To assemble Section B, begin by joining Unit 10 to Unit 11 and Unit 12 to Unit 13. Join 10-11 to top of 12-13. Add Unit 14 to bottom of this unit as a diagonal corner. Join Unit 15 to bottom of combined unit. Next, join two of Unit 16 to Unit 17 as shown; then join 16-17 unit to bottom of Unit 15. Join Unit 18 to right side of combined unit to complete Section B.

7. To assemble Section C, begin by joining units 20, 21, and 22 in a row as shown. Join this row to bottom of Unit 19. Add Unit 23 to right side of combined row to complete Section C.

8. Join sections B and C. Join Unit 24 to side of combined sections as shown; then add Section A to top. Join Unit 25 to bottom to complete Block E. Make two of Block E.

9. Block F is made in the same manner as Block E, but it is a mirror image. Units are made exactly the same, but positions and angles of diagonal corners and diagonal ends are reversed. Make two of Block F, referring to block diagram carefully.

Piecing the Elephant Blocks

1. Referring to Block G Assembly diagram, use diagonal-corner technique to make one each of units 2, 3, 4, 7, 8, 10, and 17.

2. Using diagonal-end technique, make one each of units 5, 9, and 13.

3. To make Unit 15, add diagonal end 15a to piece 15; then add diagonal corner 15b to end of combined unit.

4. To make Unit 16, add diagonal corner 16a to top of piece 16; then add diagonal end 16b to bottom of piece 16.

5. Join Unit 1 to Unit 2 and Unit 3 to Unit 4. Join units 11 and 12; then join 11-12 to bottom of Unit 10. Set these units aside.

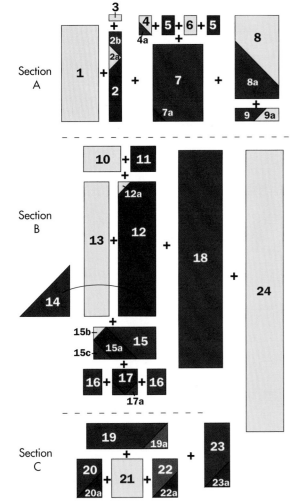

Block E Assembly

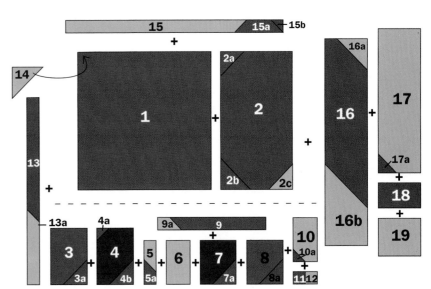

Block G Assembly

6. Join units 5, 6, 7, and 8 in a horizontal row as shown. Join this row to bottom of Unit 9. Join 3-4 unit to left side of combined row; then add 10-11-12 unit to right side.

7. Join row (units 3–12) to bottom of 1-2 unit to make body section.

8. Join Unit 13 to left side of body section. Using diagonal-corner technique, join Unit 14 to top of body. Add Unit 15 to top to complete body section.

9. Join Unit 16 to right side of body section. Next, join units 17, 18, and 19 in a vertical row as shown. Join 17-18-19 to Unit 16 to complete block. Make 14 of Block G.

Center Quilt Assembly

1. Referring to diagrams of strip sets 1, 2, and 3, assemble designated strips as shown to make one of each strip set. From these, cut 2¾"-wide segments. Cut seven segments from Strip Set 1, five segments from Strip Set 2, and four segments from Strip Set 3.

2. Referring to Block H Assembly diagram, join four segments as shown. Add Unit H-1 to top and bottom of joined segments to complete Block H. Make two of Block H for center path.

3. Referring to Center Quilt Assembly diagram, join one Block H to nose side of each turtle block, sewing a Unit 26 strip between blocks. Add remaining Unit 26 strips to tail sides of turtles.

4. Join Unit 27 strips to face sides of each lion block; then add Unit 28 strips to tail sides.

5. Referring to assembly diagram and quilt photograph for correct placement, join lion blocks to top and bottom of turtle sections.

6. Referring to Center Quilt Assembly diagram, join remaining strip set segments to make vertical center path.

7. Join animal blocks to sides of vertical path to complete Section A.

8. Referring to diagrams of strip sets 4 and 5, join designated strips as shown. Make one of Strip Set 4 and four of Strip Set 5. Cut nine 2⅜"-wide segments from Strip Set 4. Cut thirty-eight 3½"-wide segments from Strip Set 5.

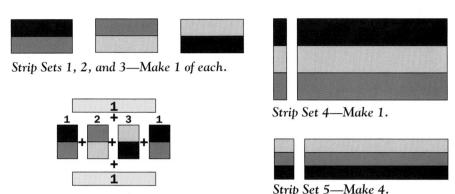

Strip Sets 1, 2, and 3—Make 1 of each.

Block H Assembly—Make 2.

Strip Set 4—Make 1.

Strip Set 5—Make 4.

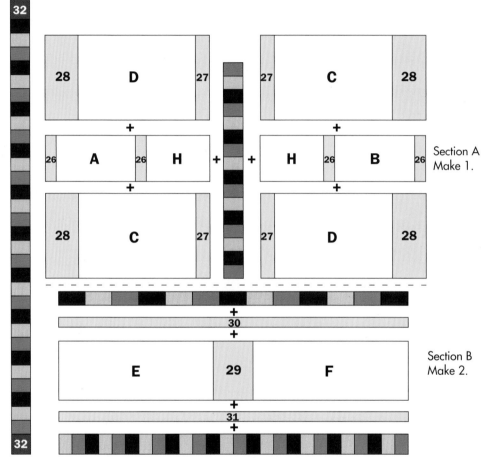

Center Quilt Assembly

9. To assemble Section B, begin by joining five Strip Set 4 segments end-to-end to make first horizontal path. Pull out seam to remove last two fabric pieces. (Use removed portion later to begin path for second Section B.)

10. Join two 2" x 25" strips of Fabric I end-to-end to make one Unit 30. Use two 1⅝" x 25" strips to make one of Unit 31 in the same manner.

11. Matching centers, join Unit 30 to horizontal path as shown.

12. Join two giraffe blocks head-to-head as shown, sewing one Unit 29

strip between blocks. Join giraffe section to bottom of Unit 30; then add Unit 31 to bottom of giraffe section.

13. For bottom horizontal path, join nine Strip Set 5 segments end-to-end. Pull out seam to remove last fabric piece. (Use removed portion later to begin outside vertical path.) Join this path to bottom of Unit 31 to complete Section B.

14. Join Section B to the bottom of Section A.

15. Repeat steps 9–13 to make a second Section B. Turn this section upside down and join it to top of Section A.

16. Use remaining Strip Set 5 segments to assemble two side vertical paths as shown in Center Quilt Assembly diagram. Add a Unit 32 square to both ends of each path. Join these to sides of center section, easing patchwork as necessary to fit paths. (See page 15 for tips on easing.)

Adding the Elephant Section

1. For each side row, join three elephant blocks (Block G), sewing Unit 35 strips between blocks as shown in Outer Quilt Assembly diagram on page 176.

2. Join two 2" x 32" strips of Fabric II end-to-end to make a border for these rows. Make four border strips. Matching centers, join border strips to long edges of both rows.

3. Referring to assembly diagram and quilt photograph, join side rows to center section.

4. For top row, join four elephant blocks, sewing Unit 34 strips between blocks. Repeat for bottom row. Add Unit 33 strips to ends of both rows.

5. Join three 2" x 29" strips of Fabric II end-to-end to make a border for these rows. Make four border strips. Matching centers, join border strips to top and bottom edges of both rows.

6. Referring to assembly diagram and quilt photograph, join top and bottom rows to center section.

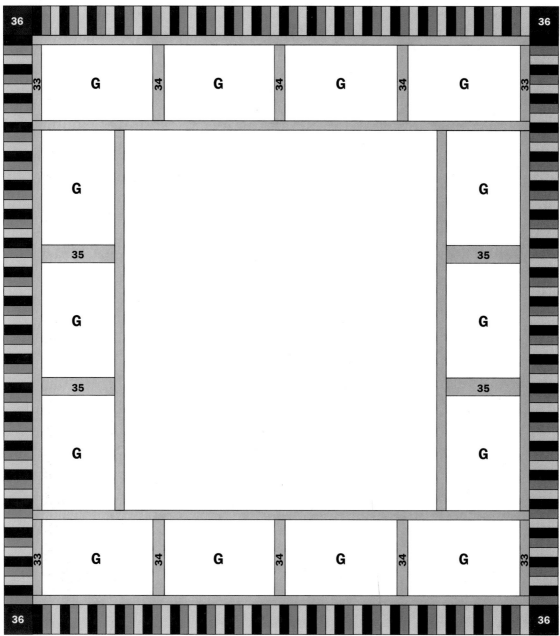

Outer Quilt Assembly

Adding Borders

1. Referring to diagram of Strip Set 6, join designated strips as shown. Make 10 strip sets. From these, cut seventy-six 5"-wide segments.

Strip Set 6—Make 10.

2. For each side, join 20 segments end-to-end. Remove one fabric piece from bottom of last segment. Join borders to quilt sides, easing quilt to fit border.

3. Join 18 segments end-to-end for top border. Add a Unit 36 square to both ends. Join border to top of quilt, easing quilt to fit. Repeat for bottom border.

4. For each middle border strip, join three 2" x 35" strips of Fabric I end-to-end, making four 104"-long border strips. Matching centers of border and quilt, join one strip to each long side of quilt. Press seam allowances toward borders; then trim excess border fabric at ends. Join remaining borders to top and bottom of quilt in the same manner.

5. For each outer border strip, join three 2½" x 36" strips of Fabric V end-to-end, making four 107"-long border strips. Join these to quilt in the same manner as middle border.

Quilting and Finishing

Mark quilting designs as desired. The quilt shown was machine-quilted with meandering lines of free-style quilting worked in the open areas around the animals. Outline-quilt patchwork; then add other quilting as desired.

Make 430" of binding. See page 23 for tips on making and applying straight-grain binding.